the DILEMMA of ACCESS

Minorities in Two Year Colleges

Michael A. Olivas

With the Assistance of Nan Alimba

Institute for the Study of
Educational Policy
Howard University

Published for ISEP by
HOWARD UNIVERSITY PRESS
Washington, D.C.
1979

LIBRARY OF CONGRESS CATALOGING IN PUBLICATION DATA

Olivas, Michael A.
    The dilemma of access.

    Bibliography: p.
    1. Minorities—Education, Higher—United States.
2. Junior colleges—United States.   I.   Alimba, Nan.
joint author.   II.   Title.
LC3727.043   378.1'543'0973   79-2575
ISBN 0-88258-079-5

Table of Contents

List of Tables

Foreword

The Institute for the Study of Educational Policy (ISEP) was established in 1974 with substantial support from the Ford Foundation to act as a national clearinghouse and a research center on the issues affecting equal opportunity for blacks in higher education. Through its reports and monographs, through its seminars and workshops and through its announcements and public testimony, ISEP attempts to fill a vacuum in the organized body of knowledge on minority participation in higher education. The primary program objective of the Institute is to issue an annual or biennial report on the status and situation of blacks in higher education. Two such reports have been published and another has been completed. These reports deal with blacks in all aspects of postsecondary education. The National Advisory Board decided that because of the emerging special and significant place of community colleges in providing access to blacks in higher education, a special report should be done on two year colleges from the minority perspective.

The Dilemma of Access is the first comprehensive study by the Institute that has tried to contain not only the black perspective, but also the perspective of other minority groups. Dr. Michael Olivas, the principal investigator for this study, in developing its research design, urged the Institute's staff and the Board to cover more than blacks in dealing with disadvantaged racial, ethnic, and minority groups. The Board approved this request, and the results can be seen in this study.

This study attempts to give a balanced review from a minority perspective of the fastest growing sector of postsecondary education. I believe that as a result of this comprehensive study, Dr. Olivas has come to better appreciate some of the problems of these institutions, and the Board has come to better appreciate the positive practices and possibilities of these institutions in assisting in the task of equalizing educational opportunity for all groups in our society. The Institute's Board hopes that this study will make a constructive contribution to the ongoing inquiries and discussions of two year and other colleges in the American educational system.

Special appreciation is extended to Dr. Michael Olivas who, when he began work on this study in September 1977, was a Research Fellow and was later promoted to Senior Fellow and Assistant to the Director for Research in recognition of the high quality of his work and service to the Institute. Finally, Howard University and the Institute gratefully acknowledge the assistance and continued support of the Ford Foundation and its Program Officer in charge of our grant, Dr. Benjamin Payton, who has been indispensable for all works of the Institute, including this study.

KENNETH S. TOLLETT
Chairman
National Advisory Board
Institute for the Study of
Educational Policy

Preface

Writers risk being misunderstood for several reasons, including those of their own making and those posed by readers' questions. In order to minimize the possibilities of misunderstanding, I have prepared a short list of what this book does *not* say, including concerns not specifically addressed.

First, I do not disparage two year institutions. These institutions have increased educational opportunities for many students, particularly a significant number of minority students. For this reason, they deserve substantial support; however, these institutions, like all organizations, can improve their services. I have, where appropriate, made recommendations that I believe would assist two year institutions in meeting the needs of minority communities. This book will provide two year college personnel with rationales for increasing their funding and for seeking equitable legislation.

Second, I do believe that two year colleges promise too much to their communities. In a rush to provide "lifelong learning" to all adults who would enroll, two year colleges risk losing their commitment to the full-time technical and transfer students who attend these institutions not as afterhours continuing students, but as enrollees seeking traditional learning experiences. To be sure, both two year and baccalaureate colleges need to provide continuing education and adult education curricula, particularly to those minority adults historically denied educational opportunities. Adult education data, however, suggest that majority adults are the major beneficiaries of the expansion of postsecondary opportunities and "lifelong learning." Therefore, diverting institutional resources to such comprehensive programs could widen the gap between majority and minority educational attainment, if mainstream program quality is sacrificed to increase "lifelong learning" enrollments.

Instead of trying to become institutions with something for everyone, two year colleges should refine their missions to accomplish what their communities and resources enable them to do. This means major investments in academic and support service programs in communities where two year colleges provide the major opportunities for minority full-time enrollments in technical or transfer programs. Additional missions should be undertaken only when they are corollaries to the central, organizational purpose and when they will not divert resources from that purpose.

Third, I do criticize senior institutions for relegating the bulk of minority education to two year institutions. The rise of two year systems in some cities raises the unmistakable impression that such systems were established in order to preserve the status quo and to enable senior institutions to remain inaccessible to minority students. Even in systems not designed to limit access to baccalaureate institutions (private or public), barriers have resulted from uncoordinated transfer practices. The deplorable underrepresentation of minority personnel in two year institutions is due, in no small part, to the failure of senior institutions to provide baccalaureate and graduate opportunities for minorities.

Fourth, it is clear that there cannot be any significant changes in postsecondary education unless the elementary and secondary school systems are upgraded. A major omission in this book is an exhaustive review of urban, public K-12 systems and their role in postsecondary access. This is a deliberate omission, one required in an attempt to restrict the study to a manageable length. I am not unmindful, however, of the extent to which equity and excellence are dependent upon adequate provisions for elementary and secondary education. I am convinced that any thoughtful approach to equity will incorporate upgraded K-12 systems and improve the pools of high school graduates.

Fifth, I have chosen not to dwell on specific issues concerning economic returns to educated persons. This is for two reasons: first, the literature is conflicting and contradictory; and second, I remain unconvinced that economic returns, *per se,* determine student choices. Of course, I am not naïve enough to believe that all things are equal, or that one does not acquire better credentials from one school than from another. Things are not equal. People do prefer more prestigious schools. However, the variables affecting lifetime incomes are so complex and so poorly understood that I have chosen not to dwell upon them. I anticipate that economists will make their findings on this topic more understandable, and that their research will sharpen and inform debates upon equity issues.

Finally, I am conscious of having wavered in my feelings toward two year colleges while writing drafts during the last year and a half: My case studies and field research contributed to this fluctuation in feelings, as did exchanges with colleagues. Throughout the writing, however, I have retained my original perception of the importance of these institutions: for whatever reasons, minorities are attending community colleges and technical institutions in significant numbers; therefore, any discussion of educational equity must address the dilemma of two year colleges.

A number of colleagues have read drafts, offered suggestions, or assisted me in this project. These people (and their institutional affiliation at the time they assisted me) include: Franco Alejandro, National Institute of Education; Pepe Barron, El Congreso Nacional de Asuntos Colegiales; Joan Brackett, Office for Civil Rights, (HEW); Florence

Brawer, Center for the Study of Community Colleges; Charles Byce, College Board; Rene Cardenas, National Rural Development and Finance Corporation; Dean Chavers, Bacone College; Frank Cummings, Atlanta University; Sandra Drake, American Association of Community and Junior Colleges; Nolen Ellison, Cuyahoga Community College; Maryse Eymonerie, American Association of University Professors; David Kent, National Scholarship Service and Fund for Negro Students; Dorothy Knoell, California Postsecondary Education Commission; Barbara Lee, Bureau of Higher and Continuing Education, U.S. Office of Education, (HEW); Beatrice Medicine, University of Wisconsin; Alan Paulsen, Los Angeles Trade and Technical College; Jeanette Poore, College of Alameda; Armando Rodriguez, East Los Angeles College; and Janet Ruyle, University of California at Berkeley.

Members of ISEP's National Advisory Board were helpful in clarifying issues; Norvel Smith, of the University of California at Berkeley, was particularly helpful in arranging for me to meet people who generously gave their time. At the Institute, Kenneth Tollett encouraged me and provided the support for this project. I shall always be grateful for the opportunity he gave me. Institute research staff members who carefully read drafts and assisted in the development of this study include John Fleming, Gerald Gill, Lorenzo Morris, and Joan Tunny. Finally, I acknowledge the considerable role of Nan Alimba, Sandra Davis, Candy Cauman, Donna Ennis, Nathaniel Johnson, and Gregory Kearse. I was helped immeasurably by the assistance graciously given me by these many people. All final flaws and conclusions are my own.

MICHAEL A. OLIVAS
*Senior Fellow and Assistant to the
Director for Research
Institute for the Study of
Educational Policy*

Minorities in Two Year Colleges

Chapter 1

Introduction,
Data Sources

᭤᭤᭤

Higher education is unable to define with precision its purposes, to measure with clarity its processes, or to quantify with certainty its outputs. Purists will insist that these inabilities are not weaknesses; they will argue that organizations, particularly those that educate, are properly ambiguous, and that such questions of definition are improperly asked. These purists may very well be correct, but in a context of shrinking resources, such persons are destined to become Cassandras, correct yet ineffectual.

The appropriate strategy, then, would appear to be a movement toward reducing ambiguity, toward educational accounting practices, toward cost-benefit analyses. One public college president, however, himself a veteran of legislative wars, scorns such talk: "I have never heard a legislator talk about 'cost-benefit' analysis" (Enarson, 1974, p. 160). While this perception may be, and most probably is, correct, it appears obvious that well-reasoned, data-based, economically plausible arguments for higher education will have a more attentive audience than will appeal to noble instincts.

This can be of no comfort to two year colleges, whose ambiguities of mission are as impenetrable as those of senior institutions. Moreover, several essential characteristics of two year colleges militate against reducing the ambiguities: In a system of rewards that honors quality, however defined, how can open door institutions overcome qualitative judgments? In a system that allocates funds according to a full-time enrollment model, how can a sector that is based upon part-time attendance obtain comparable funding? In a society that views the bachelor's degree as a minimum credential, how can an institution that offers sub-baccalaureate degrees and technical certificates avoid being labeled second-class?

These questions are not asked rhetorically, for such qualitative judgments *are* made when educational appropriations are determined; when federal education titles designate setasides for institutional types; when federal financial aid policies predicated upon financial need assume a traditional, 18 to 24-year-old dependent student; and when "urban land grant" higher education legislation is drafted with research universities in mind. This dilemma—the downgrading of two year colleges' central missions—is not merely reflective of a bias practiced by the more elite sectors of higher education. As noted, this downgrading manifests itself also in the more substantive funding priorities underpinning the mission of senior institutions.

But this dilemma, funding implications aside, is external: the way others perceive two year colleges ought not be a central concern to the educators themselves. More serious is the internal dilemma inherent in the ambiguity of the two year colleges' missions. The diversity of functions undertaken by two year colleges has led supporters and opponents alike to question what it is precisely that two year colleges do. Critics such as Burton Clark tend to view the missions with a jaundiced eye. He has argued that the purpose of two year colleges is to weed out students ("the cooling-out process") without their being aware of the process:

> Should the function become obvious, the ability of the junior college to perform it would be impaired. The realization that the junior college is a place where students reach undesired destinations would turn the pressure for college admissions back on the 'protected' colleges. The widespread identification of the junior college as principally a transfer station, aided by the ambiguity of the 'community college' label, helps keep this role reasonably opaque to public scrutiny (Clark, 1960, p. 165).

Proponents of two year colleges are less negative in their judgments, and instead stress the comprehensive nature of "community" colleges. Edmund Gleazer is representative of those educators who have encouraged two year institutions to become all things to all people, urging "a new kind of college—standing between the high school and the university—offering broad programs of experiences of value in and of themselves, neither post high school as such or precollege as such" (Gleazer, 1964, p. 49). Others view this proposed comprehensiveness as a possible threat to the collegiate nature of two year institutions. John Lombardi, for instance, warns that lifelong learning, under its various *community* guises, "has the potential of transforming the community college into a non-collegiate institution" (Lombardi, 1978, p. i).

The truth, whatever it may be, probably lies between Clark and Gleazer. Two year colleges—as do many four year institutions—do "cool-out" students, and characterizing them as "commuter" or "easy access" colleges will not hide this fact, particularly from those who are full-time students. Conversely, the easy access, part-time attendance, and open admissions do make two year institutions available to students not otherwise served by baccalaureate institutions. The number of persons who successfully make the transfer from junior to senior institutions and the number who complete technical programs justify Gleazer's optimism regarding the role community colleges can play in providing educational opportunity.

This dilemma of cooling-out versus access may be unresolvable. The question may be quantifiable, but may not be measurable with certainty. For instance, does attendance at two year colleges depress aspirations, lowering the sights of students in attendance? Would two year students attend baccalaureate institutions away from home if there were not commuter schools more available? Are there qualitative differences between the educations received by students in two year and four year institutions? If these questions, and others comparing two year colleges to four year colleges, cannot be answered, what then justifies this book?

Several reasons justify this study. First is the importance of compiling and analyzing systematically the assortment of research findings on the topic of minority students in two year colleges. As the following chapters and bibliography illustrate, there is no shortage of research—however useful it may be for evaluating programs designed to assist minority participation in two year colleges, or for making policy recommendations to improve such participation. Second, policy decisions affecting access to higher education are so incremental and piecemeal that no coherent policy has evolved to coordinate approaches to achieving equity in postsecondary education. Most large-scale programs specifically designed to assist minorities (e.g., Minority Biomedical Support, Graduate and Professional Opportunities, Strengthening Developing Institutions) target senior institutions rather than the institutions in which the largest proportion of minority students enroll. Perhaps symbolic of this failure to direct resources to two year colleges is Title X of the Higher Education Act of 1965 (Establishment and Expansion of Community Colleges), which has never been funded. Third is the need to discuss the accuracy and interpretation of data. Data used by policymakers to make informed judgments are frequently inadequate, particularly those based upon racial and ethnic enrollment patterns, especially at two year institutions.

This book attempts to describe existing patterns of minority partici- pation in higher education and to make recommendations in that connection, based on the premise that access has been accorded minority students in higher education only into two year institutions within a few large, urban, public systems. This premise is squarely in the tradition of scholarship that calls for a redefinition of "access," one that incorporates the corollary concept of "distribution." It is undeniable that minority students have increased their access into higher education, if one defines access as "ability to get into some college, somewhere." However, the necessary corollary of access—distribution—is strikingly skewed against minority students and raises a *prima facie* assumption of inequitable distribution within the system. This assumption is examined in the following four chapters, which include detailed investigations into the status of minorities in two year colleges: institutional and student characteristics; faculty, administrator, and trustee characteristics; aca- demic programs and support services. The summary chapter analyzes major policy issues and offers recommendations for policymakers at the institutional, systemwide, state, and federal levels.

The following chapters are built, in large part, upon previous research efforts and current federal data sources. For this reason, an introductory aside is necessary: analyses and conclusions drawn from racial and ethnic data should, as a rule, explain the origins of those data. In the case of racial and ethnic educational data, such explanations are particularly appropriate, for data used by policymakers constitute a significant policy arena in themselves, one no less subject to political considerations or manipulation by advocates than more traditional policy arenas, such as public works projects or congressional redistricting. Indeed, because of the peculiar nature of educational statistics—and their malleability for those who would employ them to their own purposes—educational statistics and attendant data issues are concerns which necessitate analysis. Therefore, this introduction will consider several of these technical, conceptual, and political issues involved in racial and ethnic educational data, and the concluding chapter will include recommendations aimed at improving the collection and utility of such data.

Major data sources on two year college enrollments are the Office for Civil Rights (OCR) and the National Center for Educational Statistics (NCES), both administered by the Department of Health, Education, and Welfare; the Bureau of the Census, Department of Commerce; the American Association of Community and Junior Colleges (AACJC); and the American College Testing Program (ACT, or the Parker survey). Those federal and state agencies and private associations that conduct higher education surveys do so for varying and sometimes conflicting purposes. Federal and state agencies request from institutions racial and ethnic data for employment records, financial aid programs, construction and housing contract applications, court-ordered affirmative action or desegregation compliance, and other purposes. Some federal data collectors make requests for purposes primarily related to education; for others, education is a secondary concern, significant only in its impact upon other governmental concerns. In these cases, knowledge of educational data makes understanding them, and understanding other specified phenomena, easier.

The Department of Health, Education, and Welfare (HEW) derives its responsibility for collecting higher education statistics from its multiple missions to fund programs, institutions, and students. Aggregate surveys of institutional data, conducted by the two HEW authorities, OCR and NCES, could accurately be termed quality or oversight control mechanisms for monitoring HEW's funded constituencies. These surveys also serve legislative data and primary data base functions for a host of governmental and private sector uses. OCR collects racial and ethnic postsecondary enrollment data on a biennial basis, monitoring all institutions that receive federal financial assistance to determine their continued eligibility for these funds. NCES, as a primary annual data source, gathers and disseminates data on enrollment and other related aspects of higher education. Through annual digests, NCES also compiles current data from other sources and, through occasional papers, sponsors research from its own and other data bases.*

Education and educational statistics also significantly influence other national concerns. The Bureau of the Census, in monitoring the economic and demographic condition of the country, surveys the population for educational attainment and enrollment statistics.** These data are relevant to the Commerce Department, because educational attainment affects economic growth, the labor force, and other economic sectors appreciably. Higher education, in this context, is a commodity or commercial enterprise. The Census Bureau data also have racial and ethnic implications for political redistricting, revenue sharing, and similar programs determined by demographic formula.

---

* "The purpose of the center shall be to collect and disseminate statistics and other data related to education in the United States and in other nations. The center shall . . . collect, collate, and, from time to time, report full and complete statistics on the condition of education in the United States; [and] conduct and publish reports on specialized analyses of the meaning and significance of such statistics. . . ." (20 U.S.C. 1221e-1)

** See Hernandez *et al.* (1973) and Abramowitz, ed. (1976), for analyses of conceptual and political issues concerning racial and ethnic data, which include Census Bureau data.

Major privately funded collections of two year enrollment data include those of AACJC and ACT. Although neither survey instrument is sensitive to minorities, their annual statistics are widely recognized and used by policy makers. The AACJC survey is more than a membership roster, and attempts to include all sub-baccalaureate institutions, most of which are affiliates of the association. The ACT survey, conducted annually by Garland Parker, tends to sacrifice accuracy for timeliness, as its avowed purpose is "to collect, report, and interpret American two-year college enrollment data as early in the academic year as possible and release a preview of these findings in early press releases. . . ." This leads to considerable variation between preliminary and final figures, and between ACT and NCES figures in final form. Nevertheless, for defining subgroups and constituencies, private and association enrollment data sources continue to show the diversity within postsecondary education.

What these surveys mean to institutions, however, is that several major data requests must be made each year, requiring considerable time. Much of what is being collected by various survey instruments overlaps, while persons responsible for completing the forms have conflicting perceptions of each survey's purpose. There is a strong tendency to perceive racial and ethnic data requests as needlessly repetitive, and undue delays between the time of gathering and publishing data may lead institutions to question the data's usefulness. Additionally, several federal and state efforts to streamline paperwork have deleted racial and ethnic data requirements in programs, and frequently caused uneven data collation within the same institution. For example, the Office of Management and Budget (OMB) has recommended that TRIO programs not maintain racial or income data files, a policy somewhat at odds with avowed legislative purpose of the program: to deliver services to disadvantaged students, most of whom are minorities.* Chapter Five contains several recommendations to consolidate data collection efforts.

In addition to the diverse and sometimes conflicting reasons for gathering enrollment data, there are the more complex conceptual and operational problems of acquisition and enumeration. Most postsecondary enrollment data are collected either by institutional surveys, e.g., OCR, NCES, ACT, AACJC, or by querying informants, e.g., Census Bureau, Current Population Surveys (CPS). Surveys, whether of interest at the primary or secondary education level, require differences in sampling procedures. Conceptualizing and defining the sample, and

---

* Discussions with OMB, U.S. Office of Education (USOE) staffs. TRIO programs include Talent Search, Upward Bound, and Special Services for Disadvantaged Students.

applying appropriate statistical controls to the sample are crucial elements of the data collection process, as the accuracy of this process renders the data more or less useful. All data sources define their universe to be sampled differently in terms of institutional categories and student characteristics. Just how representative the sample will be for generalization depends on the universe from which it is to be drawn. For instance, OCR, NCES, and AACJC define their two year universe more narrowly and clearly than ACT or the Census Bureau. Those surveyors that chose a broader universe included many different types of postsecondary institutions and students. Parker's survey includes all schools that fall under the two year rubric, without defining institutional size and category. The universe he is defining appears unclear, and this makes his survey results unclear. The results derived from these samples cannot be weighted; the universe is unclear, and those who would use these data for higher education enrollment analysis cannot tell which part of the two year universe the estimates most accurately describe. It is especially important when analyzing racial and ethnic enrollments that the universe be clearly defined. Failure to do so distorts the picture of minority participation in postsecondary education.

There are additional definitional problems inherent in categorizing ethnic institutions, particularly black institutions, problems that have conceptual and political roots. Black institutions have been variously described as "historically black," "traditionally black," and "newer predominantly black."* On the surface, these classifications would appear to have little relevance to data issues, except that many surveys (e.g., ACE's annual Freshman Profiles) separate black enrollments by institutional type, necessitating a clear understanding of the categories into which the racial data are separated.

Definitional problems also exist in using sampled data to measure educational attainment. In addition to the statistical difficulties encountered in sampling minority populations, which may reveal the enumerator's unfamiliarity with the respondent's language or culture, there are understandable possibilities of error in educational definitions. Two such examples are the failure of Census Bureau or Current Population Survey (CPS) questionnaires to distinguish between collegiate and proprietary enrollments and, for collegiate enrollees, to distinguish between transfer or technical coursework. The assumption of these questionnaires is that household respondents possess accurate information regarding the type of institution attended by and status of a family member enrolled in a postsecondary institution. There may also be a tendency for family members to inflate their family's educational attainment.

---

* See, for example, NACBHEBCU (1978) and Turner and Michael (1978) for discussions for definitional issues concerning black institutions.

Thus far, this catalog of potential errors has been limited to technical and conceptual problems in the gathering of racial and ethnic data. Another major category of data error includes reporting errors or problems associated with actually disseminating gathered data. For example, NCES data from the same period are cited differently by NCES reports. *The Condition of Education, 1977* from NCES reports fall 1974 and fall 1975 total enrollments in two year institutions as 3,312,000 and 3,871,000 respectively, while *The Condition of Education, 1978,* reports enrollments for the same two years as 3,404,000 and 3,970,000 respectively.* Such discrepancies make it very difficult for policy makers or researchers to validate the accuracy of these statistics without purchasing the tapes and making expensive computer runs.

For all the difficulties facing those who would use existing data, the most problematic need may be for data not yet collected. Missing data seem a minor problem when contrasted with the major difficulties already detailed for collected and reported data, and yet missing data create gaps for those who would make informed judgments on higher education policy. Some of these problems of omission have been alluded to, as in the OMB requirement for TRIO to discontinue record keeping by racial and income categories.** One NCES project to recommend statistical needs suggested the following large categories of missing data: equal educational opportunity, equal choice, retention, personnel needs, recurrent education, and educational diversity (Christoffel and Rice, 1975). Thus, ironically, researchers and policy makers are faced with too much and too little data, including large amounts of data of questionable utility and large amounts of potentially useful data that are not being collected. Throughout the remaining chapters this irony will be explored, as inadequate or missing data are noted.

While the most obvious starting point for a coherent racial data policy is at the federal level, an equally important focus for implementing change is the state level, which coordinates or governs most institutional planning policies. However, an ISEP survey of state data policies revealed that few states have taken initiatives to coordinate racial and ethnic data practices to streamline collection or dissemination procedures. Of particular interest was how few state agencies responsible for higher

---

* Compare Tables 3-3 (*The Condition of Education, 1977*) and 3-4 (*The Condition of Education, 1978*).

** Such categorizing occurs in the private sector as well, even in organizations that continue to collect racial and ethnic data. The National Research Council (NRC), for instance, has combined its disaggregated Hispanic groupings into one "Hispanic" category, ignoring the National Board on Graduate Education (NBGE 1976) recommendations that NCR maintain disaggregated data on doctorates.

education planning—those having vested interests in accurate and comprehensive data—maintained racial and ethnic data records. Of the forty-nine responding state commissions, only twenty (41%) collect and analyze racial and ethnic institutional data.*

Most state boards collect data for purposes of planning, review of enrollment trends, or legislative (or agency) oversight. Several states, notably those involved in civil rights litigation, do so in compliance with court-ordered mandates to monitor equal access. Few commissions maintain a staff whose sole responsibility is to gather and compile institutional data, although several that have not invested in full-time staff have apportioned responsibilities to several administrators to coordinate and make available comprehensive data. In Illinois, for example, the *Data Book on Illinois Higher Education* is maintained to "minimize the reporting burden on the institutions." Similarly, other states have employed standing committees or directed mail systems to reduce duplication of existing information and to assign requests for information. This centralization of data helps reduce the institutional burden by facilitating responses to many research and public information requests.

Inasmuch as all respondent states collect data on student and institutional characteristics, the failure of some agencies to analyze racial and ethnic data may suggest some indifference to minority needs. In many instances, it would only require minor modifications in existing survey designs to accommodate analyses of race and ethnicity for items already being measured. Surprisingly, several states had not even collated institutional data already collected by OCR and Higher Education General Information Survey (HEGIS). These states apparently remain unaware of the potential usefulness to themselves of the data the individual institutions are required to collect. The existing federal requirements provide states with an adequate base for racial and ethnic analyses, and it is surprising that such important planning tasks continue to be performed perfunctorily or not at all.

---

* Questionnaires were sent to all 1202 state commissions or, in states without designated planning commissions, to the state coordinating or governing agency. Only Rhode Island did not respond to the survey.

Chapter 2

Institutional and Student Characteristics

༡ ༡ ༡

In analyzing data or recommending policy options, it is easy to lapse into generalizations and to oversimplify complex interrelationships, particularly when the concepts at issue are amorphous, as "equity," "access," and "opportunity" undeniably are. Nevertheless, in assessing the maldistribution of minority students in two year institutions, it is necessary to affix labels to these concepts, imperfect though both labels and concepts may be. An understanding of this maldistribution requires analyses of a number of factors including institutional, enrollment, and student characteristics. These factors are inextricably linked, and any separation must seem artificial and contrived. However, when assembling large amounts of data in order to understand complex interrelationships, it is helpful to conceptualize the elements separately. To this end, Chapter Two displays data, many previously unpublished, that show patterns of growth and change in two year institutions. Fundamental institutional characteristics are analyzed, including size, type, location, residential facilities, and financing. Enrollment patterns are examined, with particular focus upon minority students. Special purpose two year institutions are examined briefly, including historically black two year institutions, Bureau of Indian Affairs-sponsored colleges, and proprietary institutions. Characteristics of two year college students, persistence, withdrawal rates, and financial aid data are also examined for racial and ethnic patterns.

An unmistakable trend in statewide coordination and governance is worth noting. Appendix A reports individual state statutory planning and coordinating responsibilities for higher education institutions. Forty-three states exercise these responsibilities for public junior colleges, and twenty-nine states exercise these responsibilities for public vocational and technical institutions.[1] Those states that do not exercise planning and coordinating responsibilities either have no such institutions in the state, or have colleges held in public trusts by institutional boards of trustees.[2] The importance of state boards in higher education policy making has been widely researched (Berdahl, 1971; Millard, 1976), and merits further attention. Of particular note will be the role of state boards in student financial aid policies and in statewide desegregation efforts in public higher education (Haynes, 1978). It must suffice to say that these two subjects, as well as others concerning minorities in higher education, suggest statewide boards as appropriate loci for effecting changes in statewide systems of public—and, in some states, private—higher education.

Institutional Characteristics

Perhaps no single phrase summarizes the two year colleges better than does "rapidly grown." While the number of private two year colleges remained constant from 1958 to 1974, the number of public two year institutions nearly tripled, from 309 to 901 (Table 2-1). The period between 1966 and 1974 saw more than one new public two year institution open each week, more than doubling the existing number of institutions. Not only were many institutions opened, but existing institutions grew larger (Table 2-2). The number of small institutions (under 1,000 students) declined from 452 in 1968 to 389 in 1976, while the number of large institutions (over 10,000 students) grew from 33 (4% of all two year institutions) to 89 (8%) during the same period.

As noted in Chapter One, the two year rubric is often unsatisfactory for data analysis, and variations in definitions often preclude comparative study. Table 2-3 reinforces points made earlier about the inability to compare data from different sources. The tabular data, previously unpublished, were gathered in a survey of AACJC membership. Mem-

---

[1] By contrast, 48 state agencies exercise these responsibilities for public senior institutions, 23 for private institutions, and 12 for proprietary schools. Eleven states control these responsibilities for all five institutional types and sectors.

[2] These trustee boards are examined in more detail in Chapter Three. For an analysis of 1202 commissions, see Salazar and Martorana, 1978, esp. Table 2.

TABLE 2-1

**2-Year Institutions by Control
Selected Years, 1958–76**

Control	Number of Institutions						
	1958	1962	1966	1970	1974	1975	1976
Total	557	628	685	897	1,151	1,151	1,141
Public	309	366	408	659	901	901	901
Private	248	262	277	238	250	250	240

Source: NCES, The Condition of Education 1976 Edition, Table 1.18 thru 1974; 1978 Edition, Table 3.9 to 1976.

bership in the association is voluntary and exceeds the NCES two year institution counts due to varying unit definitions.[3] The table is important, however, for the heterogeneity of administrative structures it reports; only sixty percent report themselves in the prototypical category, that of community and junior colleges. Even allowing for overlapping or inconsistent categories, it is clear that any definition of the two year college can exist only as a model or construct. One final gauge of size would be the comparison of two year colleges to four year institutions, particularly the largest systems of public higher education. Appendix B lists the sixty largest campuses in the country, including ten, two year college systems. Of the two year systems, only the largest, Miami-Dade, enrolls more full-time than part-time students. As with variations in institutional mission, variations in size render discussions of a prototypical two year college difficult. Deep Springs College, near the Nevada-California border, and its 26 students surely have little in common with Miami-Dade and its nearly 40,000 students, save that both offer the associate degree as their highest degree.

Access, strictly considered, is an index of student financial charges and institutional selectivity. Accessibility and proximity to students are corollary concerns, particularly to commuter students. Early studies of proximity and its relationship to area college attendance rates (Koos, 1944; Willis, 1964) confirm what appears obvious: there is an "attractive pull" when an institution is readily accessible to students. The more easily a college can be attended, the more likely students are to enroll. Of course, measures of accessibility must take into account available rapid transit or public transportation, parking facilities, class schedules, and distances from home (or work) to campus. Willingham's (1970)

---

[3] Moreover, the categories are not mutually exclusive. A number of community and junior colleges are multi-unit (Palola and Oswald, 1972).

TABLE 2-2

2-Year Institutions by Enrollment Size
Selected Years, 1968, 1972, and 1976

Size of Enrollment	All Institutions		2-Year Institutions	
	Number	Total Enrollment	Number	Total Enrollment
Fall 1968				
Total	2,483	7,513,091	864	1,792,822
Under 200	302	33,637	114	12,565
200 to 499	341	120,434	155	54,837
500 to 999	557	411,691	183	134,023
1,000 to 2,499	627	963,971	221	338,074
2,500 to 4,999	266	947,025	99	354,835
5,000 to 9,999	211	1,492,850	59	401,481
10,000 to 19,999	119	1,624,674	28	366,068
20,000 to 29,999	35	829,804	4	94,992
30,000 or more	25	1,089,005	1	35,947
Fall 1972				
Total	2,665	9,214,860	964	2,665,787
Under 200	262	28,947	72	9,058
200 to 499	367	130,019	152	53,810
500 to 999	542	396,178	176	127,367
1,000 to 2,499	680	1,062,698	270	423,687
2,500 to 4,999	328	1,161,428	143	509,107
5,000 to 9,999	259	1,841,726	93	634,559
10,000 to 19,999	149	2,093,994	51	718,600
20,000 to 29,999	44	1,014,850	6	142,480
30,000 or more	34	1,485,020	1	47,119
Fall 1976				
Total	3,067	11,121,426	1,143	3,916,613
1–1000	1,204	580,918	389	209,214
1,000 to 2,499	809	1,293,773	325	527,002
2,500 to 4,999	411	1,460,464	186	651,554
5,000 to 9,999	356	2,574,697	154	1,115,465
10,000–19,999	193	2,663,459	74	1,042,896
20,000 or more	94	2,548,115	15	370,482

Source: National Center for Education Statistics, *The Condition of Education,* 1976 Edition, Table 1.19 (1968, 1972); 1978 Edition, Table 3.10 (1976). ISEP staff calculations.

indices of free access commuting distances are not replicated here, although this chapter does present previously unpublished data on minority enrollment in urban two year colleges (Appendix D) in the

TABLE 2-3

2-Year Colleges by Type of Institution
1977–78

Type	Number
Community junior college	788
Vocational technical institute	153
2-year branch campus	94
Single campus of multi-campus	227
Administrative units of multi-campus	70
Total	1,332

Source: AACJC unpublished data.

discussion of minority enrollment characteristics. Table 2-4 displays data on institutional location, not held constant by size. Nor are these data controlled for geographical distribution. Willingham found wide regional variations in his analysis of college accessibility, and even within urban areas, "urban" and "suburban" characteristics may vary with the age of the city, stability of the neighborhood, or other commercial factors.

While institutional size, type, and location contribute to an understanding of two year college growth patterns, nothing so strikingly depicts the role of these institutions as do enrollment figures over time for two year colleges, particularly in the public sector. Tables 2-5 and 2-6 summarize these patterns. In 1976 two year institutions, constituting 37% of all institutions, enrolled 35% of the total enrollments. Most notably, the ratio of public to private two year enrollments exceeded the

TABLE 2-4

2-Year Institutions by Primary Location
1977–78*

Location	Number
Urban	336 (27%)
Suburban	343 (28%)
Rural	550 (45%)
Total	1,229

Source: AACJC unpublished data.

* Excludes unreported institutions.

TABLE 2-5

Higher Education Enrollment (in Thousands)
1972–76

Type and Control of Institution	Fall of Year				
	1972	1973	1974	1975	1976
All institutions	9,215	9,602	10,224	11,185	11,012
4-year institutions	6,459	6,592	6,820	7,215	7,129
Universities	2,621	2,630	2,702	2,838	2,780
Other 4-year institutions	3,838	3,962	4,117	4,376	4,349
2-year institutions	2,756	3,010	3,404	3,970	3,883
Public institutions	7,071	7,420	7,988	8,835	8,653
4-year institutions	4,430	4,530	4,703	4,998	4,902
Universities	1,941	1,951	2,007	2,124	2,080
Other 4-year institutions	2,489	2,579	2,696	2,874	2,822
2-year institutions	2,641	2,890	3,285	3,836	3,752
Private institutions	2,144	2,183	2,235	2,350	2,359
4-year institutions	2,029	2,062	2,117	2,217	2,227
Universities	680	679	696	714	700
Other 4-year institutions	1,349	1,383	1,421	1,503	1,527
2-year institutions	115	120	119	134	132

Source: NCES, *The Condition of Education*, 1978 Edition, Table 3.4.

ratio of public to private four year and graduate institutions: public two year enrollments accounted for 97% of all two year enrollments in 1976, an increase from the 1972 level of 96%. At the same time, the number of private two year colleges dropped from 270 in 1970 to 240 in 1976 (*The Condition of Education, 1978,* Table 3-9). Thus, the shrinking number of private two year institutions is accompanied by a shrinking proportional share of enrollments, despite slightly increased total private enrollment. This overall decline of private two year institutions will affect residential patterns in the two year institutions. Few public two year institutions provide on-campus student housing, whereas private two year institutions more often do.

Figure 2-1 indicates the small extent to which public two year institutions provide student housing. Despite the general lack of residential facilities in two year colleges, significant numbers of students in these institutions enroll full-time. Of course, "full-time" and "residential" student designations are not synonymous, despite traditional notions of the "typical student" as a full-time resident. Nor are commuter students exclusive to two year institutions; a number of urban upper division colleges have specific missions to serve part-time and commuter students

TABLE 2-6

**Institutions of Higher Education: Number and Enrollment
1976**

Type of Institution	Number	Public	Private	Public as Percent of Total Number
	Number of Institutions			
Total	3,067 (100%)	1,465	1,602	48
University	161 (5%)	96	65	60
4-year	1,763 (57%)	462	1,301	26
2-year	1,143 (37%)	907	236	79
	Enrollment (in thousands)			
Total	11,012 (100%)	8,653	2,359	79
University	2,780 (25%)	2,080	700	75
4-year	4,349 (39%)	2,822	1,527	65
2-year	3,883 (35%)	3,752	132	97

Source: National Center for Education Statistics, The Condition of Education, 1978 Edition, Tables 3.4 and 3.10. ISEP staff calculations.

Note: Figures may not total 100% because of rounding.

(Dash and Riley, 1977).[4] The commuter nature of two year institutions is best shown by tables indicating proportions of part-time enrollments, and by a table supplementing 2-4, detailing enrollments by institutional location. Table 2-7 reports Census Bureau data on two year college enrollments in suburban institutions. In 1976, 46% of all two year students were enrolled in suburban two year colleges, which also had proportionately fewer full-time students than did central city or rural institutions.

Before exploring minority enrollment patterns, two additional considerations are necessary to provide a statistical portrait of two year colleges: income and expenditure patterns. An analysis of higher education finance or economic issues is well beyond the scope of this book; however, comparative income and expenditure data will help clarify the differences in institutional missions and in the resources among institutional missions.[5] Tables 2-8 and 2-9 detail income and expenditure patterns for academic year 1975-76.

---

[4] Six of the baccalaureate institutions listed in Appendix B have larger part-time than full-time enrollments.

[5] For detailed analysis of these issues, see Gladieux, 1975; Garms, 1977; Breneman and Finn, eds., 1978; Nelson, 1978a, 1978c.

FIGURE 2-1

Percentage Distribution of Assignable Areas in Buildings of Higher Education Institutions 1970

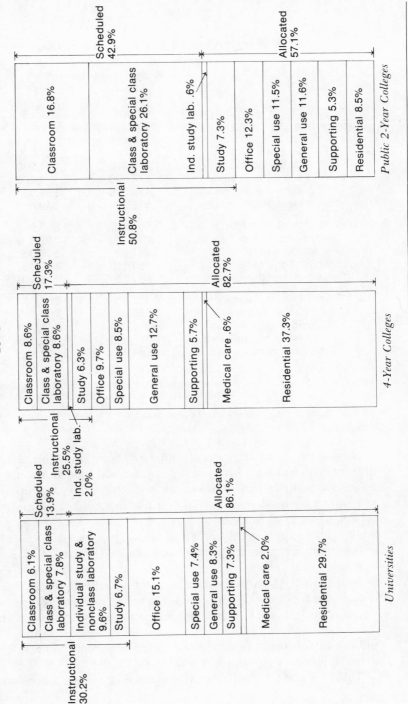

Source: Halstead, 1974, p. 420.

TABLE 2-7

2-Year Enrollment Size by Metropolitan, Non-metropolitan Areas 1974-76

Residence	Total Enrolled	Attending Full-Time	
		Number	Percent
1976 2-year total enrollment	2,435,000	1,430,000	58.7
Metropolitan areas	1,899,000	1,061,000	55.9
Inside central cities	777,000	472,000	60.7
Outside central cities	1,122,000	589,000	52.5
Non-metropolitan areas	536,000	369,000	68.8
1975 2-year total enrollment	2,561,000	1,567,000	61.2
Metropolitan areas	2,007,000	1,192,000	59.4
Inside central cities	844,000	508,000	60.2
Outside central cities	1,163,000	684,000	58.8
Non-metropolitan areas	554,000	376,000	67.8
1974 2-year total enrollment	2,072,000	1,237,000	59.7
Metropolitan areas	1,686,000	966,000	57.3
Inside central cities	675,000	401,000	59.4
Outside central cities	1,011,000	565,000	55.9
Non-metropolitan areas	386,000	272,000	70.4

Source: U.S. Census Bureau, Social and Economic Characteristics of Students, October 1974, Series P-20, No. 286, 1975. U.S. Census Bureau, Social and Economic Characteristics of Students, October 1975, Series P-20, No. 303, 1976. U.S. Census Bureau, Social and Economic Characteristics of Students, October 1975, Series P-20, No. 319, 1978.

Most notable in the income patterns shown in Table 2-10 is the difference in sources of income by institutional type and sector. In the public sector, two year institutions are slightly more reliant upon tuition as a source of income than are senior institutions, but far more heavily reliant upon local, unrestricted appropriations. Two year institutions are less able to generate income by "sales and services," in part because of fewer income-generating health services, and in part because of fewer dormitory and refectory enterprises. In the private sector, differences by institutional type also occur, most notably in the higher reliance upon tuition and fees by two year schools than that by senior colleges. Private two year institutions, like their public counterparts, are less reliant upon federal sources of funding than are senior institutions, although, unlike public two year institutions, they do raise a large portion of their income through auxiliary (dormitory) enterprises.

Table 2-8 and 2-9 show the effect of mission upon resource allocation.

In both the public and private sector, two year institutions spent the largest share for "student education," an amount roughly equivalent to instructional costs. The missions of research and public service in senior institutions reveal resource patterns that are not central to two year institutions; for most two year colleges, "community" or "public" service means delivery of instruction, not the extensive clinical or research programs generally sponsored by baccalaureate and graduate institutions. As before, spending patterns for residence facilities and the auxiliary enterprises differed by sector in the two year institutions.

These figures are judgment-free, although they do reveal institutional characteristics. Table 2-10 is more judgmental in two respects. First, it separates resource data to allow comparison among institutional types, and second, it reflects legislative judgments concerning the value of different institutional types, as inferred from per capita expenditures. Although some states have used program budgets to "equalize" appropriations for similar programs at different types of institutions (e.g., × dollars per full-time equivalent (FTE) student for English composition classes at technical institutes or state universities), there remain major differences between the educational resources allocated to two year colleges and to senior institutions.

Table 2-10, a composite of Alexander Astin's research (1975a), shows the extent to which educational resources allocated per FTE student differ by public institutional type. With respect to educational and general expenditures, financial aid, and libraries and facilities, two year colleges receive less money per FTE student than do senior colleges. The summary category, "subsidy," combines educational and general expenditures and financial aid packages, from which tuition is subtracted. Like the measures of expenditures, this measure of subsidy (i.e., the extent to which different institutional types subsidize the educational costs for their students) indicates that two year institutions receive less subsidy and return less subsidy to their students. The hierarchical nature of public systems of higher education, arguably defensible on grounds of efficiency, is less defensible in its distribution of resources. Astin has noted such hierarchical systems:

In one sense, these data provide strong support for the notion that "them that has, gets." More important, they show clearly that 'educational opportunity,' as measured by the amount contributed to that student's education through public funds, is by no means equivalent in different types of public institutions. Here again is another important side effect of a hierarchically arranged public system based on selective admissions: students who are denied access to the universities and more selective four-year colleges

TABLE 2-8

Current Funds and Revenues of Institutions of Higher Education
(in Thousands)
1975–76

| | Public | | | |
| | Universities | | Other 4-year | |
Source	Amount	Per-cent	Amount	Per-cent
Total	$11,321,977	100.0	$10,519,424	100.0
Tuition and fees from students	1,438,651	12.7	1,309,623	12.5
Federal government	2,007,136	17.7	1,597,005	15.2
Unrestricted appropriations	265,268	2.3	402,863	3.8
Unrestricted grants and contracts	204,766	1.8	98,915	0.9
Restricted grants and contracts	1,339,737	11.8	894,707	8.5
Independent operations (FFRDC)[1]	197,365	1.7	200,520	1.9
State governments	4,723,670	41.7	5,000,755	47.5
Unrestricted appropriations	4,536,725	40.1	4,874,528	46.3
Unrestricted grants and contracts	12,030	0.1	9,355	[2]
Restricted grants and contracts	174,915	1.5	116,872	1.1
Local governments	48,582	0.4	266,538	2.5
Unrestricted appropriations	27,195	0.2	219,598	2.1
Unrestricted grants and contracts	1,601	[2]	1,841	[2]
Restricted grants and contracts	19,786	0.2	45,099	0.4
Private gifts, grants, and contracts	403,720	3.6	189,223	1.8
Unrestricted	32,294	0.3	17,974	0.2
Restricted	371,426	3.3	171,249	1.6
Endowment income	66,026	0.6	28,599	0.3
Unrestricted	28,672	0.3	13,718	0.1
Restricted	37,354	0.3	14,881	0.1
Sales and services	2,410,198	21.3	1,958,089	18.6
Educational activities	279,703	2.5	124,118	1.2
Auxiliary enterprises	1,465,763	12.9	1,125,304	10.7
Hospitals	664,732	5.9	708,667	6.7
Other sources	223,994	2.0	169,592	1.6

Source: NCES, The Condition of Education, 1978 Edition, Table 5.2.

Note: Details may not add to totals because of rounding.

[1] Generally includes only those revenues associated with major federally funded research and development centers.

[2] Less than 0.05 percent.

		Private					
2-year		Universities		Other 4-year		2-year	
Amount	Per-cent	Amount	Per-cent	Amount	Per-cent	Amount	Per-cent
$4,993,497	100.0	$6,061,835	100.0	$6,495,804	100.0	$310,629	100.0
729,292	14.6	1,681,092	27.7	2,847,025	43.8	166,259	53.5
396,981	8.0	1,645,020	27.1	812,562	12.5	18,476	5.9
113,747	2.3	69,155	1.1	52,511	0.8	2,933	0.9
19,343	0.4	231,917	3.8	65,856	1.0	1,881	0.6
263,828	5.3	958,428	15.8	414,345	6.4	13,650	4.4
63	[²]	385,520	6.4	279,850	4.3	12	[²]
2,233,912	44.7	137,858	2.3	150,982	2.3	8,709	2.8
2,153,811	43.1	72,343	1.2	94,546	1.5	4,046	1.3
13,527	0.3	6,066	0.1	13,955	0.2	2,432	0.8
66,574	1.3	59,449	1.0	42,481	0.7	2,231	0.7
1,184,408	23.7	76,110	1.3	38,986	0.6	2,351	0.8
1,168,800	23.4	74	[²]	2,304	[²]	1,573	0.5
3,816	[²]	7,469	0.1	3,006	[²]	413	0.1
11,792	0.2	68,567	1.1	33,676	0.5	365	0.1
23,466	0.5	558,407	9.2	704,340	10.8	37,880	12.2
8,782	0.2	182,622	3.0	521,379	8.0	33,318	10.7
14,684	0.3	375,785	6.2	182,961	2.8	4,562	1.5
2,373	[²]	325,847	5.4	259,639	4.0	4,987	1.6
2,199	[²]	148,148	2.4	170,899	2.6	4,304	1.4
173	[²]	177,699	2.9	88,740	1.4	683	0.2
317,882	6.4	1,474,718	24.3	1,464,887	22.6	61,607	19.8
19,437	0.4	170,180	2.8	49,959	0.8	2,022	0.7
298,445	6.0	568,945	9.4	1,029,579	15.9	59,585	19.2
0	0.0	735,593	12.1	385,349	5.9	0	0.0
100,184	2.0	162,784	2.7	217,886	3.4	10,359	3.3

TABLE 2-9

Current Expenditures and Mandatory Transfers
of Institutions of Higher Education (in Thousands)
1975–76

	Public					
	Universities		Other 4-year		2-year	
Purpose	Amount	Per-cent	Amount	Per-cent	Amount	Per-cent
Total	$11,081,437	100.0	$10,310,430	100.0	$4,792,089	100.0
Educational and general	8,715,556	78.7	8,078,014	78.3	4,489,432	93.7
Student education[1]	5,953,472	53.7	6,817,843	66.1	4,147,979	86.6
Research[2]	1,565,659	14.1	574,046	5.6	14,736	0.3
Scholarships and fellowships[3]	355,164	3.2	305,669	3.0	137,682	2.9
Public service	728,537	6.6	226,798	2.2	80,373	1.7
Mandatory transfers[4]	112,725	1.0	153,657	1.5	108,656	2.3
Auxiliary enterprises[5]	1,406,845	12.7	1,118,757	10.9	302,514	6.3
Hospitals and independent operations[6]	959,032	8.7	1,113,659	10.8	143	[7]

Source: NCES, The Condition of Education, 1970 Edition, Table 5.1.

Note: Details may not add to totals because of rounding.

[1] Includes instruction, academic support, libraries, institutional support, student services and operation and maintenance of the plant. These are the items most nearly comparable to "student education" expenditures reported prior to 1974–75.

[2] Includes all sponsored research and other separately budgeted research with the exception of federally funded research and development centers which are included under "independent operations."

| | Universities | | Private | | | |
| | | | Other 4-year | | 2-year | |
	Amount	Per-cent	Amount	Per-cent	Amount	Per-cent
	$5,996,450	100.0	$6,422,901	100.0	$299,869	100.0
	4,336,017	72.3	4,733,462	73.7	246,204	82.1
	2,924,103	48.8	3,830,663	59.6	216,299	72.1
	925,223	15.4	206,777	3.2	922	0.3
	349,920	5.8	468,732	7.3	18,692	6.2
	88,744	1.5	111,863	1.7	2,284	0.8
	48,027	0.8	115,426	1.8	8,007	2.7
	577,242	9.6	1,017,818	15.8	53,665	17.9
	1,083,192	18.1	671,621	10.5	0.0	0.0

³ Monies given in the form of outright grants and trainee stipends to individuals enrolled in formal coursework, either for credit or not, includes aid in the form of tuition or fee remissions. Prior to 1974–75 this category was entitled "student aid" and was not an educational and general item.

⁴ Mandatory transfers from current funds are those that must be made to fulfill a binding legal obligation of the institution. Includes debt service provisions relating to academic buildings, including amounts set aside for debt retirement and interest, and required provisions for renewal and replacements to the extent not financed from other sources.

⁵ Includes residence halls, food services, college store, and intercollegiate athletics. Includes mandatory transfers from auxiliary enterprises.

⁶ Includes expenditures for hospitals and for "independent operations" which are generally limited to expenditures of federally funded research and development centers. Includes mandatory transfers from hospitals and independent operations.

⁷ Less than 0.05 percent.

TABLE 2-10

Educational Resources and Benefits of Different Public Institutions

Type of Institution	Dollars Per Full Time Student					
	Educational and General Expenditures	Value of Buildings, Land, and Equipment	Library Ex-penditures	Expenditures for Financial Aid	Tuition	"Subsidy" (Educational and General Plus Aid Expenditures Minus Tuition)
2-year colleges	1,533	3,982	71	60	385	1,208
4-year colleges						
Low selectivity	1,534	5,514	83	77	358	1,253
Medium selectivity	1,758	6,467	98	94	404	1,448
High selectivity	2,523	7,875	104	129	473	2,179
Universities						
Low selectivity	3,101	7,710	109	133	490	2,744
Medium selectivity	3,230	8,453	116	190	564	2,850
High selectivity	5,408	12,320	212	316	519	5,205

Source: Astin, 1975a, Tables 3, 4.

(including a disproportionate share of the low-income and minority students) receive substantially less public subsidy for their postsecondary education than do students who manage to enter the more selective public colleges and universities (Astin 1975a, pp. 7–8).

One additional point about financing needs to be made: the volatility of student aid programs. Unlike state appropriations, which tend to fluctuate moderately and are usually adjusted slightly upward for inflation,* student aid programs are subject to federal legislation that can have significant impact upon programs, program eligibility, and funding levels—for example, the GI Bill and the discontinuation of the Vietnam War. Appendix C shows sources of direct student aid by institutional type and control. It is noteworthy that over 86% of federal student aid to public two year institutions in 1974–75 was administered through the GI Bill, compared to 64% in four year institutions. The 1976 change in GI Bill benefits (Nelson, 1978b, p. 81) will undoubtedly affect this source of funding for institutions, as would any major change in social security educational benefits (Fitt, 1977). Additional data on student aid programs that have a bearing on two year colleges are discussed in the following section on student characteristics.** Before detailing student characteristics, however, this chapter presents minority enrollment data for consideration.

Table 2-11 reports unpublished OCR figures for 1976. The table is busy, but it contains many data that bear directly upon the extent to which minority students have access to the lowest tier of postsecondary education. The most obvious evidence of the data is the overwhelming presence of minority students in these institutions. Minority students accounted for over 20% of all enrollments in two year colleges. A better index of their presence is each minority group's two year enrollment as a percentage of that group's total undergraduate enrollments. This calculation graphically depicts the role of two year institutions in providing educational access to minority students. Blacks enroll 50% of their students in two year institutions; Asians, 52%; Hispanics, 59%; American Indians, 67%. White students, who constitute 79% of all two year enrollments, concentrate 45% of their numbers in these institutions.

These figures, striking as they are, report only aggregate minority

---

* A proper consideration of Proposition 13 and its economic implications for public two year colleges is beyond the scope of this book, although it appears clear that local and state tax bases cannot be considered "stable" sources of support.

** AACJC was the only major higher education association to support the legislation calling for tuition tax credits, and did so because two year college students tend to be older and part time, and it was felt that such credits would especially benefit this clientele (ISEP conversations with AACJC staff member).

TABLE 2-11

Racial/Ethnic Enrollments
1976

Race/Ethnicity	Total Undergraduate		2-Year Undergraduate		2-Year Undergraduate as Percent of Total Undergraduate	2-Year Full-Time as Percent of Undergraduate Full-Time
	Full-Time	Part-Time	Full-Time	Part-Time		
White	4,820,716 (81.2%)	2,070,377 (80.3%)	1,280,872	1,799,927	44	26
Black	605,116 (10.1%)	261,199 (10.1%)	221,874	207,849	49	36
Hispanic	263,982 (4.4%)	145,682 (5.6%)	119,444	122,565	59	45
Asian	103,247 (1.7%)	51,700 (2.0%)	33,908	46,510	51	32
American Indian	38,420 (.6%)	22,996 (.8%)	18,424	22,820	67	47
Total						
Minority	1,010,765 (17.0%)	481,577 (18.6%)	393,650	399,744	53	38
Non-resident alien	104,421 (1.7%)	25,454 (1.0%)	16,253	26,172	32	15
Aggregate	5,935,902	2,577,408	1,690,775	2,225,843	46	28

Source: Unpublished data, Office for Civil Rights; National Center for Education Statistics, *The Condition of Education,* 1978 Edition, Table 3.6; *Higher Education Daily,* 6. No. 59 (March 1978), pp. 1–2. ISEP staff calculations.

group enrollments, which are not separated by full-time and part-time attendance status. A closer examination of minority full-time attendance in two year institutions reveals disturbing patterns. Clearly, access to two year colleges has not been for part-time, nontraditional students, but instead, for a disproportionately large number of minority traditional students. For Asians, 33% of their full-time students are enrolled in two year institutions; blacks, 37%; Hispanics, 45%; American Indians, 48%. Only 27% of full-time white students are enrolled in two year institutions. To be sure, some of the historically black two year colleges and federal and tribal Indian two year colleges are residential, mitigating somewhat the adverse effects of commuter institutions. However, this maldistribution of minorities in two year institutions suggests a distressing lack of minority access to senior baccalaureate institutions.

Appendices D and E should be read in tandem with Table 2-12, as all three report the concentration of minority students in two year institutions. Table 2-12, as noted, reports aggregate minority enrollment patterns in two year colleges, and the resulting disproportionate concentration of full-time students. In Appendix D, the concentration and location of minority students are examined in the 150 institutions that have the heaviest concentrations of minority enrollments. Appendix E

TABLE 2-12

Black Enrollment in Historically Black 2-Year Institutions

Institution	Black Enrollment		Total Enrollment
U Lawson St. College	1,315	(98.8%)	1,331
R Lomax-Hannon Junior College	125	(99.2%)	126
U S.D. Bishop St. Junior College	1,340	(88.0%)	1,523
U Alabama Lutheran	130	(94.9%)	137
U Shorter College	189	(95.0%)	199
U Southern University—Shreveport	973	(99.9%)	974
R Coahoma Junior College	1,362	(94.2%)	1,446
R Prentiss Normal Industrial Institute	137	(98.6%)	139
R Utica Junior College	990	(99.6%)	994
R Mary Holmes College	619	(100.0%)	619
U Friendship Junior College	155	(80.7%)	192
R Clinton Junior College	208	(100%)	208
S Morristown College	173	(98.3%)	176
U Virginia College	239	(98.8%)	242
S Southwestern Christian College	371	(93.0%)	341
Total	8,326		8,647

Source: OCR, Racial and Ethnic Enrollment Data 1976, prepublication release. ISEP calculations.
Key: U = Urban, R = Rural, S = Suburban.

examines the list in further depth, separating the urban institutions from Appendix D.

The formula employed to determine minority institutional concentrations in Appendix D was the following:

Black:	40% black enrollments *or* 1,000 black students
Hispanic:	40% Hispanic enrollments *or* 10% Hispanic enrollments of 3,000 total students
American Indian:	40% Indian enrollments *or* 10% Indian enrollments of 3,000 total students
Asian:	40% Asian enrollments *or* 10% Asian enrollments of 3,000 total students
or	total 1,000 minority students
or	20% total minority students of 15,000 total students
or	50% total minority

These 11 rules sorted out 150 institutions with significant minority enrollments. The 150 institutions represent 13% of all two year institutions in the OCR data, and include colleges in 29 states. Fifty-seven colleges in the list are located in California.

Over half of Appendix D represents urban campuses, analyzed in more detail in Appendix E. The number of states shrank from 29 to 23, while California's colleges dropped from 57 to 35. Nonetheless, these 83 urban two year institutions represent over 40% of minority two year enrollments: 21% American Indian, 43% black, 43% Hispanic, and 45% Asian. These concentrations are an important key to understanding minority access to postsecondary education. Minority students are as maldistributed throughout the two year tier* as they are throughout the postsecondary hierarchy. Seven percent of the two year institutions enroll 42% of the minority two year students. This minority concentration in a small number of urban institutions gives the illusion of access. These 83 urban two year colleges, less than 3% of all postsecondary institutions, enroll nearly 23% of all undergraduate minority students; thus, urban enrollments inflate two year minority proportions which, in turn, inflate postsecondary figures.

Declarations of minority progress hinge upon relative improvements over previous figures, historically at low levels, and upon channeled access to relatively few two year colleges. Minority housing patterns are largely metropolitan and central city (U.S. Commission on Civil Rights,

---

* This chapter does not analyze institutional characteristics of proprietary, or noncollegiate, schools. Appendix F, however, reports the extent to which this sector overlaps the two year sector.

1976); therefore, one would expect a disproportionately high concentration of minority students in urban public institutions, if these institutions were serving their communities. In this regard, two year institutions face a "no-win" dilemma: as community-based service organizations they must serve the community clientele, but if attendance patterns and school locations serve a segregated housing area, then those schools will tend to reflect those housing patterns. One president of a two year college has called this dilemma "being accessible to the community, as opposed to mechanically promoting racial balance among adults attending the institution in non-compulsory education programs" (Middleton, 1978).

This dilemma, somewhat reminiscent of K-12 desegregation theories, must not lull policy makers or educators into inaction concerning access and distribution of minority students. Previously analyzed data indicate the maldistribution of students in one tier (two year institutions), and within this tier, into a very small number of schools: Table 2-4 shows that rural areas have the largest number of institutions, and Table 2-7 shows that suburban two year colleges enroll the largest number of students. Multi-unit districts must examine campus locations for disproportional racial impact, and schools not serving minority students, when minority populations are proximate, must evaluate their policies to eradicate admission barriers. Strong *prima facie* evidence of inequitable access is available, and civil rights groups are increasingly vigilant in higher education issues (Mexican American Legal Defense and Education Fund, 1978; Middleton, 1978).

Ironically, those institutions without barriers to minority students find themselves threatened by public perceptions concerning minority access. Historically minority institutions, always underfinanced, are increasingly under attack as anachronisms. Higher education desegregation litigation, most recently the Adams case,* has called into question the rights of institutions established to serve minority students. Resulting state plans to desegregate public systems of higher education threaten the status of the historically black two year colleges, listed in Table 2-12 (Haynes, 1978). The network of traditionally Indian two year institutions is reported in Table 2-13.** Additional federal funding is authorized by Congress and disbursed to tribal two year institutions ("Carter Signs," 1978; see also Appendix K). There is no formal network of historically Hispanic two year institutions, although there have recently emerged alternative schools (Southwest Network, 1974; Arce, 1978) and an identifiably Puerto Rican two year college in New York, Hostos Com-

---

* *Adams v. Califano*, 356 F. Supp. 92 (D.D.C. 1973).

** Only two of the thirty-two campuses are baccalaureate institutions.

TABLE 2-13

Indian Colleges

Institution	AIHEC Membership[a]	Indian Colleges in U.S.[b]	AACTE[c]	AIHEC Testimony[d]	AIPRC[e]
American Indian Community College Winnebago, Nebraska		X			
American Indian Satellite Community College Norfolk, Nebraska	X		X	X	X
Bacone College Muskogee, Oklahoma		X			
Blackfeet Community College Browning, Montana	X	X		X	
Cheyenne River Community College Eagle Butte, South Dakota	X	X	X	X	X
College of Ganado Ganado, Arizona		X			
Dull Knife Memorial College Lame Deer, Montana		X			
Flaming Rainbow University Stilwell, Oklahoma		X			
Flathead Community College Kalispell, Montana		X			
Fort Berthold College Center New Town, North Dakota	X	X	X	X	X
Haskell Indian Junior College Lawrence, Kansas		X			X
Hehaka Sapa College at D-Q University Davis, California	X	X	X	X	X
Institute of American Indian Arts Santa Fe, New Mexico		X			X

Institution	AIHEC Membership[a]	Indian Colleges in U.S.[b]	AACTE[c]	AIHEC Testimony[d]	AIPRC[e]
*Inupiat University of Arctic Barrow, Alaska	X	X		X	X
Kuskokwim Community College Bethel, Alaska		X			
Little Bighorn Community College Crow Agency, Montana				X	
Little Hoop Community College Fort Totten, North Dakota	X	X		X	
Lummi School of Aquaculture Lummi Island, Washington		X			
Native American Educational Services Chicago, Illinois		X			
Navajo Community College Tsaile, Arizona	X	X	X	X	X
Navajo Community College Branch Shiprock, New Mexico	X			X	X
Northwest Community College Nome, Alaska		X			
Oglala Sioux Community College Pine Ridge, South Dakota	X	X		X	X
Ojibwa College Bemidji, Minnesota		X			
Salish-Kootenai Community College Roman, Montana	X				
*Sheldon Jackson College Sitka, Alaska				X	

Institution	AIHEC Membership[a]	Indian Colleges in U.S.[b]	AACTE[c]	AIHEC Testimony[d]	AIPRC[e]
Sinte Gleska College Center Rosebud, South Dakota	X	X	X	X	X
Sisseton-Wahpeton Community College Sisseton, South Dakota	X	X	X	X	X
Southwestern Indian Polytechnic Institute Albuquerque, New Mexico		X			X
Standing Rock Community College Fort Yates, North Dakota	X	X	X	X	X
Tanana Chiefs Land Claim College Fairbanks, Alaska		X			
Turtle Mountain Community College Belcourt, North Dakota	X	X	X	X	X

* Inupiat University and Sheldon Jackson College are baccalaureate institutions.

[a] AIHEC, 1978.

[b] Chavers, 1979.

[c] Thompson, ed., 1978, Appendix III.

[d] Nichols, 1979.

[e] Report on Indian Education, 1976, Table 6, Appendix M.

Key: AIHEC—American Indian Higher Education Consortium.
   AACTE—American Association of Colleges for Teacher Education.
   AIPRC—American Indian Policy Review Commission.

munity College (Castro, 1975). The two year system in Hawaii is, in effect, a network of Asian institutions.

Ethnic institutions have emerged as alternatives to the mainstream educational system, which is perceived by minority communities as being unresponsive to their students' needs. As argued earlier in this chapter, it is questionable whether the majority of institutions have evidenced commitment to access for minority students, or whether the schools into which they have access are funded equitably. If a case of first impressions can be made suggesting a systemic lack of access and inequitable distribution, the burden of proving otherwise would fall upon those policy makers and educators who administer postsecondary educational institutions. Additional evidence toward such a case is presented in the second half of this chapter, an examination of student characteristics.

Student Characteristics

The first half of this chapter examined in detail patterns of minority student enrollments and characteristics of the institutions in which these students enrolled. Alternative definitions of access were proposed, incorporating a corollary component of distribution. By these criteria, the data reported unmistakable findings of maldistribution throughout the system and skewness toward urban public two year institutions. The clearest evidence of this maldistribution was the disproportionately large number of minority full-time students who gain access into two year nonresidential institutions, and that these institutions received markedly lower per capita appropriations and subsidies than did senior institutions. Additionally, it was noted that a small percentage of institutions was enrolling the bulk of these students, creating the illusion of representative access in the aggregate. This half of chapter two examines the members of educational institutions, notably students. Racial and ethnic student data are presented, if available, by institutional type. Specific studies of two year student retention and attrition are examined, as are available results of ongoing longitudinal student research.

Several cautions are in order. First, the concerns about data expressed in chapter one are more appropriate to student data than to institutional data. The major federally sponsored student survey is the National Longitudinal Study of High School Seniors (NLS) and its follow-up studies. By definition, the study charts the educational plans and progress of students over time. Inherent in this type of research and similar private sector research, e.g., the American Council on Education/Co-operative Institutional Research Program (ACE/CIRP), is the attrition in sample size over the time period. This attrition causes peculiar difficulties in studying minority populations within the sample (Astin, in Abramowitz, ed., 1976). Second, with few exceptions, the major research on students has been conducted in senior institutions and on majority students; no large-scale study of racial and ethnic minority students in two year institutions has been undertaken yet. Third, while senior institutions control their admissions processes, enabling them to screen students with predetermined characteristics, open door institutions enroll any student with basic age or diploma prerequisites. Thus, the range of student abilities (and other characteristics) in two year institutions is likely to be greater than it would be in selective institutions. This makes it easy to generalize, but difficult, if not impossible, to conceptualize student variables. Finally, as noted in the discussion of institutional characteristics, the typology of two year institutions reduces many of them to a single sub-baccalaureate model, when in actuality the institutional environments vary considerably.

These cautions notwithstanding, it is possible to draw important inferences from available student data. Foremost, two year students are more likely than four year students to be members of racial and ethnic minority groups. Table 2-14, an NLS follow-up study, indicates the activity status of 1973 respondents one year after high school graduation. Whereas 47.2% of whites were engaged in some level of study, only 40.3% of blacks and 35.6% of the Hispanics in the sample were students. But these figures do not tell the entire story of college attendance patterns, as several studies from the Center for Social Organization of Schools indicate. These studies, reanalyzing NLS data, found that when whites and blacks had similar family socio-economic status (SES) and academic ability measures, blacks were more likely to attend college than whites (Thomas, Alexander, and Eckland, 1977). When these factors were held constant, the researchers found what they termed a "black advantage in terms of college attendance." The analysis showed that "the higher attendance rates of blacks than whites is largely attributed to the higher performance of blacks on 'school process' measures, the greater level of moral and social support that blacks receive from 'significant others,' and their higher educational expectations" (Thomas, 1977, p. 13). Even with higher attendance rates, however, proportionally fewer blacks (23.8%) and Hispanics (14.5%) attended senior institutions than did whites (28.5%).

These figures support the thesis articulated in the first half of this chapter: minorities have increased their access, but that access has been to two year institutions. Other attendance patterns in Table 2-14 appear to confirm Karabel's (1972) thesis that SES and class distinctions are evidenced in the hierarchical arrangement of institutions. Students from high SES families are far more likely to attend senior than junior institutions or vocational schools. Additional evidence of this economic determination of access follows in Table 2-15, which reports previously unpublished ACE/CIRP data on enrollments and income.

Despite the establishment of new federal financial aid programs since 1972, the gap between the family income of two year students and that of four year students has not closed, which suggests only partial success for attempts to reduce economic restrictions to college attendance. In 1972, the difference between incomes under $15,000 of families with two year students (73.3%) and those of families with university students (50.5%) was 22.8%; by 1976, this gap had narrowed only to 21.2%. The effect of federal and state programs upon this gap remains unknown. Need-based programs, theoretically, would be weighted toward low SES families, a disproportionate number of which are minority; a recent study of financial aid packaging noted that federal policies favored low income and minority families (Wagner and Rice, 1977, Chapter VI). The study also documented parental contribution percentages, and concluded that minority families contribute higher proportions of educational expenses than do majority families (Chapter VIII). Appendix G includes more detailed data from this study.

Table 2-14, presented earlier, contains NLS data on other student characteristics, including regional factors. The regional findings are of some significance because equality of opportunity is frequently perceived in global, aggregate terms rather than in local or regional contexts. This regional distribution was alluded to in the previous section that analyzed institutional location patterns, where state and metropolitan data showed that minority students were intensely concentrated in a small number of urban two year institutions.

California's extensive public two year system and its large minority population, which includes significant percentages of the four major minority groupings (black, Hispanics, American Indian, Asian), combine to inflate the western proportion of the aggregate (Table 2-14). Analysis of geographical considerations for minority access to postsecondary education (e.g., Richards, Rand, and Rand, 1969; Crain and Mahard, 1978) is beyond the scope of this book, although such analysis is clearly important for determining educational policy. The most obvious conclusion to be drawn from these data is that in the absence of a comprehensive federal policy concerning access, the major actors in establishing equitable access or distribution will be local institutional and state officials.

Two other factors in Table 2-14 have implications for institutional policy makers: high school program emphasis and academic ability. Postsecondary educational institutions are the focus of this chapter, but these two elements, high school curriculum and ability, considered "givens" at the time of application to college, require looking backward into high school preparation and into traditional measures of ability. Without reviewing the extensive literature on desegregation or minority elementary and secondary schooling, it can be suggested that inequality in public K-12 systems results in unequal opportunities and outcomes for a disproportionate number of minority children (U.S. Commission on Civil Rights, 1971; National Assessment of Educational Programs [NAEP], 1977; Crain and Mahard, 1977). These unequal conditions in turn render less precise the usual indices of academic ability, particularly for nontraditional students, whose conceptual skills may be inadequately measured by traditional means of evaluation.

Table 2-14 clearly shows that students in academic (college preparatory) curricula and those with high academic ability are more likely to attend college than are students in vocational or general curricula or those with lower academic ability, measured by grades and class rank. Correspondingly high proportions of vocational students took full-time employment, which, with military service and full-time homemaking,

TABLE 2-14

Activity Status Frequency Distributions (in Percentages) October, 1972

October 1972 Activity Status	All Persons	High School Program			Academic Ability		
		Votech	General	Academic	Low	Medium	High
Total percentage¹	100.0	100.0	100.0	100.0	100.0	100.0	100.0
4-year college only	16.6	2.8	8.3	30.7	4.7	13.3	33.4
4-year college and work	10.8	2.2	5.9	19.3	2.7	8.9	22.2
2-year college only	4.4	2.5	5.0	5.1	3.6	5.2	3.8
2-year college and work	8.5	5.8	7.4	10.7	5.6	10.0	8.8
Votech school only	2.3	2.2	2.4	2.2	2.5	3.1	1.6
Votech school and work	3.1	3.7	3.0	2.8	3.3	3.5	2.5
Other study	0.5	0.6	0.4	0.5	0.3	0.5	0.3
Work full-time only	39.0	59.9	48.2	20.0	55.8	41.3	19.0
Work part-time only	4.4	6.5	5.2	2.7	6.3	4.4	2.6
Military service only	1.7	1.6	2.6	1.1	2.5	1.5	1.0
Homemaker only	4.2	7.0	5.5	1.6	6.3	3.8	2.1
Look for work only	2.1	2.5	2.9	1.3	3.2	1.9	1.0
Other	2.6	2.6	3.1	2.1	3.2	2.6	1.8
Total sample size	20,599	4,922	7,167	8,344	4,147	6,403	3,834

October 1972 Activity Status	Socioeconomic Status			Race/Ethnicity		
	Low	Medium	High	White	Black	Hispanic
Total percentage¹	100.0	100.0	100.0	100.0	100.0	100.0
4-year college only	7.1	13.1	34.1	17.3	14.2	8.2
4-year college and work	5.7	9.8	18.2	11.2	9.6	6.3
2-year college only	3.0	4.6	5.8	4.3	4.7	6.4
2-year college and work	5.4	9.6	9.5	8.6	5.4	10.2

	Male	Female	NE	NC	South	West
Votech school only	2.6	2.4	1.8	2.2	2.8	2.4
Votech school and work	3.1	3.7	1.7	3.1	3.3	1.8
Other study	0.4	0.6	0.4	0.5	0.3	0.3
Work full-time only	50.6	41.4	20.2	39.1	37.1	43.1
Work part-time only	5.5	4.8	2.9	4.1	5.9	6.3
Military service only	2.6	1.7	0.7	1.5	3.1	2.5
Homemaker only	7.1	4.1	1.3	4.1	4.3	5.7
Look for work only	3.8	1.8	1.1	1.6	5.3	3.8
Other	3.1	2.5	2.2	2.4	4.0	3.0
Total sample size	6,133	9,354	4,611	14,831	2,559	819

October 1972 Activity Status	Sex		Region (High School Location)			
	Male	Female	NE	NC	South	West
Total percentage[1]	100.0	100.0	100.0	100.0	100.0	100.0
4-year college only	17.6	15.7	19.9	16.3	16.2	12.7
4-year college and work	11.1	10.4	11.9	11.7	10.2	8.4
2-year college only	4.3	4.5	4.2	2.6	4.4	7.9
2-year college and work	9.6	7.3	7.2	7.4	7.2	14.4
Votech school only	1.7	2.9	2.8	2.3	2.0	1.9
Votech school and work	3.4	2.7	3.0	4.1	2.9	1.8
Other study	0.4	0.5	0.5	0.6	0.3	0.4
Work full-time only	42.0	36.1	37.3	40.7	41.9	34.0
Work part-time only	2.9	5.8	3.9	4.9	3.7	5.4
Military service only	3.2	0.2	1.3	1.7	1.9	1.9
Homemaker only	0.0	8.2	3.4	3.9	4.7	4.8
Look for work only	1.6	2.6	2.0	1.6	2.3	2.6
Other	2.1	3.0	2.6	2.1	2.3	3.8
Total sample size	10,072	10,489	4,353	5,363	7,365	3,518

Source: Fetters et al., 1977, Table 3.

[1] Details may not add to 100.0 because of rounding.

TABLE 2-15

**Enrollments by Family and Median Income (in Percentages)
1972–76**

Type of Institution	Total Percent	$0–4,000	$4,000–10,000	$10,000–15,000	$15,000–20,000	$20,000–25,000	$25,000 and Over	Median Income Constant $ (1972)
1972								
2-year	100.0	11.6	30.2	31.5	12.6	6.3	7.9	$11,126
4-year	100.0	7.0	22.5	29.4	15.7	9.5	14.9	13,153
University	100.0	3.4	17.6	29.5	17.0	12.2	20.3	14,908
1974								
2-year	100.0	9.1	22.8	31.5	14.3	10.3	12.2	11,056
4-year	100.0	6.8	18.8	26.4	15.6	11.9	20.4	12,559
University	100.0	3.6	14.0	26.2	17.0	14.0	25.2	14,419
1976								
2-year	100.0	8.3	18.5	26.3	17.3	12.4	17.1	10,635
4-year	100.0	5.9	14.8	22.3	17.1	13.7	26.3	11,777
University	100.0	3.2	9.8	18.9	17.2	15.6	35.3	14,911

Source: Unpublished ACE/CIRP data; CEEB staff calculations.

form the major alternatives to enrolling in school. Further, it is not assumed that everyone will want to attend college. If no disproportionate racial impact occurs *before* application to college, measures of curricular track or academic ability are appropriate indices if they reveal no systemic inequalities that would preclude minority access to higher education.*

In controversial educational issues, racial and ethnic patterns emerge when one looks beneath the surface. In the case of academic ability, however defined or measured, these patterns usually emerge in the context of the need to maintain "standards" in what is perceived to be an egalitarian system of access to higher education. In an operational sense, these patterns arise in the context of attempts to match students with institutions. Thus, there is a logic in the use of indices that will measure, in Astin's terms, "dropout proneness" (Astin, 1975b).

In a literature with little universal agreement, one near-universal predictor of college attendance and retention stands out: academic ability. Engin Holstrom's study of low achievers concluded that students with low high school grades (C+ or lower) are less likely to graduate from college than are students with greater academic ability (Holstrom, 1973). Astin concludes, "By far the greatest predictive factor is the student's past academic record and academic ability" (Astin, 1975b, p. 45) Thomas *et al.* (1977) reached similar conclusions concerning the use of high school grades to predict college success.

Measurements of academic ability are crucial, though not perfectly understood determinants of minority access to and distribution within higher educational institutions; however, the methods of measuring or testing ability require analysis, even for open door, noncompetitive admissions practices.** Comparative measures of school achievement are problematic for several reasons, yet comparative indices such as testing, rank in class, and curricular program track are frequently employed by admissions personnel to determine access to the more selective institutions of postsecondary education.

Thomas' findings, while confirming the utility of measuring academic ability, challenge overreliance upon quantifiable indices:

> . . . the prime role of curriculum, class rank, educational expec-
> tations and to a lesser extent 'significant others' in mediating the
> direct influence of structural background variables (i.e., SES,
> mental ability, race and sex) on college attendance implies that
> currently the internal stratification processes within the schools,

---

* For a discussion of black high school eligibility pools, see ISEP, 1976, pp. 28-38.
** As chapter four notes, admission to two year programs, particularly choice technical curricula, has been quite competitive in some institutions.

coupled with students' educational goal orientations and to a lesser extent 'significant others,' may be more influential in directly affecting various educational outcomes than [are] external societal stratification processes. . . . For race differences, both expectations and curriculum placement were more influential in affecting white attendance than black attendance (Thomas, 1977, p. 22).

Thomas suggests research into normative school structures and other environmental variables to understand college attendance patterns. Her analysis, however, does not differentiate between mere access and distribution; therefore, access at all levels is treated similarly, despite the demonstrably dissimilar opportunities to be gained from access at different levels.

Crain and Mahard's work—like Thomas' research, derived from NLS data—distinguishes among levels of the system and between North and South as regional variables. After documenting a strong relationship between grades, class rank, and attendance at a senior institution, they note:

It is widely recognized that high school grades are an important predictor of college performance. However, it is this very reliance upon grades which seems to explain why black students from predominantly white schools do not have more of an advantage over blacks who attend predominantly black schools. A lower relative class standing for blacks in white schools operates directly to reduce their chances of attending and surviving in college. Class rank also affects black college outcomes indirectly. Poor grades mean two year colleges and no scholarships. Obviously, to boost black college attendance and survival rates we have to find a way around the problem of class rank (Crain and Mahard, 1977, p. 88).

The authors go on to suggest that black counselors play a major role in influencing black college attendance and retention, a point that is reiterated in chapter three. The authors' contributions to an understanding of two year college minority enrollment patterns are in their suggestion that comparative measures of academic ability have regional context or validity, and that institutional type is a major variable in persistence.*

This detailed analysis of two year student characteristics, particularly minority student characteristics, is necessary as a transition to considerations of persistence and retention, the final focus of this chapter.

---

* For a study of Hispanic student achievement and drop-out proneness, see Iwamoto et al., 1976.

Discussions of high attrition rates in two year colleges, indeed in all of higher education, resemble the chicken-and-egg argument: do two year colleges cause dropouts, or do dropout-prone students gravitate toward two year institutions? A large school of thought disdains questions of failure or the negative value judgment normally attached to dropping out. Brawer, for instance, feels that the concept of attrition is misunderstood: "Indeed, the premises themselves are in error. A system that judges its worth by its 'finished products' and a society that views certification as evidence of knowledge—these are the causes of the 'dropout problem.' If education were viewed in other ways, the problems would disappear. Indeed, the idea of viewing students as 'input' and 'output' of an educational system is offensive—both in principle and practice" (Brawer, 1973, p. 20).

If one were to grant Brawer her thesis—and it is an entirely plausible and noble defense of education as a societal good and as an end in itself—it is still necessary to investigate institutional characteristics that facilitate persistence. ACE/CIRP data on the impact of the type of institution upon retention suggest that the chances of freshmen persisting are greatly improved when they attend senior institutions (Chickering, 1974). Astin notes that attendance by baccalaureate-aspiring students at a two year college reduces their chances of completing the degree by 12% (Astin, 1975a, Table 3-1). He attributes much of the lowered likelihood of completion to the lack of residential facilities at two year colleges, problems inherent in transferring to a four year school, and reduced opportunities for financial assistance (Astin, 1975b).

When one analyzes the disproportionately high concentration of minority full-time students in two year institutions (Table 2-11), the systemic nature of the maldistribution becomes clear: for whatever reasons, minorities are overwhelmingly enrolled in the tier in which fewest students persist. The available data on minority student undergraduate degree patterns—associate, technical, or baccalaureate—allow only one reasonable inference: by quantifiable indices, minority students do not fare as well as do majority students.

That two year colleges may be a systemic barrier to quantifiably demonstrable minority parity is illustrated by the following:

Chicano college freshmen have a somewhat greater chance of dropping out than do white students or even other ethnic minorities. A closer inspection of the data, however, reveals that this difference is entirely attributable to the heavy concentration of Chicanos in community colleges. Among community college students, Chicanos have the same probability of dropping out as do other students. Among students entering four year colleges and universities, the drop-out rate among Chicanos is actually slightly less than the drop-out rate for other students. These differences dramatize how the demography of Chicanos can affect their subsequent educational attainment (Astin, in Perez, ed., 1977, p. 17).

To a greater or lesser extent, the same is true of other minority groups. But demography alone cannot explain disparities in educational access; regional data show variations in patterns far more complex than would be evidenced merely by demographic factors.

In an attempt to understand these patterns of retention and their implications for minority students, the final section of this chapter examines in more detail the NLS data and analyzes research findings concerning persistence and withdrawal. Tables 2-16 through 2-19 report NLS data, which, unfortunately, have limited utility for judging racial and ethnic patterns. The group of minority students in the NLS sample is small, and the follow-up studies, while more useful for understanding aggregate patterns of persistence, are to be interpreted cautiously for inferences about minorities.

Aggregate patterns of persistence reduce complex motivations to numbers. NLS data, for example, indicate that by 1974, attrition had begun to take its toll upon the high school class of 1972 that attended college: 7% of those who had entered senior institutions and 6% of those who enrolled in two year institutions had dropped out of college. These figures, when adjusted for college attendance rates by type of institution, reveal that within two years, the four year class had shrunk by 23% and the two year class by 39%. Transfers further complicate the persistence patterns, as many students transfer between institutional types and among colleges within each type (Willingham, 1972; Menacker, 1975; Brimm and Achilles, 1976). Despite ambiguity inherent in the complex transfer patterns, two trends are clear in Table 2-16: students with high ability and aptitude persist, transfer upward (two to four year institutions), and graduate in rates higher than those for lower ability students; and students with higher aspirations tend to persist, transfer upward, and graduate in rates higher than those of students with lower aspirations.

The aggregate patterns tend to homogenize the internal data, for it is clear that dropping out, like enrolling, is a simple activity that results from complex motivations and conditions. For instance, studies have found that dropouts and persisters frequently resemble each other statistically, and that characteristics of both groups may be virtually identical (Pandey, 1973). Measures of alienation or noninvolvement often have limited value in identifying dropout-proneness (Brawer, 1973; Morgan, 1974; Astin, 1975b; Baumgart and Johnstone, 1977). National Longitudinal Study data, from disaggregated findings that

TABLE 2-16

Persistence Rates for 1972 Freshmen

Characteristics of Students	Number in Sample	Percentage Distribution, by Enrollment Status in 1974				
		Total	Persister	4 → 4 Transfer	4 → 2 Transfer	Dropout
4-Year College Freshmen in 1972						
Aptitude						
Low	368	100.0	37.71	15.32	3.54	43.43
Middle	1,627	100.0	53.10	14.96	3.92	28.02
High	2,274	100.0	63.48	17.31	2.62	16.60
Educational aspiration						
Less than college	211	100.0	12.57	4.89	4.06	78.47
2-year college	146	100.0	21.14	5.39	8.27	65.20
4-year college or beyond	5,478	100.0	60.27	16.78	3.03	19.91

Characteristics of Students	Number in Sample	Percentage Distribution, by Enrollment Status in 1974					
		Total	2 → 4 Transfer	Graduate	Persister	2 → 2 Transfer	Dropout
2-Year College Freshmen in 1972							
Aptitude							
Low	441	100.0	13.91	8.58	19.02	5.68	52.80
Middle	1,091	100.0	22.37	13.54	20.89	4.68	38.52
High	517	100.0	35.91	14.30	17.75	2.18	29.87
Educational aspiration							
Less than college	443	100.0	4.44	15.33	10.65	2.38	67.20
2-year college	473	100.0	8.36	24.76	17.85	4.92	44.12
4-year college or beyond	1,928	100.0	33.42	9.41	22.00	4.26	30.91

Source: U.S. Department of Health, Education, and Welfare, National Center for Education Statistics, National Longitudinal Study of the High School Class of 1972, *Transfer Students in Institutions of Higher Education.*

TABLE 2-17

Total Percentage of Withdrawal, by Sex and Race, of Persons Entering College Fall, 1973

Type of Withdrawal	Male			Female		
	Black	Hispanic	White	Black	Hispanic	White
4-Year College						
Total	27.03	27.90	22.66	27.40	21.20	23.93
Academic withdrawal	5.88	4.45	6.18	6.76	4.81	3.99
Nonacademic withdrawal	21.15	23.45	16.47	20.64	16.39	19.94
Number of students	294	88	2,769	453	75	2,476
2-Year College						
Total	53.60	47.11	38.72*	43.77	43.36	37.81
Academic withdrawal	6.28	12.67	6.33	6.85	5.06	4.53
Nonacademic withdrawal	47.32	34.44	32.39*	36.92	38.30	33.28
Number of students	145	110	1,405	214	100	1,238

Source: National Center for Education Statistics, Withdrawal From Institutions of Higher Education, National Longitudinal Study, 1977.

* The percentage for blacks was significantly greater than that for whites ($|Z| > 2.33$, $p < .01$).

analyze withdrawal, suggest that different groups of students are motivated to leave school for different reasons.

In each case, except for Hispanic females in senior institutions, white persistence surpasses minority persistence.* Persistence patterns in four year colleges do not reveal statistically significant racial and ethnic differences, although minorities (except Hispanic women) cite nonacademic reasons for withdrawal more frequently than do majority students. Minority male students give academic rationales for withdrawal less frequently than do majority men.

The persistence patterns in two year colleges, however, show very different results. Withdrawal rates for females do not vary significantly; however, black and Hispanic male rates of retention do vary significantly, though in different patterns from each other. Black men cite nonacademic reasons nearly 50% more often than do majority men. Hispanic males more closely resemble the majority; however, the academic

---

* The Hispanic female persistence pattern, if accurate, corroborates Munoz and Garcia-Bahne's finding (1978) that Mexican-American women encounter significant stress in college, but cope with the stress better than do Mexican-American men.

withdrawal rates for Hispanic men is double that for majority males, which were close to black male percentages. These findings, tentative though they may be, suggest that different groups may require different retention strategies.

TABLE 2-18

Withdrawals and Reentry Patterns
1974

Reason Cited[a] for Withdrawal	*Percent Citing Reason*	
	4-Year College	*2-Year College*
Nonacademic Withdrawal[b]		
Financial difficulties	32	25
Marriage	28	14
Desire to get practical experience	28	35
School work not relevant	21	17
Offered a good job	16	33
Other	47	49
Academic Withdrawals		
Failing or not doing well	87	82
Courses too hard	25	21
Desire to get practical experience	42	30
Financial difficulties	38	32
School work not relevant	28	20
Offered a good job	23	22
Other	33	31

Type of Institution Reentered	*Reentry Rate (in Percents)*			
	Academic Withdrawal		*Nonacademic Withdrawal*	
	4-Year College	*2-Year College*	*4-Year College*	*2-Year College*
4-year college	18	3	28	6
2-year college	5	15	5	13
Total	23	18	33	19

Source: NCES, "Self-Reported," 1977.

[a] Respondents were allowed to indicate more than one reason for withdrawal, so percentages may not be added.

[b] Nonacademic withdrawals are defined as those who had a self-reported GPA of C or better and who gave no indication of academic reasons (failing or not doing well or courses too hard) for withdrawal on the survey questionnaire.

Academic and nonacademic withdrawal patterns suggest that attrition has many causes. Tables 2-18 and 2-19 convey in more detail self-reported reasons for withdrawal, showing patterns in withdrawal rates that vary by institutional type. A notable feature in these findings is the extent to which nonacademic reasons overshadow academic withdrawal reasons: in four year colleges, the rate is two to one; in two year colleges, it is four to one (NCES, "Self-Reported," 1977, p. 1). In actuality, the reasons for withdrawal are unlikely to be as discrete as implied by the NLS data, even allowing for the nonadditive nature of the questionnaire. However, patterns emerge that reflect the different purposes for which students enter four and two year institutions.

In nonacademic withdrawals, employment considerations appeared to influence two year students more than they did four year students; job offers and the desire to get practical experience more frequently influenced two year students. Financial difficulties and marriage more frequently caused dropout for four year than for two year students, a surprising finding in light of the poor availability of financial aid in two year institutions (Table 2-10; Gladieux, 1975). Table 2-19 gives evidence that adequate financial aid increases the likelihood of college persistence for recipient students, particularly for minority students.* For those who withdrew for academic reasons, a different pattern emerged; a larger percentage of four year students expressed vocational and practical concerns. Forty-two percent of the four year students cited the desire to get practical experience as a reason for leaving, while thirty percent of the two year students expressed the same reason. Not surprisingly, over 80% of both student groups cited failing grades or poor academic work as their reason for withdrawing.

It was clear from earlier tables (e.g., Table 2-16) and from research that persistence, ostensibly static, is actually a dynamic process involving transfers across and within institutional types and "stopping-out," attendance on an intermittent basis. Table 2-18 shows re-entry data that form several patterns. First, students who leave and return are likely to return to the same type of institution, whether they left for academic or nonacademic reasons. Second, students who leave senior institutions are more likely to return than are students who leave two year institutions. Third, the type of student most likely to return after having left school is the student who leaves a senior institution for a nonacademic reason. These findings suggest the importance of exit interviews with students who withdraw, so that the reasons for withdrawal can be identified and the students advised on re-entry procedures.

---

* In this table, only black students are reported. Wagner and Rice's (1977) findings suggest that similar retention patterns could be expected for other minority aid recipients as well.

TABLE 2-19

Total Withdrawal Rate[1] and Graduation Rate for 2-Year College Students[2]
1974

| Student Characteristic | Total Withdrawal Rate[3] | | | | Graduation Rate for 2-Year College Students | |
| | 4-Year College Students | | 2-Year College Students | | | |
	Aided	Not Aided	Aided	Not Aided	Aided	Not Aided
Ability						
Low	37.0 (26.5)	53.4 (44.9)	53.1 (40.6)	63.3 (54.8)	11.0	4.1
Middle	26.0 (19.6)	35.1 (27.7)	39.3 (33.7)	47.8 (40.9)	21.3	11.7
High	14.4 (11.1)	21.6 (17.2)	18.6 (15.1)	43.2 (37.7)	31.3	16.2
Race						
White	20.9 (15.6)	29.0 (22.5)	34.0 (25.5)	49.1 (42.4)	25.5	12.2
Black	24.4 (18.4)	46.2 (37.5)	43.5 (33.5)	67.1 (58.0)	11.0	4.1
Educational aspirations						
Vocational-technical school	73.3 (53.0)	79.9 (66.3)	62.8 (48.4)	79.5 (69.9)	13.1	5.1
2-year college	53.8 (45.3)	74.1 (51.8)	60.0 (44.4)	60.4 (51.7)	20.7	10.7
4-year college	25.8 (19.9)	30.9 (25.2)	34.5 (29.3)	41.8 (35.5)	24.2	11.3
Graduate school	14.9 (10.9)	20.2 (15.0)	21.6 (16.0)	36.0 (30.8)	22.7	15.7
Socioeconomic status						
Low	30.8 (22.8)	52.6 (43.0)	46.7 (38.7)	64.3 (56.3)	15.8	6.4
Middle	22.6 (16.7)	37.5 (30.2)	34.5 (29.3)	55.1 (46.6)	25.0	10.4
High	14.4 (10.9)	22.2 (16.4)	25.0 (17.3)	38.6 (33.3)	22.6	13.8

Source: National Center for Education Statistics, *The Condition of Education*, 1978 Edition, Table 3.14.

[1] Percentage of those in a given enrollment and financial aid status, who have withdrawn.

[2] Includes those attending college in 1972 or 1973, but not in 1974.

[3] Includes those who withdrew for academic and nonacademic reasons. Figures in parentheses are nonacademic withdrawal rate; subtracting these figures from the ones preceding them will give academic withdrawal rates for that subgroup.

Focus upon re-entry patterns must not obscure the considerable wastage inherent in minority attrition. The fact that large numbers of majority students also withdraw from college is no solace, for minority groups have not yet achieved equal opportunities, and dropping out— even at majority attrition levels—would cause minority groups to fall farther behind. Nor can the promise of adult and continuing education, an increasing concern within postsecondary education, be expected to provide access for previously excluded minority adults; data on adult education show that minority enrollments in these programs have declined from 9% of the aggregate in 1969 to 8% in 1975 (Boaz, 1978). Therefore, unless major changes in minority access to adult education occur, educators may not expect this sector of postsecondary education to provide learning alternatives for minorities.

As long as two year colleges continue to be the major point of entry for minority students, retention in these institutions and transfer to senior institutions must be high priorities for policy makers concerned with equalizing opportunities. Astin has summarized intervention strategies aimed at involving students in institutional activities; unfortunately, many of these activities are nonexistent in commuter, nonresidential institutions (including most public two year colleges):

> If ways can be found to involve students more in the life and environment of the institution, their chances of staying in college are improved. A number of mechanisms are available to most institutions to bring about student participation: academic programs, admissions, freshman orientation, counseling and advisement, financial aid, work opportunities, extracurricular activities, and housing and student services (Astin 1975b, p. 148).

Other writers, acknowledging the need to involve students in the institutional environment, have suggested additional ways to do so. These methods include reorganizing the administrative and governance structure to reduce incongruency between the students and their community (Alfred, 1975), diagnosing dropout proneness and advising students more competently than they are advised now (Brawer, 1973), and concentrating more institutional resources upon comprehensive counseling and remedial instruction programs (Moore, 1970; 1976a).

Whether one views two year institutions as tracking systems or as appropriate means of access, it is evident that public two year colleges enroll the largest concentration of minority students. Further, whether one views college attrition as normal and healthy or as wastage, large numbers of minority students are withdrawing from college and not taking associate or baccalaureate degrees.

The maldistribution of minority students poses questions beyond mere access, including what access is accorded minority students, and what practices could improve the quality of education in the institutions now affording access. To this end, chapter three examines personnel practices in two year institutions, and chapter four examines enrollment patterns and student services.

Chapter 3

Teaching Faculty, Trustees, and Administrators

༪ ༪ ༪

Several commonly held assumptions about two year college personnel require closer scrutiny. These views, widely accepted by educators and researchers, include presumptions about competence, professional direction, and representation of personnel in two year colleges *vis-à-vis* personnel in baccalaureate and graduate institutions. The myths include:

1. Two year faculty are more representative of racial and ethnic minority populations than are their four year counterparts.

2. Two year trustees are more representative of racial and ethnic minority populations than are their four year counterparts.

3. Two year administrators are more representative of racial and ethnic minority populations than are their four year counterparts.

Inquiry into these statements dictates two strategies, one essentially quantitative and the other, qualitative. Analysis of available research studies of two year college faculty demographics leads inescapably to the conclusion that racial and ethnic minorities fare no better in these institutions than they do in upper level college faculties; indeed, in proportion to minority enrollments in two year colleges, minority faculty are even more poorly represented in two year colleges than in upper level institutions. Qualitative data on the teaching ability and predilections of two year faculty are less dramatic, but appear neither to confirm nor deny the assumption that two year faculty members are better teachers than baccalaureate or graduate faculty members. This chapter analyzes the major research on faculty conducted since 1970, with particular attention paid to data containing racial and ethnic compositions of two year faculty. Additionally, the chapter analyzes administrative and trustee data, similarly noting minority underrepresentation at these levels of decision making.

Faculty

It must be noted that research on college faculty is scanty; in many cases, this dearth of original research data leads to frequent re-citing of the relatively few national studies. Similarly, racial and ethnic data on graduate enrollments have only recently become a scholarly concern as federal legislation mandating affirmative action guidelines necessitated more complete and reliable data. The National Board of Graduate Education (NBGE), while deploring the inadequacies of such enrollment and degree data, noted that 1970 was the year in which data on minority education began to be collected systematically (NBGE, 1976, p. 42–51). Racial and ethnic data on doctoral recipients were not collected until 1973, when the National Research Council redesigned its Survey of Earned Doctorates questionnaire to reflect self-reported racial and ethnic status.

In 1969, the Carnegie Commission on the Future of Higher Education and the American Council on Education sponsored a national survey of faculty members that, for all practical purposes, was the benchmark study of American college and university faculty, including minority faculty (Bayer, 1970). The institutions were selected and weighted to render respondents' answers to the twelve-page questionnaire "applicable to the entire population of institutions of higher education" (Bayer, 1970, p. 3; see also Creager, 1968). The racial and ethnic data, self-reported by respondents, are reported in Table 3-2. It should be noted that the senior colleges included several large historically black institutions that made the aggregate appear to be more integrated than it was. Even so, two year colleges had the lowest proportion of minority faculty.

In 1970, the year Bayer reported his findings (which showed 1.6% minority faculty in two year colleges), AACJC sponsored a study of minority students, faculty, and programming in its 1,091 two year institutions (Goodrich et al., 1972/73). The findings indicated a more diverse faculty in two year institutions than had the Bayer study.

The apparent percentage increase in two year college minority faculty from 1969 to 1970 (1.6% to 5.0%) almost certainly reflected differences

TABLE 3-1

Recent National Faculty Research Conducted Including 2-Year Faculty

Date Published	Author (Sponsoring Agency)	Date Conducted
	Research Containing Racial/Ethnic Data	
1970	Bayer (ACE)	1969
1972/73	Goodrich et al. (AACJC)	1970
1973	Bushnell (Project FOCUS)	1970–71
[1977]	Goodrich (unpublished)	1971–72
1973	Bayer (ACE)	1972–73
1974	Moore and Wagstaff (Ohio State)	1972–73
1974	Bayer (ACE) in Change	1972–73
1976	Moore in ACCJCJ	1972–73
1976	Freeman (reanalysis of ACE data)	1969, 1972
1977	Cohen and Brawer	1975
	Research Not Containing Racial/Ethnic Data	
1973	Baldridge et al. (SPAG) in JHE	1971
1977	Baldridge et al. (SPAG) in JHE	1971
1975	Carnegie Council	1974–75
1975	Cartter and Salter (NBGE)	1974
[1976]	NEA in Fact Book	1975–76
[1976]	NCES, HEGIS in Fact Book	1972, 1975
[1976]	AAUP in Fact Book	1970, 1975
1978	Tuckman and Vogler (AAUP)	1977

in reporting rather than major breakthroughs in minority hiring practices. Goodrich did not report Asian faculty, although Bayer had found .5% of minority two year faculty to be Asian. However, the Goodrich· study did include Hispanics (separate entries for Chicanos and Puerto Ricans) and American Indians; the Bayer study did not. These groups constituted over 25% of the minority faculty in two year institutions in 1970.

Another AACJC-sponsored study conducted in 1970–71, Project Focus, reported dissimilar minority faculty data (Bushnell, 1973). The dissimilarities in the racial and ethnic distribution of two year faculty are interesting inasmuch as the Goodrich et al. project surveyed all AACJC member institutions (with a 63% return rate), while Bushnell's Project Focus employed weighting and sampling techniques in its survey of 92 AACJC member institutions, and eliminated branch campuses of baccalaureate-granting colleges. Further, it was narrowed to include only the continental forty-eight states, certainly reducing figures for Puerto Ricans (not separately listed), and Asian-Americans, groups

TABLE 3-2

Minority Faculty By Percentage
1968–69

Race	All Institutions			2-Year			4-Year			Universities		
	Male	Female	Total	Male	Female	Total	Male	Female	Total	Male	Female	Total
White	96.6	94.7	96.3	99.1	96.7	98.4	94.2	91.3	93.5	97.7	97.7	97.7
Black	1.8	3.9	2.2	.5	1.4	.7	4.2	7.4	5.0	.4	1.0	.5
Oriental	1.3	1.1	1.3	.2	1.4	.5	1.2	.9	1.2	1.6	1.0	1.6
Other	.3	.3	.3	.2	.5	.3	.4	.3	.4	.3	.2	.3
Total minority			3.7			1.6			6.5			2.3

Source: Bayer, 1970.

TABLE 3-3

Minority Faculty Status in 2-Year Institutions
1970–71

Race/Ethnicity	Full-Time		Part-Time		Total	
	Number	Percent of Total	Number	Percent of Total	Total	Percent of Total
White	43,328	95.6	24,854	94.1	68,292	95.0
Black	1,451	3.2	1,117	4.2	2,568	3.6
Chicano	385	.8	365	1.4	740	1.0
Puerto Rican	43	.1	20	.1	63	.1
American Indian	129	.3	51	.2	180	.3
		[4.4]		[5.9]		[5.0]
Total Faculty	45,436		26,407		71,843	

Source: Goodrich et al., 1972/73, Table 6.

Note: Bracketed figures are ISEP calculations.

which would have surfaced had the report been calibrated to recognize these identities or had the questionnaire been administered to AACJC faculty in Alaska, Hawaii, and Puerto Rico.

While differences in the reporting options and survey techniques obviously account for dissimilarities in the two AACJC-sponsored projects, full-time faculty aggregate percentages for the three comparable racial and ethnic groups reported in both studies are almost equal.* Goodrich et al. reported that 4.3% of the respondent full-time faculty members were either black (3.2%), Chicano (.8%), or American Indian (.3%). Bushnell's data reported 4.2% for the same three groups: black (1.7%), Chicano (1.4%), and American Indian (1.1%). These comparisons indicate, if anything, an arbitrariness in racial and ethnic data collection that calls for care in making inferences from such data.

Goodrich, in a second survey of AACJC membership, documented a slight decline in the number of minority faculty the following year, 1971 (Goodrich, 1977). In his follow-up study, with a 69% return rate, he solicited information in terms of primarily teaching and nonteaching rather than full-time or part-time faculty. He also included "American Oriental" as a category, absent from his 1970–71 survey.

What is particularly striking, given the increased response rate, is the decline in reported minority faculty as a percentage of total faculty in each case, and a decline in real numbers in every case but black faculty.

---

* Project Focus data were also analyzed in another AACJC report (Gleazer, 1973).

TABLE 3-4

Racial/Ethnic Breakdown of Full-Time 2-Year Faculty, by Academic and Occupational Appointment (in Percentages) 1970–71

Race/Ethnicity	Academic	Occupational	Unclassified	Total
White	92.0	93.5	83.8	92.1
Black	1.7	.9	1.3	1.5
American Indian	1.1	.3	3.4	1.0
Mexican/Spanish American	1.4	.8	5.5	1.4
Oriental American	.8	1.6	2.1	1.0
Other Minority	1.3	1.2	1.3	1.3*
Not responding	1.7	1.6	2.5	1.7
Weighted N in thousands	48.4	15.5	2.4	66.3

Source: Bushnell, 1973, Table 2.24; ISEP Staff calculations.

* Reported Minority Total: 4.9.

TABLE 3-5

Racial/Ethnic Breakdown of 2-Year Teaching and Non-Teaching Minority Faculty 1971–72

Race/Ethnicity	Minority Teaching Faculty		Minority Non-Teaching Faculty		Total Minority Faculty	
	Number	Percent of AACJC	Number	Percent of AACJC	Number	Percent of AACJC
Black	2,330	2.6	449	.5	2,779	3.1
Mexican American	610	.6	114	.1	724	.8
Puerto Rican	40	.04	9	.01	49	.05
American Indian	112	.1	29	.03	141	.1
American Oriental	398	.4	63	.07	461	.5
Total	3,490	3.9	664	.7	4,154	4.7

Source: Goodrich, 1977, Table 9.

Note: Total AACJC faculty from respondent institutions: 87,880. Data from Junior College Directory, 1972.

The increase in aggregate faculty size in AACJC institutions from 1970 to 1971 (71,843 to 87,880)* occurred at a time when affirmative action policies were being initiated and when minority graduate enrollments were increasing (NBGE, 1976; National Research Council, 1977), which would lead one to expect an increase not only in numbers of minority faculty, but in percentages of total faculty as well. Yet Goodrich's previously unreported data reveal the opposite, as this figure** shows.

	1970–71		1971–72	
Race	Number	Percent	Number	Percent
Black	2,568	3.6	2,779	3.1
Chicano	740	1.0	724	.8
Puerto Rican	63	.1	49	.05
American Indian	180	.3	141	.1
American Oriental	N/A		461	.5

A follow-up study by Bayer indicated some progress in minority hiring between 1969 and 1972 (Bayer, 1973). His ACE-sponsored research again weighted institutions and sampled faculty in those

TABLE 3-6

Minority Faculty Status in AACJC Institution Sample, by Transfer Area 1971–72

Academic Area	Total Faculty	Minority Faculty	Percentage
Pre-teaching	250	33	13.2
Pre-law	82	8	9.8
Pre-medicine	122	14	11.5
Pre-engineering	91	12	13.2
Business	309	25	8.1
Social Science	762	84	11.0
Math	196	14	7.1
English	343	23	6.7
General Studies	1,416	93	6.6
Total	3,571	306	8.6

Source: Goodrich, 1977, Table 12. (Adjusted for aggregate faculty in respondent institutions.)

* Goodrich reported total faculty only from respondent institutions.
** See Tables 3.3 and 3.5.

TABLE 3-7

**Minority Faculty in AACJC Institutions Sample,
by Occupational Area
1971–72**

Program Area	Total Faculty	Minority Faculty	Percent of Total
Agri. Business	51	0	0
Allied Health	695	65	9.4
Applied Arts	40	0	0
Business and Related (Sales and Secretarial)	823	63	7.7
Engineering Technologies	488	25	5.1
Public Services	251	29	11.6
Total	2,341	162	6.9

Source: Goodrich, 1977, Table 14. (Adjusted for aggregate faculty in respondent institutions.)

institutions; the number of two-year colleges in 1969 was 57, while in 1972, he sampled faculty in 42 two year institutions. In his overview of findings, Bayer cites the slight increase in hiring of blacks and speculates that the incremental gain is due to institutional resistance, insufficient numbers of minority graduate students, or the skewing of minority hiring toward noninstructional staff (Bayer, 1973, p. 14). Minority participation in administrative positions is examined in the final part of this chapter, and this supposed redistribution does not appear to have occurred.

If gathering racial and ethnic data requires sensitivities, reporting such data may require another set of sensitivities. Two reports by Bayer on the 1972–73 ACE survey results illustrate this point. In his August 1973 ACE Research Report, Bayer cited the increase in black faculty (2.2% to 2.9%) and women faculty (19.1% to 20.0%) as modest: "Thus, affirmative action plans designed to increase the proportions of minorities and women on college and university faculties seem to be moving at a slow pace" (Bayer, 1973, p. 14). In a second reporting of the same data, in *Change* magazine, Bayer appeared more optimistic about the increases:

Another item of importance to the academic community is the changing proportion of faculty who were minority group members or women. In 1968–69, 2.2 percent of all college and university faculty were Blacks, and 19.1 percent were women. While their representation among faculties is still meager, relative to their representation in the general population, the *rate* of growth in the

TABLE 3-8

Racial/Ethnic Breakdown of Teaching Faculty in Academe
(in Percentages)
1972–73

Race/Ethnicity	All Institutions			2-Year			4-Year			Universities		
	Male	Female	Total	Male	Female	Total	Male	Female	Total	Male	Female	Total
White	95.1	93.6	94.8	97.1	93.3	96.1	92.1	91.3	91.9	97.0	96.6	96.9
Black	2.4	4.8	2.9	1.3	4.2	2.1	4.6	8.1	5.4	.9	1.2	.9
American Indian	.8	.9	.8	.9	.8	.9	.8	1.1	.8	.7	.6	.7
Oriental	1.4	1.7	1.5	.6	3.3	1.3	1.5	.8	1.4	1.6	1.8	1.6
Chicano	.3	.2	.3	.7	.4	.6	.2	.1	.2	.3	0.0	.2
Puerto Rican	.3	.3	.3	.1	.3	.1	.7	.4	.6	.1	.3	.1
Other	1.5	1.1	1.4	1.3	1.6	1.3	2.1	1.2	1.9	1.1	.6	1.0
Total minority			5.8			5.0			8.4			3.5

Source: Bayer, 1973.

Note: Data exclude "no response."

recruitment of women and Blacks has been substantial over the period. Clearly, some progress has been made in the recruitment of these groups despite the low turnover in college faculties and the allegations that the pool of qualified minorities and women may be limited (Bayer, 1974, p. 50) [emphasis in the original].

Even had the Goodrich follow-up study not shown decreases in both aggregate numbers of minority two year faculty and rates of minority faculty in the two year faculty total, these inconsistent tones used in reporting the same data would have been disturbing. Comparisons of white faculty in Bayer's two studies reveal the extent to which institutions hired minority faculty in the academic years 1968–69 through 1972–73.*

	Percentage of White Faculty					
	All Institutions			*2-Year*		
Year	*Male*	*Female*	*Total*	*Male*	*Female*	*Total*
1968–69	96.6	94.7	96.3	99.1	96.7	98.4
1972–73	95.1	93.6	94.8	97.1	93.3	96.1
Rate of change		(−1.5)			(−2.3)	

	4-Year			*Universities*		
1968–69	94.2	91.3	93.5	97.7	97.7	97.7
1972–73	92.1	91.3	91.9	97.0	96.6	96.9
Rate of change		(−1.6)			(−.8)	

These figures indicate either the "slow pace" (Bayer, 1973) or the "substantial" rate of growth (Bayer, 1974) in black and female faculty hirings over the four years. While this is clearly a half-full or half-empty portrayal, it is unusual to find the same research contrarily characterized by an author.**

It was to such *half-full* or *half-empty* perceptions that William Moore, Jr., and Lonnie Wagstaff addressed their 1974 study, *Black Educators in White Colleges*. Their questionnaire, sent to black professionals identified through college presidents and informal black contacts, was completed by more than 3,000 black faculty members and administrators in white institutions (Moore and Wagstaff, 1974).

---

* See Tables 3-2 and 3-6.

** Bayer's 1972–73 racial and ethnic data exceed 100% in the totals, ranging from 101.4% to 102.4%. With small groups, such totals over 100%, even if rounded, should be noted; each group percentage is slightly inflated as reported.

In their cover letter to faculty, the researchers cited claims by others that the cup was half-full in minority hiring:

> College and university administrators, in predominantly white institutions at all levels, have been announcing significant progress in the recruitment and hiring of black professionals . . . As black professors, we want to find out for ourselves if the claims being made by college and university officials are true . . . (Moore and Wagstaff, 1972 letter to faculty).

In addition to surveying identified black educators, Moore and Wagstaff also polled all predominantly white college presidents to determine whether their institutions employed black faculty members or administrators. In two year colleges 81% percent of the presidents responded to this survey; in four year colleges, 74% of the presidents responded (Moore and Wagstaff, 1974, p. 4).

The results of both these surveys shattered the myth—already called into question by the previous faculty research examined in this chapter—that minority faculty members were more frequently hired in two year institutions than in four year institutions. Because predominantly black institutions were excluded from data, Moore and Wagstaff's study provides the clearest comparison between two year and four year college minority hiring practices, both for faculty and administrators. They concluded that the cup was half-empty.

The data are extremely telling in that they reveal the absence of even token black administrators or faculty in nearly half the two year colleges and nearly a third of the four year institutions (31%). The final column of Table 3-9, a derivative calculation, shows that 49% of two year institutions had at least one black faculty member, and that 65% of four year institutions had one black faculty member. Inasmuch as the study excluded black institutions, it shows the relative position of black faculty in two year colleges to be worse than in four year and graduate institutions.

Moore and Wagstaff also reported the full-time and part-time status of black faculty in their study, noting that less than half of the respondents (42.5%) held full-time, regular faculty appointments. The number of full-time black faculty members in two year institutions totaled 493 (46.8%), while they totaled 897 (40.4%) in four year colleges. In Goodrich et al.'s study of the previous year's two year faculty (Table 3-3), full-time black faculty accounted for 57% of all black faculty in two year colleges.

In examining black faculty in white institutions, Moore and Wagstaff, and Moore in a follow-up report (Moore, 1976), noted that research on black women in higher education has been comparatively scarce. Research on women in higher education is relatively recent (H. Astin, 1969; H. Astin and Bayer, 1972; Bernard, 1964; Kreps, 1971; Rossi and

TABLE 3-9

Predominantly White Institutions Employing Black Faculty or Administrators
1972–73

Type of Institu- tion	Total Re- spondents	Black Faculty and Adminis- trators	No Black Faculty or Ad- min- istrators	Black Faculty, No Black Adminis- trators	Black Adminis- trators, No Black Faculty	At Least One Black Faculty Member
2-year	872	236 (.27)	416 (.48)	192 (.22)	28 (.03)	428 (.49)
4-year	892	439 (.49)	273 (.31)	137 (.15)	43 (.05)	576 (.65)
Total	1,764	675 (.38)	686 (.39)	329 (.19)	71 (.04)	1,004 (.57)

Source: Moore and Wagstaff, 1974, Table 1.

Note: Percentages calculated by ISEP staff.

Calderwood, 1973), and the male-female analyses clearly outline the underrepresentation of women at all levels and in all institutional types. Increasingly, these data are being analyzed for racial and ethnic issues as well (Epstein, 1973; National Board of Graduate Education, 1976), as they were in Bayer's 1968–69 and 1972–73 ACE study. Bayer noted that the proportion of black women holding faculty appointments was greater than that of black men, for all institutional types, as seen in this figure.*

Faculty	All Insti- tutions	2-Year	4-Year	University
Black male faculty (as percent of male faculty), 1968–69	1.8	.5	4.2	.4
Black female faculty (as percent of female faculty), 1968–69	3.9	1.4	7.4	1.0
Black male faculty, 1972–73	2.4	1.3	4.6	.9
Black female faculty, 1972–73	4.8	4.2	8.1	1.2

Moore and Wagstaff's conclusions, drawn from their sample (41.7% of two year respondents and 29.1% of four year respondents were female), appear incorrect when they write: "Black career women constitute a larger proportion of the black professional community than women in the white professional world (Epstein, 1973, p. 916) but not

* See Tables 3.2 and 3.8.

as faculty members and administrators in predominantly white colleges and universities" (p. 162). Their return indicated, for example, that 60% of the female respondents in two year institutions were full-time faculty (p. 166), whereas only 46% of the male respondents were full-time faculty (p. 150).

In light of white male to white female ratios in teaching positions at all institutional types, especially two year institutions, Moore and Wagstaff's analysis is not supported by other data, notably Bayer's ACE studies. As the following figure* indicates, white female faculty percentages are less than white male faculty percentages, whereas the previous figure showed that black female faculty percentages surpass black male faculty percentages.

Faculty	All Institutions	2-Year	4-Year	University
White male faculty (as percent of male faculty), 1968–69	96.6	99.1	94.2	97.2
White female faculty (as percent of female faculty), 1968–69	94.7	96.7	91.3	97.7
White male faculty, 1972–73	95.1	97.1	92.1	97.0
White female faculty, 1972–73	93.6	93.3	91.3	96.6

This disparity is especially true in the two year college, where the rate of black female appointments was three times the appointment rate of black male faculty in both 1968–69 (1.4% to .5%), and 1972–73 (4.2% to 1.3%). Thus, Epstein's (1973) thesis appears to be corroborated, particularly by the two year faculty data. This 3 to 1 ratio may remain constant or increase if percentages of women hired in two year institutions increase. As an example of this trend, NCES data from 1972–73 and 1974–75 showed a slight increase in the percentage of female full-time faculty members in two year institutions (from 32.9% to 33.3%).

A word needs to be said about several other faculty studies, the findings of which are corollaries to this assessment of research on the racial and ethnic composition of two year faculties. These include studies by Richard Freeman (Freeman, 1976), Carnegie Council (CCPSHE, 1975), the Census Bureau (U.S. Census, 1976), and several recent reports on part-time faculty. The Freeman analysis of ACE faculty data is included in this chapter, which outlines the distribution patterns of minority faculty. The Carnegie Council report, *Making Affirmative Action Work in Higher Education,* "did not receive data from enough two year colleges to provide reliable information on the racial composition of their faculties" (CCPSHE, 1975, p. 29). Census Bureau faculty data from

---

* See Tables 3.2 and 3.8.

TABLE 3-10

**Women as a Percentage of Full-Time Faculty
1972–73 and 1974–75**

Institutional Type and Faculty Rank	1972–73	1974–75
All Institutions	22.3	24.1
Professors	9.8	10.3
Associate professors	16.3	16.9
Assistant professors	23.8	27.1
Instructors, other	38.0	39.4
Universities	16.4	18.5
Professors	6.3	6.3
Associate professors	12.5	13.3
Assistant professors	19.8	23.9
Instructors, other	44.4	46.4
4-year	23.4	25.0
Professors	12.5	12.9
Associate professors	18.1	18.7
Assistant professors	25.1	28.1
Instructors, other	43.1	45.5
2-year	32.9	33.3
Professors	22.1	24.8
Associate professors	25.0	24.9
Assistant professors	31.9	34.4
Instructors, other	35.9	34.9

Source: Carnegie Council, 1975, pp. 21–22.

1970 estimate that 3.3% of college teachers were black (with the categories limited to black and non-black); however, these data were not analyzed by institutional type, and therefore report the total universe rather than a two year and four year comparison, which would be more useful for the present study.

The part-time data are becoming increasingly important as institutions turn to temporary and less than full-time faculty for economic and other reasons. The importance of considering part-time two year faculty in a survey of racial and ethnic data becomes clearer when it is known that in California during 1974–75, there were 14,000 full-time and 20,000 part-time faculty members in two year institutions (Sewell *et al.*, 1976, p. 5); in all AACJC member institutions, the 1976 data showed 56% of total faculty members were part-time (AACJC, 1977, Table II).* These

---

* In 1970, part-time faculty members were 37% of the total in respondent institutions (Table 3.3).

data and research studies that analyze the implications for two year personnel policies (Abel, 1977; Fryer, 1977; Tuckman and Vogler, 1978) have not begun to determine the impact of part-time faculty hirings upon affirmative action and minority faculty hiring practices. A commitment not previously in evidence will be required to increase the representation of minority faculty when fewer full-time openings are filled (Fleming, Gill, and Swinton, 1978).

A summary of the studies that produce racial and ethnic two year college faculty data will serve two purposes here: to synthesize the plethora of data presented in the previous pages, with particular emphasis upon the myth of higher minority participation rates in two year colleges, and to clarify the statistical context for a discussion of two year qualitative research. The following figure reprints the minority faculty findings from the previously discussed faculty reports.

Table	Source	All Institutions	2-Year
3.2	Bayer, 1968–69	3.7%	1.6%
3.3	Goodrich et al., 1970		5.0%
3.4	Bushnell, 1970		4.9%
3.5	Goodrich, 1971		4.7%
3.6	Bayer, 1972–73	5.2%	3.9%

Despite the varying methodologies, the changing and noncomparable classifications, and the cultural and technical problems associated with collecting racial and ethnic data, the studies appear remarkably consistent in hovering about the 4–5% minority faculty level. These data have been corroborated (or cited with approval) by the Carnegie Council (CCPSHE, 1975, pp. 28–29), Moore and Wagstaff's studies (Moore and Wagstaff, 1974, p. 6; Moore, 1976b, p. 18), and numerous other researchers and policy makers.

Consistent through the studies is the refutation of a commonly held assumption that two year institutions, being newer and less prestigious employers, hire a greater percentage of minority faculty than their four year counterparts.* The reverse appears to be true, even while excluding historically black colleges. The following table illustrates the extent to which black faculty in predominantly black colleges, particularly in four year institutions, inflate the total percentage. Column II, which controls

---

* A 1974 listing of Chicano faculty and administrators drawn from an informal Hispanic network reported nearly 400 faculty and staff members (self-reported survey respondents): 26% (98) were employed by two year institutions, 72% (274) by four year and graduate schools, and 2% (8) by noninstitutional educational organizations (Macias and Gomez-Quinones, eds., 1974).

for black faculty in black institutions, indicates the meager levels of integration in predominantly white colleges and universities. It is significant to note that this recalculation halves Bayer's estimates for the aggregate. This review of quantitative studies forms the backdrop for an analysis of qualitative research on two year faculty.

In the first section of this chapter on minority faculty in two year colleges, it was necessary to set the quantitative background for a closer examination into qualitative faculty characteristics. Keeping in mind the previous research (and its implications) that suggests that minority faculty members in two year colleges are less than 5% of total two year faculty, this section examines research findings concerning faculty credentials, activities, and perceptions. Faculty effects upon students will also be examined. The data, some of which grow out of studies discussed in the first section of this chapter, have limitations similar to those associated with survey and research data. In particular, two year faculty baseline data are sketchy and impressionistic. This paucity of baseline data is particularly acute for two year minority faculty, forcing a researcher to utilize data gathered as a subset of all college faculty data, or to compare scant available racial and ethnic data with non-race-specific faculty research.

It would be helpful to summarize the evolution of faculty research, the growing attention to social science tools being employed to examine faculty, and the increasing focus on professionalization and specialization within faculty research. One thread tying these seemingly disparate areas of research together is the almost unanimous and significant finding that minority faculty are underrepresented in every field and in every institutional type, and that this situation has been historically observable. Less unanimity exists over root causes or remedies for the situation.

The college faculty has evolved into a subject of study in the twenty years since publication of *The Academic Marketplace* (Caplow and McGee, 1958). Markets for faculty services grew as American priorities in scientific and professional training necessitated a larger supply of college teachers and researchers (Jencks and Riesman, 1968). *The Mobile Professors* (Brown, 1967) ignored racial and ethnic compositions of faculties (as had the Caplow and McGee study)*, and concentrated upon the marketability of the professoriate. Other research (e.g., March, ed., 1965; Cohen, March, and Olsen, 1972; Hind, 1971) has also focused increasingly upon concepts of professionalism and evaluation.

This increase in faculty research was accompanied by the use of social science methodologies and paradigms, especially organizational theory;

---

* The only mention of race or ethnicity is on p. 194: "Discrimination on the basis of race appears to be nearly absolute."

TABLE 3-11

Faculty by Type of Institution and Race
1972–73

Faculty	All Institutions	All Institutions, Predominantly White	All 2-Year	All 4-Year	Predominantly White 4-Year[c]	Universities
Total	518,849	506,240[a]	94,475	202,719	190,110	221,655
Black faculty	15,046	7,373[b]	1,988	11,068	3,381	1,995
Percent black faculty	2.9	1.46	2.1	5.4	1.78	.9

Source: ISEP Reanalysis of Bayer, 1973 Data Published in Fleming, *et al.*, Table 7.1.

[a] (Bayer, 1973), Table 1, Col. 3 (Total) *minus* Table 1, Col. 3 (predominantly Negro College).

[b] (Freeman, 1976, Table 77), Number of Black Faculty in predominantly Black Colleges, male and female, 1973; [51% *times* total Black Faculty] subtracted from total Black faculty.

[c] Fleming, *et al.*, 1978, p. 214.

investigations into the effects of collective bargaining upon governance; and the attention paid to professional traits and characteristics within individual professions. In particular, this third line of inquiry—investigation of faculty members within a given professional field of study—has led to racial and ethnic considerations of the field's membership. Research into ethnic groupings of faculty and institutions, as well as the inquiry into female representation, have contributed to the growth of research on faculties.

The contributions of social science to faculty research are most evident when recent studies are compared to the anecdotal, descriptive research conducted earlier. As an example, the idyllic "community of scholars" perspective, described in *The Academic Man* (Wilson, 1942) and *The Academic Community* (Millett, 1962), has given way to the more research and social science-based, theoretical *Handbook of Research on Teaching* (Gage, ed., 1963), *Academic Governance: Research on Institutional Politics and Decision Making* (Baldridge, ed., 1971), and *Governing Academic Organizations* (Riley and Baldridge, eds., 1977).

One researcher on collective bargaining and faculty unionism has noted the evolution of collective bargaining literature from administrative "handwringing" and scare tactics to more sophisticated legal analyses, political theory, and conflict research to determine effects upon professionalism, governance, and resource allocation (Lee, 1978). Representative faculty collective bargaining literature includes *Professors, Unions, and American Higher Education* (Ladd and Lipset, 1973), *Faculty Tenure* (Commission on Academic Tenure, 1973), and *Unions on Campus* (Kemerer and Baldridge, 1975).

Increased scholarly attention has been paid to the nature of professionalism and specialized academic authority (e.g., Gross and Grambsch, 1968), and to the effects of institutional characteristics upon the professional autonomy of faculty (Baldridge, *et al.*, 1973; 1977). However, the examination of professionalism has been directed less at two year college faculty (exceptions include Cohen, 1974; Cohen and Brawer, 1977) than at assembling statistical profiles of faculty in the aggregate, by white ethnic origin, and by academic field or discipline.

As did the ACE studies examined earlier (Bayer, 1970; Bayer, 1973), the annual Ladd-Lipset surveys report demographic, professional, and attitudinal characteristics, in the aggregate, of the American professoriate. These findings are published regularly in the *Chronicle of Higher Education* (e.g., "Professors' Religious and Ethnic Backgrounds," 22 September 1975; "The Big Differences Among Faculty Unions," 13 March 1978). Ladd and Lipset have also reported their findings on faculty in the aggregate (*The Divided Academy,* 1975a), and in more specialized populations that include natural scientists and engineers (1972) and political scientists (1971).

White ethnic faculty members have been examined in several contexts, including institutions of Catholic higher education (Greeley and Rossi, 1966; Greeley, 1969); studies of British faculty (Halsey and Trow, 1971); Jewish academics (Lipset and Ladd, 1971); and Jewish and Catholic faculty (Steinberg, 1974). These studies, particularly those of Jewish and Catholic faculty, reveal a past history of bigotry and anti-Semitism.

In addition to the increasing use of social science techniques in faculty research concurrent with studies of white ethnic faculty, there has been a healthy tendency to investigate career patterns and professional characteristics within individual disciplines and academic fields. These studies of a profession becoming increasingly introspective (and, it might be said, of a profession more subject to external scrutiny than it once was), have provided the most striking and consistent evidence of underrepresentation of minority faculty in all institutional types. This branch of research on faculties has focused on two areas: intense scrutiny of the professoriate in a given field, and philosophical analyses of ethnicity and ethnic perspectives within a given field. These two developing areas, of course, are not mutually exclusive. Attempts to analyze the conceptual frameworks of academic fields and researchers within the fields include Myrdal's *Objectivity in Social Research* (1969), Richter's *Science as a Cultural Process* (1972), and Finn's *Scholars, Dollars, and Bureaucrats* (1978). The former branch of research, concentrating upon single disciplines, includes studies of the professoriate in sociology (Morgan, 1970; Oromaner, 1970), political science (Ladd and Lipset, 1971), higher education (Rogers, 1969; Harcleroad, ed., 1974; Dressel and Mayhew, 1975; Kellams, 1978), natural science and engineering (Ladd and Lipset, 1972), and educational administration (Willower and Culbertson, eds., 1964; Campbell and Newell, 1973). Scholars who have examined their own ranks for racial and ethnic membership have frequently concluded that those ranks are overwhelmingly white and male.

Campbell and Newell, in their study of professors of educational administration, discovered 98% of their respondents to be men, and 97% to be white. They concluded:

> Professors of educational administration, in the main, are part of middle class America. They are relatively young, white, and married . . . Due, perhaps, to the public nature of the practice of educational administration, from which most professors have come, there appears to be an alarming homogeneity within the professorship. The number of mavericks, those who are distinguished by great independence of thought and action, seems to be very small. One wonders if any academic field can thrive unless it makes a place

for, and reckons with the sting of, constructive, provocative critics within its own ranks (Campbell and Newell, 1973, pp. 136–137).

These scholars who have chosen to analyze more thoroughly the latter area of the professoriate—to focus upon ethnic issues within disciplines—agree with the perspective of Campbell and Newell and advance theories for both increased participation in their field (and all fields) by minority faculty and increased attention by *all* faculty to ethnic issues within their fields. In *Black Educators in White Colleges*, Moore and Wagstaff (1974) advance conclusions harsher than Campbell and Newell's. They conclude:

> The academic community is filled with discrimination and racism. Some argue that it does not consciously produce it. Others contradict this argument strenuously. Nonetheless, whether it produces it or not, it does distill it, use it, and provide it in the purest form (research is one such form) for the many in a society who do consciously discriminate. Although we can identify few cases of overt discrimination in many colleges, blacks perceive it as always being there; like relative humidity, it is present, penetrating, oppressive, encompassing, and pervasive (Moore and Wagstaff, 1974, p. 205).

Researchers who are investigating racial and ethnic faculty membership and professional issues have concentrated upon black scholarship: in sociology (Blackwell and Janowitz, eds., 1974; Staples, 1976); in science and engineering (Wilburn, 1974); in psychology (Wispe *et al.*, 1969; Boxley and Wagner, 1971), and in other disciplines. Researchers who are analyzing ethnic issues for other minority groups have identified underrepresentation of Chicanos (Valverde, 1976; de los Santos, 1974); Puerto Ricans (Vazquez, 1969; Betances, 1974); and Native Americans (Thornton, 1977; Locke, ed., 1978) on college and university faculties. Asian–American faculty and educational data reflect participation in excess of other minority rates of participation (National Board of Graduate Education, 1976, p. 28; U.S. Commission on Civil Rights, 1978; see also Sung, 1975; Montero, 1978).

Given the increasing amount of attention being paid to ethnic and professional issues within academia and within academic disciplines, it is startling to note the scant attention paid to the two year college instructorship. Almost exclusively, research dwells on professional issues central to four year and graduate faculty, notably graduate education and research issues. This introspection does not encompass those members of the profession in two year institutions. Their relative obscurity is due, in no small part, to the disinclination of two year college faculty to conduct research on themselves. The bulk of research on two year college faculties has concentrated, not on demographic or professional characteristics, but rather on self-perceptions and personality traits (Garrison, 1967; Brawer, 1968); values (Park, 1971, Brawer, 1971); or instructional techniques and pedagogical issues (Kelley and Wilbur, 1970). Cohen and Brawer are perhaps the most trenchant critics of faculties in two year colleges. In *The Two-Year College Instructor Today* (1977), they note the provincialism, anti-intellectualism, and uncertainty with which many two year college faculty perform their tasks. Garrison's characterization of two year faculty, intended to portray the uniqueness and uncertainty of two year faculties *vis-a-vis* four year faculties, could more properly portray today's minority faculty member in these institutions:

> He is the servant of several demanding masters, and he is groping to bring such demands into a compatibility, a coherence, that will command his loyalty and his long-range commitment (Garrison, 1967, p. 15).

Who are these servants of such demanding taskmasters? What are their credentials? How do they spend their professional time? What are their perceptions of themselves? Of their students? Do minority faculty members exhibit similar characteristics? Do four year faculty members exhibit similar characteristics? These questions, important in any discussion of qualitative judgments regarding faculty, take on additional importance in an evaluation of the effectiveness of the institutions in educating the students, majority and minority.

The examination of two year college faculty credentials, activities, and perceptions leads one to question even more the striking underrepresentation of minority faculty in these institutions. Such underrepresentation is all the more mystifying when arguments against affirmative action principles are made concerning higher education faculty in the aggregate (e.g., Glazer, 1975). Even if one assumes the validity of arguments which justify the lack of minority Ph.D. holders, the specialized needs of research institutions, and the tendency of minorities to cluster in relatively few graduate fields, two year institutions ought not be so drastically unrepresentative of minority populations. Two year faculties differ considerably from their four year counterparts, as do their institutions and their professional development opportunities.

Considering the historic lack of opportunity available to minorities, one might expect that these differences would have led to more minority faculty members in two year institutions than in four year or graduate institutions. Trend data, however, such as Freeman's reanalysis of Bayer's 1969 and 1973 ACE studies, show recent shifts in black faculties from two year to baccalaureate institutions. The redistribution is marked for black males (25% to 42%), and less so for black females (25% to 31%). An increasing proportion of blacks are being hired by senior institutions. The apparent "upgrading" of black faculty positions must be considered cautiously, for the aggregate numbers of black faculty are small, and, as previously noted, the data are questionable.

Nevertheless, comparisons between two year and four year faculties unanimously show higher paper credentials, more access to resources, and more professional development activities as characteristics of baccalaureate faculties. These overwhelming factors would seem to answer the "supply" argument of critics of affirmative action: there are fewer minority faculty because there are fewer minority doctorate holders. Although ·there are fewer minority Ph.D. holders, this argument is inadequate as an explanation for minority underrepresentation in two year institutions.

The following figures, compiled from several sources, show both the comparisons between doctorate holders as a percentage of two and four year faculties, and Moore and Wagstaff's findings from their black faculty project. The Stanford Project on Academic Governance (SPAG) ranked institutional types on a modified Carnegie classification and found that in 1972, 15% of public two year college faculty members held doctorates, compared to 12% of private two year faculty members.

TABLE 3-12

Percentage of Black and White Employed Faculty, by Sex
Selected Years, 1969 and 1972

Type of Institution	1969–70		1972–73	
	Black	White	Black	White
Male				
Universities	10	51	18	44
Colleges	15	36	24	36*
Black colleges	71	1	51	1
2-year	4	12	7	19
Female				
Universities	10	41	10	37
Colleges	15	40	21	37
Black colleges	70	1	51	1
2-year	5	18	18	25

Source: Freeman, 1976, p. 210.

* Typographical error corrected.

These percentages are well below those of faculty members in other institutions.

These low percentages of doctorate–holding faculty members appear to be corroborated by additional data, including AACJC internal figures estimating 10% (75% holding a master's degree) in 1977 (AACJC, "Faculty in Two-Year Colleges" 1977). If these figures are accurate,* they reverse a trend toward *lower* percentages of Ph.D.-holding two year faculty, as reported by Cartter and Salter (1975), from AACJC figures.

TABLE 3-13

Percentage of Faculty with Doctorate
1973

Type of Institution	Percentage
2-year private	12
2-year public	15
Public liberal arts colleges	44
Public colleges	55
Public comprehensive	53
Elite liberal arts colleges	69
Public multiversity	77
Private multiversity	82
Average for all institutions	39

Source: Baldridge *et al.,* 1977, Table 2.

TABLE 3-14

Tenure Status of Black Faculty
in Predominantly White Institutions
1972–73

Black Faculty	2-Year	4-Year
Hold tenure	340 (32%)	430 (20%)
In tenure–accruing position	355 (34%)	685 (32%)
Not in tenure–accruing position	319 (30%)	968 (44%)
No response	36 (3%)	91 (4%)

Source: Moore and Wagstaff, 1974, p. 153; Moore, 1976, p. 20.

---

* The figures are derivative estimates, according to the Director of Research Information, AACJC (personal conversation). A recent survey indicated that 11% of new two year faculty members held a doctorate or planned to complete the doctorate within two years (Atelsek and Gomberg, 1978).

TABLE 3-15

Percentage of 2-Year College Faculty with the Doctorate
Selected Years, 1959–70

Year	Percentage with Doctorate
1959–60	8.37
1962–63	8.32
1966–67	7.12
1969–70	6.30

Source: Cartter and Salter, 1975, Table 4.

The reversal of this trend can be seen in Bayer's studies of the years 1969 and 1973, in which he reported 6.7% (Bayer, 1970, p. 13) and 6.9% (Bayer, 1973, p. 26). These percentages included Ph.D., Ed.D., and "other doctorate" holders, presumably including B.A. holders as well.

Bushnell's study of 1971 faculty confirmed these estimates, and subdivided two year faculty members by academic and occupational subject. As one might expect, academic or transfer curricula faculty held higher degrees than their technical or terminal counterparts.

Moore and Wagstaff's data are not comparable here, because their sample was not weighted. They do note, however, that 64% of their two year respondents, and 7.3% of their responding black faculty *and* administrators, held the doctorate (Moore and Wagstaff, 1974, p. 46). Sixty-six percent of the blacks working in two year colleges held master's degrees (p. 46). In a reanalysis of the 1972–73 data, Moore noted that black women in two year institutions had degree characteristics similar to those of black men (Moore, 1976b, p. 19). Freeman's reanalysis of Bayer's data showed the opposite, namely, that black men, in all institutional types, were more likely than black women (23% to 12% in 1969; 20% to 7% in 1973) to hold the doctorate (Freeman, 1976, Table 73).

This discussion of degrees has been lengthy, for degree holders serve as the supply half of the faculty equation, the demand half being the number of annual openings advertised or, more precisely, the number of hirings each year. Cartter and Salter, in their analysis of faculty hiring trends, predict that "the two year college sector is not likely to represent a vast new untapped market for doctorates being trained by the nation's graduate schools" (Cartter and Salter, 1975, p. 40). This prediction echoes Huther's prediction that two year college faculties will prove to be only a small market for doctorate holders (Huther, 1972).

TABLE 3-16

Highest Degree Held by Full-Time Faculty (in Percentages)
1971

Degree	Academic	Occupational	Unclassified	Total
High school	0.7	11.6	5.4	3.4
Associate	0.6	6.9	4.2	2.2
Bachelor's	9.2	29.4	10.3	13.9
Master's	82.6	51.6	71.7	75.0
Doctorate	6.9	0.5	8.4	5.5
Weighted N in Thousands	48.5	15.3	2.6	66.4

Source: Bushnell, 1973, Table 2.19.

These predictions, if accurate, appear to augur well for minority faculty hiring in two year institutions, for minorities received a higher percentage of MA degrees in 1975–76 (10.7%) than Ph.D. degrees (6.9%) in the same year (OCR, 1978). However, the available data do not indicate a trend toward rectifying the imbalance, although there could be significant change in the hiring of minority faculty by two year institutions in that holding a doctorate is not a prerequisite for teaching in two year colleges (in fact, is a rarity), and the two year college sector is the only growth sector in significantly increasing enrollments (see, e.g., chapter two, Cartter and Salter, 1975). It is clear that more concerted efforts in planning (see, e.g. Cartter, 1975), hiring practices (Carnegie Commission, 1975; Fleming, Swinton, and Gill, 1978), and graduate education (National Board on Graduate Education, 1976; Martorana, Toombs, and Breneman, eds., 1975) will be necessary to identify and to hire minority faculty. It is inaccurate to suggest that the golden opportunity for minority faculty hiring has passed. Such defeatism could lull institutions into not pressing for minority faculty, and could lead minority faculty to discontinue applying for available positions. It is equally defeatist, however, to suggest that parity of any kind exists already, even in these institutions on the lowest prestige end of the higher education continuum.

What additional factors, other than doctorate percentages per faculty, characterize two year college faculty, and do these factors explain the underrepresentation of minority faculty? Do existing minority faculty differ in these personal characteristics? Parents' SES measures, and parents' educational attainment data, both suggest that minorities who are more likely to come from low-SES families would be more likely to join faculties in two year institutions (and to have attended two year institutions) than to join faculties in baccalaureate or graduate institutions. The following table offers evidence that children of highly educated fathers (and for 1972-73, mothers) are more likely to join four year or graduate faculties than two year faculties.

The impact of social class upon the professoriate and upon institutional affiliation has been noted by Ladd and Lipset, who theorized that socio-economic status, ethnic group culture, and discrimination interact to produce the religious and ethnic composition of faculties (Ladd and Lipset, 1975b). They note also that, with the exception of high Jewish participation and modestly increased Catholic (although not Latin American) representation, "little has happened to the American professoriate, in terms of its ethnic and religious makeup, in the years since World War II. There has been extraordinary growth, but the succeeding waves of newcomers closely resemble those who came before" (p. 2).

In *The Academic Melting Pot*, Steinberg (1974) examined religious

TABLE 3-17

Father's Educational Attainment for Faculty (in Percentages) Selected Years, 1969 and 1972

Educational Attainment	Type of Institution Employing Faculty		
	2-Year	4-Year	Universities
1969[a]			
Eighth grade or less	37.1	30.5	26.1
Some high school	15.1	15.0	13.5
Completed high school	19.3	17.1	17.3
Some college	12.1	12.2	13.1
College graduate	6.5	9.0	11.0
Some graduate school	3.2	5.6	5.8
Advanced degree	6.6	10.7	13.1
1972[b]			
Eighth grade or less	34.0 (23.2)	30.4 (23.9)	25.2 (19.6)
Some high school	16.5 (17.5)	13.8 (14.1)	13.0 (13.4)
Completed high school	19.7 (31.4)	18.2 (29.7)	18.7 (30.2)
Some college	12.8 (14.2)	11.9 (14.7)	13.2 (16.6)
College graduate	8.0 (9.1)	9.1 (11.1)	11.7 (13.1)
Some graduate school	2.8 (2.4)	5.1 (3.0)	5.4 (3.2)
Advanced degree	6.2 (2.2)	11.5 (3.6)	12.9 (3.9)

Note: Numbers in parentheses indicate mother's educational attainment.

[a] Bayer, 1970, p. 12. Total figures, including male and female faculty.

[b] Bayer, 1973, p. 31. Total figures, including male and female faculty. Excludes "no response."

backgrounds of faculty. He documented class origins and hypothesized that the relative over- or underrepresentation of ethnic groups on faculties was due, in large measure, to the social class and professional backgrounds of immigrants (see especially his Tables 9, 10, and 12).* The stratification of college faculties by religious and ethnic origins resembles the "submerged class conflict" thesis of Karabel (1972), in which he suggests that two year colleges foster inequality by tracking working class students into the least prestigious institutions.

The analogy is not entirely appropriate. Although aggregate minority enrollments are high in two year institutions, aggregate minority faculty percentages are disproportionately low in these institutions, as well as in institutions with high minority populations (Moore and Wagstaff, 1974, pp. 4–7; Moore, 1976b). As with doctoral percentages, the tendency of two year college faculties to be populated by persons from working class backgrounds would lead observers to expect significantly more minority faculty members in these institutions.

If one expects minority faculty hirings will increase because few two year college faculty members hold the doctorate, because professional prestige in these institutions is the lowest in the hierarchy of American higher education, or because these faculties are drawn from the lowest socio-economic classes, that expectation will not be met—at least not if current trends continue. Although isolated instances of increased minority recruiting do occur—as in California, where, due to sheer size of the system, any minority hirings will substantially affect the national aggregate—trend data for two year colleges show few gains and, in fact, show erosion from previous levels. For instance, in the north central region of the country (nineteen states), 96% of new full-time two year college faculty members hired in 1973 were white (Brown, 1975), a record that would not even maintain present levels, much less increase the percentages of minority faculty.

Freeman suggests that, as a result of affirmative action and the "new market" for minorities, notably blacks, black faculty members have begun to receive disproportionately high rewards for published research, relative to whites (Freeman, 1976). Assuming that Freeman's reanalysis of Bayer's ACE data is correct (and, given the small sample of blacks, inferences from the ACE data must be made cautiously), this phenomenon of the new marketplace would affect the two year college marketplace—where publications are rare and relatively small percentages of

---

* For an example of the passion generated by such scholarship, see the acrimonious exchange of comments by Andrew Greeley, Robert Wuthnow, and Steinberg in *The Sociology of Education,* January 1977, July 1977, October 1977, and January 1978.

two year faculty publish books or articles—less than the four year marketplace.

Clearly, in an environment where the reward system does not include publication, a "bullish" marketplace model predicated upon publications will be less useful than it might be for a four year environment. If Freeman's analysis is correct, its implications for two year faculty will be toward redistribution, i.e., the tendency for blacks to be redistributed upward from two year to more senior institutions. Freeman's data appear to confirm, at least at first glance, the "black brain drain theory," the belief that desegregation has created a market situation in which black faculty members are free to pursue positions in institutions other than predominantly black colleges and universities (Poinsett, 1970; Rafky, 1972; Mommsen, 1973; 1974). His data noted the shift not only *into* senior institutions, but *from* predominantly black colleges (see Table 3.12; Freeman, 1976, Table 77). This shift, however, is the movement of relatively few pawns in a much larger game. With so few black faculty (15,046) in so large a universe (518,849), any shifts *within* the black faculty across institutional types will be notable.

Yet nearly 90% of Moore and Wagstaff's respondents (entirely drawn from predominantly white institutions) indicated they had *not* worked previously in black institutions (Moore and Wagstaff, 1974, pp. 133–135; Moore, 1976b, pp. 18–19). These data do not corroborate any findings of a black brain drain. Given hardening attitudes toward minority hiring (see Jones, 1977) and fewer projected hirings (Cartter and Salter, 1975; Fleming *et al.*, 1978) the minority brain drain may well be in the negative impact of detenuring, reductions-in-force, and last-in-first-out seniority practices upon the minority faculty already hired.* Moore and Wagstaff's study found, for example, that not only were significant numbers of black professionals untenured, but an alarming number were in non-tenure-accruing positions (see Table 3.14). Because these numbers are not comparable to the aggregate number of national faculty, the conclusions are unclear. Some of those holding non-tenure-accruing positions are administrators. The last section of this chapter, however, documents an underrepresentation of minorities in administrative positions at least as serious as that of faculty in these institutions. It would seem likely that the blacks who responded to the Moore and Wagstaff

---

* In part to deal with the increased competition for tenured position, the National Chicano Council on Higher Education (NCCHE), with funding by the Ford Foundation, has begun a modest program of post-doctoral fellowships for Chicano academics in tenure-accruing positions in research universities. This program, targeted as it is for senior college faculty, will not affect Chicano faculty in two year colleges.

TABLE 3-18

Percentage of Faculty with Publications

Study (Data Collected)	Article			Book		
	2-Year	4-Year	University	2-Year	4-Year	University
Bayer (1969)[a] ("Professional Writings")	23.7	48.9	71.5	25.1	33.1	50.4
Bayer (1972)[b]	23.8	52.4	76.0			
Baldridge et al. (1972)[c] Public	5.0			10.0		
Private	7.0			6.0		
Cohen and Brawer (1975)[d] (Humanities Faculty Only)	29.0			12.5		

[a] Bayer, 1970, p. 15. ISEP staff calculations.

[b] Bayer, 1973, p. 28.

[c] Baldridge, et al., Table 2. (Use Modified Carnegie Classifications.)

[d] Cohen and Brawer, 1977, p. 140.

survey hold a variety of non-tenure-accruing positions without significant promises of security.

The area of two year college faculty perceptions merits further examination. It has already been noted that no comparative data exist to differentiate between majority and minority faculty members in two year institutions with regard to credentials or tasks performed. However, there is evidence across institutional types of at least four perceptions of two year college faculties *vis-a-vis* four year faculties and *vis-a-vis* minorities. These perceptions include student-centeredness, attitudes toward teaching, attitudes toward open admissions, and attitudes toward affirmative action and hiring practices.

These attitudes are not as inextricable or independent as questionnaires and research instruments would indicate. Together they form a nexus of attitudes that undoubtedly influences institutional tasks and institutional receptivity to minorities. Much of the research evidence is only suggestive, and aggregate figures level the extremes. It is noteworthy, however, that different researchers, employing varied techniques and sampling different faculty populations, have reached similar conclusions concerning faculty attitudes and perceptions.

Faculty perceptions of students and of the teaching task (one component of professional work activities, which would include research, service, professional development, advising, administration, and other activities) appear to be a function of institutional type and mission. There is, however, considerable incongruity between reward systems and job requirements, evidenced by the standard university requirement that young faculty members develop courses while being evaluated primarily for research and publications, and by the increasing complexity and professionalism of academic disciplines which demand multiple loyalties from faculty members (Lewis, 1967; Ladd and Lipset, 1973).

Such incongruity is less evident in the two year college, where the only criterion for hiring and tenure appears to be teaching skill (Cohen and Brawer, 1977; Blank, 1978). One might expect to find professional conflict among doctorate-holding faculty in two year colleges (those few employed in these institutions), for their academic training presumably prepared them to conduct research in their discipline—an activity neither highly prized nor highly rewarded. This expected conflict finds mixed support in the available literature. Indeed, Cohen and Brawer's findings suggest that the opposite is true: humanities faculty members with a "research orientation"* exhibited higher concern for students and for curriculum development than nonresearch-oriented faculty

---

* This construct included weighted responses to questions concerning interest and participation in research and publication, external funding, time spent reading, etc. (Cohen and Brawer, 1977, Chapter 8).

members. This lends evidence to the theory that research and teaching are mutually reinforcing, rather than dichotomous (see also Cohen, 1974). Cohen and Brawer's Ph.D.-holding respondents showed less concern for students and for teaching than did the group of respondents as a whole *or* than the group of respondents who were characterized as "research-oriented" (chapter eleven). This finding, coupled with the suggestion that research reinforces teaching attitudes, could lead faculty development administrators to encourage staff training and research activities, but to discourage Ph.D. hiring in two year colleges (Centra, 1978).

These data can only be regarded as preliminary and, in any case, the percentage of doctorate holders hired or doctorates earned within ranks is likely to increase only slightly (Cohen and Brawer, 1977, p. 74; Atelsek and Gomberg, 1978), regardless of shifts in perception that may accompany the additional training. But more studies have focused upon the perceptions of faculty toward students, and upon the differences among faculty groups across institutional types, and it is this body of research that has implications for institutional staff development and recruitment, particularly for two year college faculties.

Consistently, research has identified the tendency of two year faculties to be more student-oriented than their senior college counterparts (Cohen, 1974). Wilson and his associates argue that undergraduate teaching, in contrast to graduate teaching, is more student-centered (Wilson et al., 1975), and that two year college faculty are more student-centered than four year faculty (pp. 20-21). Such student-centeredness may be due to the nature of the teaching responsibilities in two year colleges and the increased student-faculty contact in these institutions (Bayer, 1970, p. 14; 1973, pp. 17, 24; 1974, p. 50), although the type of control and whether an institution is public or private also appear to affect student-centeredness (El-Khawas, 1976, pp. 38-41).

Student-centeredness is increasingly viewed as an important variable in attrition studies and theoretical models of student persistence. Spady (1970), Tinto (1975), and Pascarella and Terenzini (1976; 1977) have evolved theories suggesting that involvement between students and faculty *outside* the classroom significantly increases the likelihood that students will remain enrolled in the institution. Although Astin does not measure faculty contact as a variable, his work (1975) in retention policies would recommend such interaction: "If ways can be found to involve students more in the life and environment of the institution, their chances of staying in college are improved" (p. 148).

Garrison's early work (1967) theorized that two year college faculties were more student-centered than were four year faculties. Cohen and Brawer constructed a series of questionnaire items to determine "concern for students," items clustered as a "concept of functional equality between faculty and students" (1977, pp. 45-51). They found minority faculties to be more empathetic than their majority counterparts, and women more empathetic than men (p. 48). Moore and Wagstaff (1974) did not ask black faculty members about their student perceptions, but they did note that 64.1% of their two year faculty females and 71.6% of two year faculty males indicated that they would take professional stances antagonistic toward a stance of black students (p. 113). Notably absent from most research on professions and perceptions of professionals is the issue of whether divisions of professional loyalties occur between institutional goals and minority student demands.

Such conflicts clearly exist and have been described (e.g., Mommsen, 1973; Moore and Wagstaff, 1974), but minority faculty members in majority institutions have not been researched systematically to determine perceptions of prejudice or conflict.* Because of the increasing significance of two year colleges in educating minority students, it is important that any two year faculty research agenda include investigation into professional conflicts inherent in executing institutional tasks such as teaching or advising.

A disturbing aspect of two year faculty perceptions has been the finding that some instructors do not embrace institutional commitments to open access—the one characteristic that, perhaps more than any other, distinguishes two year colleges (Cross, 1976; Baldridge *et al.*, 1977). The observation was made by Medsker in 1960 that the perceptions of some two year faculty members were at variance with the stated goals of their institutions. These views have been explained as remnants of the secondary school experience of many faculty (Cross, 1970), or the inadequate preparation programs in universities, which train graduate students for the primary task of research (see Martorana, Toombs, and Breneman, eds., 1975).

While these reasons may have been true, and in some cases may continue to be true, the preparation of two year faculty with public school system experience is decreasing (Cohen and Brawer, 1977, pp. 118, 136) and, as noted earlier, only a small number of two year faculty members are trained as researchers. Admittedly, universities may still be training graduates to perform tasks not appropriate to the two year college, but it is unclear just how teachers can be trained in institutions that tend to de-emphasize the teaching task. Further, faculty development programs are well-established in two year institutions (Centra,

---

* A study by Schlesinger (1979) that reanalyzed Cohen and Brawer's data (1978) does attempt to do this. However, it was published too late for inclusion in this chapter.

1978), a sign that a significant portion of the pedagogical training (as opposed to subject-matter training) is occurring under the auspices of two year institutions themselves.

One is forced to confront the data suggesting that two year faculties are more conservative than senior institution counterparts, and that their conservative characteristics, to some extent, may explain the disproportionately small presence of minority faculty members in these institutions. That faculties in more prestigious and research-oriented institutions are more liberal than their colleagues in less prestigious institutions has been noted for a number of years (for example, Lazarsfeld and Thilens, 1958; Ladd and Lipset, 1973; Fen, 1973).

This tendency for faculty in lower prestige institutions to reflect conservative values can also be seen in political self-designations and in perceptions of social issues, as reported in the Bayer studies, as shown in the following tables.

But it must be conceded that political preferences and social attitudes on given issues can be held, quite apart from professional preferences. Responses to such stock questions are, at best, imperfect arbiters. However, when asked their opinion of philosophical issues pertaining to affirmative action, two year humanities faculty members interviewed by Cohen and Brawer showed exceptional conservativism.

Cohen and Brawer note that the most opposition to affirmative action comes from older white males, both full-time and part-time (p. 118). Inasmuch as these faculty members hold influential formal and informal leadership positions in the institutions, it appears clear that faculty resistance constitutes a major impediment to increasing minorities on professional staffs. Although the relative liberalism of university and four year faculties has not led to significant desegregation in these institutions (see Table 3-11), issues of undersupply, merit, and specialization* raised in senior institutions cannot be raised to explain the underrepresentation of minority faculty in two year colleges.** Rather, prejudice and resistance to change more likely account for this disproportionately small number.

This conservatism directed toward minority faculty is itself mirrored in two year faculty perceptions of the open-door mission of their institutions. Bushnell's research identified a strong current of dissatis-

---

* In law, one of the most specialized academic disciplines, black faculty (including faculty in predominantly black law schools) constitute 4.5% of the total full-time faculty (see Abramson and Moss, 1977, note 27).

** This should not be construed to lend credence to excuses advanced by senior institutions to rationalize their segregated faculties. Certainly institutions that train graduate students are responsible in large part for any undersupply of minority students (see Fleming, 1976).

TABLE 3-19

Position of Faculty on Liberalism-to-Conservatism Scale
(in Percentages)
1969

Quality of Institution	Very Liberal	Liberal	Middle of the Road	Conserva- tive	Very Con- servative
A (elite)	27	28	17	17	12
B	19	22	17	23	20
C	14	19	18	26	22
D (lowest tier)	13	17	18	27	25

Source: Ladd and Lipset, 1973, Table 9.

TABLE 3-20

Political Preferences of the American College Faculty
(Percentage Distribution)
1969 and 1972

Current Politics	All Institutions	2-Year	4-Year	Universities
1969[a]				
Left	4.9	2.5	5.4	5.1
Liberal	39.8	29.1	41.2	41.5
Middle of road	27.1	32.9	27.0	25.7
Moderately conservative	25.5	32.1	23.9	25.0
Conservative	2.7	3.5	2.5	2.7
1972[b]				
Percent indicating *strongly agree* or *agree with reservations:* "I consider myself politically conservative."	44.0	54.4	41.9	41.3

Note: Male and female responses combined by institutional type.

[a] Bayer, 1970, p. 20.

[b] Bayer, 1973, p. 30.

faction with open admissions; nearly one-third of the respondents felt that students in the two year colleges ought to be screened for admissions (Bushnell, 1973, p. 39). Bushnell summarized curtly: "Faculty members

TABLE 3-21

Attitudes of American College Faculty Toward Major Social Issues (in Percentages Indicating *Strongly Agree* or *Agree with Reservations*) Selected Years, 1969 and 1972

Statement	All Institutions	2-Year	4-Year	Universities
1969[a]				
"Where de facto segregation exists, black people should be assured control over their own schools."	64.3	62.8	65.7	63.6
"Racial integration of the public elementary schools should be achieved even if it requires busing."	44.3	36.5	46.1	45.0
"The main cause of Negro riots in the cities is white racism."	44.3	38.1	46.9	44.1
1972[b]				
"There should be preferential hiring for minority faculty at this institution."	33.6	28.7	33.8	35.5
"There should be preferential hiring for women faculty at this institution."	29.8	22.7	29.3	33.4

Note: Male and female responses combined.

[a] Bayer, 1970, p. 20.

[b] Bayer, 1973, p. 30.

who are unable, or do not want to accept this responsibility ought to seek work in more compatible settings" (p. 39).

These findings are uncertain; additional evidence has found two year faculty to believe strongly that access should be a priority in higher education. In the 1969 Bayer survey, for example, two year faculties were more likely than senior college faculties to agree with the statement, "Opportunities for higher education should be available to all high school graduates who want it," although over one-third of the two year faculty members in this study disagreed with measures to "lower standards" and increase the numbers of minority students (Bayer, 1970,

p. 17). Cohen and Brawer also cite evidence of substantial philosophical commitment to open access (1977, p. 19). There is evidence, despite the conflicting attitudinal surveys, of a considerable lag between theoretical acceptance of open admissions and faculty integration and actual practice in these institutions.

Although faculty attitudes comprise the largest context for hiring (save, of course, enrollment-driven demands for courses), attitudes of other personnel are important: internally, administrators and trustees; externally, statewide coordinating or governing boards and collective bargaining agents. A detailed analysis of the effects of collective bargaining upon governance of two year institutions is beyond the scope of this study; for a comprehensive review of collective bargaining and its impact upon faculty professionalism and hiring practices, see Kemerer and Baldridge, 1975; Garbarino, Feller and Finkin, 1977; Begin, Settle, and Weiss, 1977; Cohen and Brawer, 1977; Lee, 1978. Increasing tendencies toward state-level governance, coordination and planning (Berdahl, 1971; McGuinness, 1975; Berve, 1975; Millard, 1976) have made these administrative levels important in determinations of student-teacher ratios, funding levels, and program offerings. State-level decisions with regard to tenure policies (Lee, 1978) and affirmative action (Haynes, 1978) denote a necessary role for these professional and political decision makers in faculty policies.

Although the centralization of state involvement* has meant a redistribution of authority, some researchers contend that increased statewide authority and increased institutional size serve to maintain heterogeneity and autonomy, rather than to decrease them (Baldridge, *et al.,* 1973; 1977; Riley and Baldridge, eds. 1977). Administrators with a siege mentality would dispute any theory that was contrary to their perceptions, but the point worth emphasizing is that personnel decisions are not unilateral, but are made after determinations at several levels and by several actors, all of whom have varying motivations, expectations, and rates of participation.

A corollary of Baldridge's theory, and others', is that prestige and high levels of faculty specialization (and to a lesser extent, size) will allow faculty in these institutions to have more influence in making hiring decisions (Baldridge *et al.,* 1973, Table 2; 1977, Table 3). Because faculty autonomy and prestige are lower at two year colleges than at senior institutions, two year faculties will have less control over hiring. Moore (1971) also speculates that two year college administrators, many of whom have come from K-12 school administrations, hold more author-

---

* The increased scope of federal centralization also lies beyond the scope of this study (See Conrad and Cosand, 1976).

itarian, less collegial perspectives than do administrators in senior institutions, who are more likely to see themselves as faculty colleagues, frequently having been chosen from faculty ranks.

These layers of decision making are critical to any understanding of personnel practices, particularly any attempt to analyze underrepresentation of minority faculty. If faculty members do not appear favorably disposed toward minority hiring, and if the other decision makers are unenthusiastic, evolutionary changes in faculty composition are unlikely to occur. On the other hand, if decisions are made at points higher than the faculty, and if these decision makers are favorably disposed toward redressing clearly demonstrable underrepresentation, change may be more likely. Unhappily, two year trustees and those who execute trustee responsibilities, i.e., administrators, appear to be as unrepresentative and, arguably, as conservative as the faculty in their institutions.

Trustees

The statistical literature on boards of trustees is relatively recent and unanimous in its findings that such boards, designed to represent the public trust in higher education, are overwhelmingly white and male (see, generally, Rauh, 1969; Hartnett, 1969; Mills, 1972; Moore, 1973; AGB, 1975; Grafe, 1976; Drake, 1977; Gomberg and Atelsek, 1977). One earnest commentator on board-president relationships noted in apparent seriousness, "A well-structured board should represent but not be artificially slavish to the nature of the market, geographical diversity, to sex, age and ethnic considerations, etc." (Pray, 1975, p. 10). He need not have feared slavish attention either to race or to gender, as the following tables show.

The figures appear consistent with recent data that indicate two year college trustee membership to be approximately 6% black, 2% other minorities, and 92% white. Two year institutions are slightly better represented by minorities than are senior institutions, and are clearly better represented with female membership. One must question, however, the glacial rate of change over the last ten years when minority (black) membership averaged less than 2% (Hartnett, 1969). The electoral and appointive processes (half of public board members are elected, while half are appointed by governmental bodies [Drake, 1977, Table 6]) have failed to bring about significant change in board composition. In the private sector, significant numbers (an average of four seats per institution) remain unfilled at any one time (Nelson and Turk, [1971], p. 3), indicating complacency in making more representative

TABLE 3-22

Attitudes of 2-Year College Humanities Faculty (in Percentages)
1975

Statement	Strongly Agree	Some- what Agree	Don't Know, No opinion	Some- what Dis- agree	Strongly Dis- agree
"Claims of discrimina- tory practices against women and minority students in higher education have been greatly exaggerated."	10.9	23.9	19.4	23.9	21.8
"There should be pref- erential hiring for women and/or minor- ity faculty at this in- stitution."	7.1	16.1	15.9	29.9	31.0

Source: Cohen and Brawer, 1977, p. 151.

appointments.* As distressing as these figures are, even more distressing are the complacency and disinterest with which members perceive racial underrepresentation on their boards. The following study of two year trustees reported that they did not believe their boards were unrepresentative, and that they disagreed with proposals that they become more representative.

Although no data exist to compare measures of conservatism or resistance to integration across institutional types, the finding that two year board members are resistant to change has been confirmed by a more recent study. These findings with regard to institutional presidents' and trustee board chairpersons' perception of representation are noteworthy; a reanalysis of the AACJC data indicates that white representation on both private and public boards in the aggregate is identical (Table 3-22), but those polled in the independent sector disagree more with regard to their perceptions concerning underrepresentation than do presidents and chairpersons in public institutions. Any attempt to explore this apparent disagreement, however, would be futile, inasmuch

---

* Discussions with AACJC staff have suggested these vacancies *have increased* since 1971.

TABLE 3-23

Sex and Race of Trustees in 2-Year Colleges
1976 and 1977

Trustee	Public and Private, 1976[a]	
	Number	Percent
Female	161	15
Male	898	85
White	979	92
Black	68	7
Chicano	7	0.6
American Indian	3	0.2
Other	2	0.2

	Type of Control, 1977[b]				
	Public		Private		Both[c]
Trustee	Number	Percent	Number	Percent	Percent
Female	546	15	441	23	17.8
Male	3,056	85	1,503	77	82.2
Black, Non-Hispanic	202	5.6[d]	95	4.8	5.3
Hispanic	70	1.4	6	0.3	1.4
White, Non-Hispanic	3,149	87.4	1,742	87.4	87.4
Other minority	34	0.9	41	2.1	1.3
No response	147	4.1	110	5.5	4.6

[a] Grafe, 1976, pp. 4–5.

[b] Drake, 1977, Table 2. Includes local and state governing boards, single and multi-campus institutions.

[c] ISEP reanalysis of Public and Independent columns.

[d] Corrected to include non-respondents to race/ethnicity questions.

as the boards in the aggregate are representative neither of institutional minority students nor percentages of minorities in the public at large.

Thus, the lag between theoretical representation of "community," by whatever reasonable standard one applies, and the actual practice is considerable. This conclusion is strengthened by the board members' and administrators' apparent conviction that they do, indeed, represent their communities. Their conservative attitudes (Mills, 1972), their interlocking board memberships and multiple appointments (nearly 20% hold membership on more than one educational governing board [Gomberg and Atelsek, 1977, Table 5]), and their unjustified perceptions that they are representative stand in stark contrast to any notion of a

TABLE 3-24

Characteristics of Voting Members of Single-Campus Governing Boards (in Percentages)

Characteristic	Public Single-Campus Boards			Private Single-Campus Boards		
	University (N = 27)	*4-Year* (N = 114)	*2-Year* (N = 491)	*University* (N = 68)	*4-Year* (N = 1,217)	*2-Year* (N = 233)
Number of voting members	360	1,347	3,751	2,338	31,848	5,115
Gender						
Men	87.4	84.0	80.4	89.9	87.3	71.1
Women	12.6	16.0	19.6	10.1	12.7	28.9
Total	100.0	100.0	100.0	100.0	100.0	100.0
Race						
Black	5.6	24.9	6.4	3.7	5.1	6.5
Other minority	2.0	2.2	3.0	.3	.8	.5
White	92.5	72.9	90.6	96.0	94.1	92.9
Total	100.0	100.0	100.0	100.0	100.0	100.0

Source: Gomberg and Atelsek, 1977, Table 8.

TABLE 3-25

Racial Composition of Single-Campus Governing Boards
(in Percentages)
1977

Race	All Institutions	2-Year	4-Year	Universities
Black	5.9	6.5	5.9	4.0
Other minority	1.0	1.6	0.9	0.5
White	93.1	91.9	93.2	95.5

Source: ISEP reanalysis of Gomberg and Atelsek, 1977, Table 8. Includes public and private institutions.

community that embraces heterogeneity and pluralism. Proponents of minority faculty hiring should not expect two year boards of trustees to strive for such changes in personnel policies. One critic may have been correct when he caustically noted, "the board of trustees is, perhaps, the most uninformed and incompetent component in a community college structure" (Moore, 1973, p. 171).

Administrators

Nor should proponents of change look to two year administrators as catalysts, for their ranks are as white and male as those of their faculties and their board members. With few exceptions, positions of administrative responsibility are held by white males. Even in minority institutions, with predominantly black or Hispanic enrollments, administrative positions are held in disproportionate numbers by white males (Van Alstyne *et al.*, 1977), leaving thoughtful observers with only one possible conclusion: minority institutions provide significant opportunities for white leadership, while white institutions provide limited opportunities for minority administrators. This section will examine available data on racial and ethnic compositions of two year college administrative staffs and will break down key positions for further analysis.

The president, or chief executive officer, is the obvious person to pinpoint in examining two year college leadership and decision making; not surprisingly, presidents are overwhelmingly white and male. Exceptions to this rule appear as minority presidents are appointed to positions in minority institutions or institutions with significant minority enroll-

TABLE 3-26

Characteristics of Voting Members of Governing Boards (in Percentages)

Characteristic	Total Governing Boards				Public			Private	
	Total (N = 2,314)	Single-Campus (N = 2,150)	Multi-Campus (N = 92)	Multi-Campus (N = 72)	Single-Campus (N = 632)	Multi-Campus (N = 71)	Multi-Campus (N = 67)	Single-Campus (N = 1,518)	Multi-Campus (N = 26)
Number of voting members	47,138	44,759	1,368	1,011	5,458	609	846	39,301	924
Sex									
Men	84.9	84.9	85.8	85.2	81.7	84.9	84.1	85.3	87.3
Women	15.1	15.1	14.2	14.8	18.3	15.1	15.9	14.7	12.7
Total	100.0	100.0	100.0	100.0	100.0	100.0	100.0	100.0	100.0
Race									
Black	6.0	5.9	4.5	8.7	10.9	6.7	9.7	5.2	2.9
Other minority	1.0	1.0	1.2	2.4	2.7	2.1	2.9	.7	.3
White	93.0	93.1	94.3	88.9	86.4	91.1	87.4	94.0	96.8
Total	100.0	100.0	100.0	100.0	100.0	100.0	100.0	100.0	100.0

Source: Gomberg and Atelsek, 1977, Table 3.

TABLE 3-27

2-Year College Trustee Attitudes (in Percentages)
1972

Statement	Trustees strongly agreeing or agreeing
"Recent charges that boards lack 'representative' membership of youth, women, and minorities"	38
"The Board on which I serve is quite representative of our community."	72
"Membership of governing boards should be more representative of the community."	58

Source: Mills, 1972, Tables 3 and 4.

ments, and as women are appointed to presidencies of women's colleges or church-affiliated colleges. These data are rather startling in their indication of the extraordinary extent to which white males dominate higher education administration, across institutional types and missions. Scholars of the academic presidency have noted the near exclusion of minorities and women from institutional leadership positions (e.g., Cohen and March, 1974, pp. 12–13), except in minority-dominant colleges. The presidencies of minority institutions are not held entirely by minority administrators; as the figures above indicate, one-fifth of

TABLE 3-28

Attitudes of College Presidents and
Trustee Board Chairpersons About Representativeness
1977

Official	Percentage Agreeing with Statement: "This Board is well 'balanced' and representative of its community."	
	Public	Private
President	80	74
Chairperson	90	91

Source: Drake, 1977, Tables 10, 15, p; 14. (Only "agree" and "disagree" responses tabulated; "uncertain" responses not reported.)

TABLE 3-29

Race and Gender Patterns of College Presidencies (Percentage Distribution) 1975–76

Student Body Type of Institution

Race and Gender	Public, White Co-Educational	Private, White Co-Educational	Private White Women's Colleges	Public White Men's Colleges	Private White Men's Colleges	Public Minority Institutions	Private Minority Institutions
White male	95.6	95.5	68.6	100.0	100.0	21.1	0.0
Minority male	3.3	.5	0.0	0.0	0.0	78.9	95.5
White female	1.1	3.7	31.4	0.0	0.0	0.0	0.0
Minority female	0.0	0.3	0.0	0.0	0.0	0.0	4.5

Carnegie Classification

	Public, Research Universities	Private, Research Universities	Public, Comprehensive Colleges	Private, Comprehensive Colleges	Public, Liberal Art Colleges	Private, Liberal Art Colleges
White male	94.3	97.6	96.6	100.0	100.0	94.3
Minority male	3.8	0.0	2.4	0.0	0.0	0.9
White female	1.9	2.4	1.0	0.0	0.0	4.8
Minority female	0.0	0.0	0.0	0.0	0.0	0.0

	Public 2-Year Colleges	Private 2-Year Colleges	Public Specialized Institutions	Private Specialized Institutions
White male	95.1	88.6	100.0	97.6
Minority male	3.9	0.0	0.0	0.0
White female	1.0	8.6	0.0	2.4
Minority female	0.0	2.8	0.0	0.0

Source: Van Alstyne et al., 1977a, Table 5.   Note: Includes chief executive officers.

minority-institution presidencies in the public sector are held by white males (see Table 3-29; Van Alstyne *et al.*, 1977, Table 5).*

Moore and Wagstaff found in their 1972 study only four predominantly-white two year institutions to have black presidents (Moore and Wagstaff, 1974, p. 182), while Brooks and Avila, in a survey conducted the same year, found 95% of the two year college presidents to be white, 3% black, and 1% Asian–American (Brooks and Avila, 1974, p. 146). Although different explanations for the phenomenon can be advanced, figures appear to corroborate the underrepresentation of minorities in the decision making structure of two year institutions: presidents, trustees, and faculty.

The striking underrepresentation of minority chief executive officers has more than symbolic importance, although a significant portion of presidential time and tenure is spent in symbolic activities, in four year institutions (Cohen and March, 1974) and in two year colleges (Moore, 1971). The underrepresentation is particularly noteworthy because two year college presidents, more than four year presidents, theoretically control institutional events, influence institutional practices, and execute trustee policies. That this would be so is due not only to the decreasing percentage of full-time faculty who would be vying for influence, but authority is more likely to accrue to top administrators in institutions characterized by low levels of faculty prestige and autonomy (Baldridge *et al.*, 1973; 1977). Due to the residual authority structure that lingers from the original K-14 governance system, the chief executive officer may resemble the authoritative superintendent more than the collegial, *primus inter pares* president; indeed, there are still chief executive officers whose titles remain "superintendent" (Brooks and Avila, 1974, p. 47).**

In order to gain this position of influence, presidents in two year institutions, as in four year colleges and universities (Cohen and March, 1974), frequently have had previous educational leadership experience. While this does not seem to be a *sine qua non*, over 80% of the two-year presidents in a 1972 survey had held educational institution experience as their prior position (Brooks and Avila, 1974, Table 7). This principle of ascendancy makes minority representation at lower ranks important

---

* Arce (1978) notes that institutions serving predominantly Chicano student bodies have almost exclusively been headed by whites. Olivas (1978) compiled a listing of Chicano presidents, including twelve two year college executive officers; all of the presidents headed institutions located in the West or Southwest (see also Esquibel, 1976). Two institutions on the U.S. mainland have Puerto Rican presidents. Six two year colleges have Asian presidents (Barry, ed., 1978). Twenty-one Native Americans head BIA or tribal colleges.

** One interviewee, when asked whether the leadership resembled K-12 or higher education models, jokingly responded that the chancellor was a superintendent, while the campus presidents were "principals."

for future positions of administrative responsibility. Conceivably, underrepresentation of minority presidents could be a phenomenon due to historical discrimination and the small numbers of minority administrators in the ranks; under this theory, affirmative action and pressures for integration would be filling the lower ranks, the supply pipeline, with a growing number of minority and women administrators who, given their turn, will become chief executive officers.

This hopeful theory cannot find support in the data on lower level administrative ranks of two year colleges, where majority males hold disproportionate percentages of line, staff, and support positions. It has already been shown that faculty positions are seldom filled by minorities, so little "inflation" from faculty to administrative ranks can be expected to occur. Moore has noted that those blacks employed by white two year institutions have been employed only recently: 87% of his respondents had been on the staffs less than five years (Moore, 1976b, p. 19). His study, conducted in 1972, might also have predicted a rising in the ranks of these faculty and administrators.

Van Alstyne and her associates would dash this hope in their 1977 study of employment patterns and salary comparisons of women and minorities in higher education administration (Van Alstyne et al., 1977a), as they concluded,

A recent comprehensive national survey confirms what many have suspected is true—that after years of verbal commitment to affirmative action relatively few women and minorities hold top jobs in higher education administration, except at women's colleges and minority institutions. What is more, those who are so employed at white coeducational institutions are generally concentrated in lower paying jobs, and in those jobs the women are paid less than the men (Van Alstyne et al., 1977b, p. 39).

Was there progress from 1972, or the illusion of progress? Figures from the early seventies indicated a low bench mark from which to gain, but Van Alstyne's pessimistic characterization accurately portrays scant progress during the major years of affirmative action and institutional growth.

Goodrich's AACJC study of 1970–71 two year college administrative staffs indicated that 92.9% were white (Goodrich et al., 1972–73, Table 7). The following year, he noted that white two year administrators had risen to 93.8% (Goodrich, 1977, Table 10). Although not strictly comparable, these data provided the only statistical evidence of minority participation in two year college administrative staffs during the early 1970's.

Van Alstyne's study found that 93% of her 18,000 full-time administrator respondents were white (1977b, p. 40). In predominantly white

TABLE 3-30

Women Chief Executive Officers
1977

Type of Institution	Number of Women CEO									Student Body Composition 1977–78
	Member of Religious Orders			Others			Totals			
	1975	1976	1977	1975	1976	1977	1975	1976	1977	
4-year private	79	83	82	19	24	25	98	107	107	Women[a] 72 / Coed 35
2-year private	26	23	23	8	8	7	34	31	30	Women 15 / Coed 15
4-year public	0	0	0	5	3	5	5	3	5	Coed 5
2-year public	0	0	0	11	13	14	11	13	14	Coed 14
Total	105	106	105	43	48	51	148	154	156	Women 87 / Coed 69

Source: Association of Governing Boards, 1978, p. 2.
[a] At least 90% women.

TABLE 3-31

**Racial/Ethnic Breakdown of AAJC Minority Administrators
1970 and 1971**

Race/Ethnicity	1970		1971	
	Number	Percent	Number	Percent
Black	528	5.6	550	4.7
Mexican American	82	0.9	106	0.9
Puerto Rican	5	0.1	8	0.06
American Indian	46	0.5	44	0.3
American Oriental	*	*	34	0.2
White	8,657	92.9	12,045	93.84

Source: 1970 data taken from Goodrich, Lezotte, and Welch, 1972–73, Table VII; 1971 data taken from Goodrich, 1977, Table 10. (ISEP reanalysis of line/staff responsibilities. Total administrators adjusted for respondent institutions.)

Note: 1970 data reanalyzed to include full-time and part-time administrators.

* Data unavailable.

coeducational two year colleges, white men and women filled 96.1% of the chief executive positions, 95.4% of administrative affairs positions, 95.7% of academic affairs positions, 93.1% of the student affairs positions, and 93.7% of external affairs positions.

These data, the most recent and comprehensive figures for administrative distribution patterns by race and gender, confirm earlier studies by Goodrich and his associates (Tables 3-30, 3-31), and show underrepresentation across institutional types and administrative positions. What is less well-known is that minority institutions have traditionally drawn integrated talent into teaching and administrative ranks. A reanalysis of the Van Alstyne data indicates these findings. Whites comprise 11.2% of the administrative positions in public minority institutions, and 8.1% of the positions in private minority institutions; these positions include significant numbers of leadership positions as well as staff assignments (Van Alstyne et al., 1977a, Table 7).

Once again, it is important to note how two year institutions fare vis-a-vis more prestigious senior institutions. One would expect that two year colleges, at the bottom of the higher education prestige hierarchy, would be able to recruit more minority administrators than would elite institutions, whose top level executives traditionally hold a doctorate and rise through the faculty ranks (Baldridge et al., 1973; 1977; Cohen and March, 1974). Van Alstyne and her associates noted the hierarchical distribution among baccalaureate institutions, and concluded:

TABLE 3-32

Percentage of White Administrators in
White Coeducational Institutions
1975–76

Type of Institution	Research Universities (N = 104)	Compre- hensive Colleges (N = 229)	Liberal Arts Colleges (N = 211)	2-Year (N = 343)	Specialized Institutions (N = 53)
All white coeducational institutions	96.2	95.7	97.8	94.6	96.0
Public white coeducational institutions	96.3	96.6	93.2	94.5	95.4
Private white coeducational institutions	95.9	97.7	98.2	98.0	96.3

Source: ISEP reanalysis of Van Alstyne et al., 1977a, Table 3. Male and female figures combined.

The Carnegie classification system for research universities, comprehensive universities and colleges, and liberal arts colleges implies
a hierarchy. Institutions are first grouped by educational mission,
then subdivided within each category on the basis of relevant
criteria such as resources, selectivity, degrees awarded, or program
diversity. Those institutions placed in Group I rate higher in the
relative variables than those in Group II. Yet generally, Group II
institutions employed fewer women and minority administrators.
In effect, the 'best' are doing the 'worst' (Van Alstyne et al., 1977b,
p. 30; see also 1977a, Table 4).

No one can take consolation in her findings, for the data indicate that
no institutional type in either the public or private sector is reasonably
well-integrated (except, ironically, the minority institutions, which employ disproportionately high numbers of white administrators in key
positions). That the less-prestigious senior institutions do better than
elite senior institutions should not lull either level into complacency on
this issue.

The most surprising findings concerning hierarchical patterns, however, have not been commented upon by Van Alstyne. As poorly as the
more elite institutions are doing, two year institutions fare no better,
either in the private sector or in the public institutions. As the following
figures, derived from Van Alstyne's study, indicate, two year institutions

TABLE 3-33

Employment Patterns in Predominantly Minority Institutions
(Racial Distribution)
1975–76

Type of Institution	Number of Positions	White Males		Minority Males		White Females		Minority Females	
		Number	Percent	Number	Percent	Number	Percent	Number	Percent
Public institutions (N = 16)	329	29	8.8	237	72.0	8	2.4	55	16.7
Private institutions (N = 20)	332	19	5.7	194	58.4	8	2.4	111	33.2

Source: Van Alstyne et al., 1977a, Table 7.

are only slightly less white in the aggregate than are other institutional types and, when separated into sectors, are more white in some cases.

It should be increasingly clear that neither two year faculty ranks, boards of trustees, lower administrative ranks, nor executive personnel

TABLE 3-34

Racial Distribution of Administrative Positions in White Coeducational Institutions (in Percentages) 1975–76

Race and Gender	Chief Executive Officers	Adminis- trative Affairs	Academic Affairs	Student Affairs	External Affairs
Public Research Universities (N = 72)					
White male	94.3	88.2	87.8	90.4	88.7
Minority male	3.8	4.5	1.4	3.2	3.4
White female	1.9	6.0	10.5	6.0	7.9
Minority female	0.0	1.3	0.3	0.5	0.0
Private Research Universities (N = 32)					
White male	97.6	85.2	86.8	81.1	89.5
Minority male	0.0	3.3	2.9	3.8	1.5
White female	2.4	10.0	10.3	12.7	9.0
Minority female	0.0	1.5	0.0	2.4	0.0
Public Comprehensive Colleges (N = 163)					
White male	96.6	85.7	83.9	82.7	84.0
Minority male	2.4	4.1	4.1	5.3	2.3
White female	1.0	9.1	11.2	11.2	12.8
Minority female	0.0	1.1	0.8	0.8	0.9
Private Comprehensive Colleges (N = 66)					
White male	100.0	86.2	88.0	79.9	86.6
Minority male	0.0	1.8	1.2	2.4	0.7
White female	0.0	11.3	10.5	16.8	12.0
Minority female	0.0	0.8	0.3	1.0	0.7
Public White Arts Colleges (N = 13)					
White male	100.0	75.3	85.7	75.3	87.5
Minority male	0.0	7.8	1.8	6.8	0.0
White female	0.0	16.9	12.5	12.3	12.5
Minority female	0.0	0.0	0.0	5.5	0.0

Source: Van Alstyne et al., 1977a. Table 5.

have adequate representation of racial and ethnic minorities. Further, because these persons serve as primary decision makers in institutional policies, there is no nucleus for change in current levels of underrepre-

TABLE 3-34a

Employment Patterns by Type of Administrative Position: White Coeducational Institutions by Carnegie Classification (Percentage Distribution) 1975–76

Race and Gender	Chief Executive Officers	Adminis-trative Affairs	Academic Affairs	Student Affairs	External Affairs
Private Liberal Arts Colleges (N = 198)					
White male	94.3	82.1	74.0	72.8	80.7
Minority male	0.9	1.8	0.6	1.6	0.9
White female	4.8	15.7	24.8	24.8	18.4
Minority female	0.0	0.4	0.6*	0.8	0.0
Public 2-Year Colleges (N = 311)					
White male	95.1	81.0	76.4	76.7	75.5
Minority male	3.9	3.7	3.0	6.3	4.5
White female	1.0	14.4	19.3	15.4	18.2
Minority female	0.0	0.9	1.3	1.6	1.8
Private 2-Year Colleges (N = 32)					
White male	88.6	64.0	56.7	61.9	81.3
Minority male	0.0	2.3	0.0	2.4	0.0
White female	8.6	33.7	43.3	34.5	18.7
Minority female	2.8	0.0	0.0	1.2	0.0
Public Specialized Institutions (N = 15)					
White male	100.0	88.7	84.1	80.9	94.1
Minority male	0.0	4.1	1.6	6.4	0.0
White female	0.0	5.1	12.7	12.7	5.9
Minority female	0.0	2.1	1.6	0.0	0.0
Private Specialized Institutions (N = 38)					
White male	97.6	75.8	73.4	60.0	68.2
Minority male	0.0	0.8	2.1	4.8	2.3
White female	2.4	21.7	24.5	32.4	27.3
Minority female	0.0	1.7	0.0	2.8	2.2

* Typographical error corrected.

sentation. The periods of growth in two year institutions have not produced corollary growth in the percentage of minorities in positions of influence. There is considerable evidence that current levels are being eroded, and that future representation will be even less egalitarian. Even more dramatic losses would have been noticeable were it not for pressures of affirmative action to hire minorities and to establish ethnic studies components and administrative offices to coordinate minority affairs and ethnic data collection. It is cruelly ironic that the advocacy and establishment of minority-oriented administrative offices, and the relatively widespread adoption of such mechanisms for co-opting minority concerns, should mask the serious erosion of minority participation in the mainstream, and in central administrative ranks.

The following data show the extent to which minorities and women are employed in equal opportunity administration. These figures *understate* the number of women and minorities holding responsibility for affirmative action administration, as many institutions have consolidated the data collection and monitoring tasks under other personnel or administrative rubrics (see, generally, Kronovet, 1977).

The ghettoization, or concentration, of minorities within administrative ranks is unmistakable, and only the significant number of minority administrators performing affirmative action tasks has prevented additional erosion in the aggregate. Nearly 14% (74 of 539) of all minorities in public, white coeducational institutions hold Affirmative Action and Equal Employment Opportunity responsibilities; over 7% (10 of 135) of the minority staff members in the private sector hold these responsibilities. This concentration is all the more remarkable when it is noted that only 173 of the 1,037 sampled institutions (16.7%) reported having such a full-time position (Van Alstyne *et al.*, 1977b, p. 41).

This concentration has other stigmatizing characteristics as well. The uncertain nature and scope of affirmative action philosophies have made the administration of such programs conflicting and difficult. This uncertainty is reflected in the low prestige of the position, as measured by low salary scales* (Van Alstyne et al., 1977a; 1977b), high turnover, and the large number of part-time assignments (Gemmell, 1974; Kronovet, 1974; 1977; Liss, 1977). Studies of two year college AA/EEO officers in New York State and California found that fewer than 8% of these administrators were full-time (Kronovet, 1977, p. 4). In California, nearly 13% of the two year college presidents serve as the institutional affirmative action officers (Kronovet, 1977, p. 5), raising the possibility that no other institutional representative will have portfolio in order to advocate increased minority and female representation.

---

* Van Alstyne also found that male AA/EEO officers were paid more than female AA/EEO officers (1977a, Table 15).

TABLE 3-35

Employment Patterns in 2-Year Colleges
1975–76

	Male		Female	
Type of Institution	*White*	*Minority*	*White*	*Minority*
All white coeducational (N = 343)	3,539 (78.6%)	185 (4.1%)	728 (16.2%)	52 (1.1%)
Public white coeducational (N = 311)	3,339 (79.4%)	181 (4.3%)	634 (15.1%)	50 (1.2%)
Public white coeducational (N = 32)	200 (66.7%)	4 (1.3%)	94 (31.3%)	2 (0.7%)
All women's colleges (N = 8)	35 (48.0%)	0	38 (52.0%)	0
*Public women's colleges (N = 0)				
Private women's colleges (N = 8)	35 (48.0%)	0	38 (52.0%)	0
*All men's colleges (N = 0)				
*Public men's colleges (N = 0)				
*Private men's colleges (N = 0)				
All minority institutions (N = 8)	23 (25.3%)	44 (48.4%)	6 (6.6%)	18 (19.7%)
Public minority institutions (N = 4)	22 (36.1%)	27 (44.3%)	5 (8.2%)	7 (11.4%)
Private minority institutions (N = 4)	1 (3.3%)	17 (56.7%)	1 (3.3%)	11 (36.7%)

Source: Van Alstyne *et al.*, 1977a, Table 3.

* No data available.

In addition to AA/EEO officer, a second position has begun to emerge as race-specific, that of Director of Student Financial Aid. In both public and private sector white coeducational institutions, 10.4% (public: 56 of 539; private: 14 of 135) of the positions held by minorities direct student financial aid offices. This concentration is reassuring; it places minorities in a key area to affect an important component of college attendance (see chapter four, "Supportive Services"). The Van Alstyne study indicates, however, that relatively little prestige, as measured by salary, accrues to persons holding the position. In public sector white coeducational institutions, the position ranks 50th (of 52) in the ranked median salary scale; in the private sector, it ranks 47th (Van Alstyne *et al.,* 1977a, Table 10). Moreover, the issue of underparticipation in financial aid programs by two year colleges (see chapter four) may be explained, in part, by financial aid understaffing and lack of professional expertise (Gladieux, 1975), indications of the small extent to which two year colleges value this function.*

Although this chapter has singled out three administrative positions—chief executive officers, affirmative action coordinators, and financial aid directors—for scrutiny, any position across institutional missions or institutional types would have revealed racial and gender-based patterns.** Academic affairs, arguably the most important mission within higher education, is predominantly white and male (see Tables 3-28, 3-29), and constitutes what Astin has labeled, "The Hard Core of Sexism in Academe" (Astin, 1977b). Only three of nineteen academic disciplines in public white coeducational institutions (one in the private sector) have less than 95% white leadership.

These few deanships are held by minorities more often in four year institutions than they are in two year colleges. Moore and Wagstaff report that only 26% of their 67 respondent black deans were in two year colleges (38.8%), while they found no black directing an apprenticeship vocational program in a two year college (1974, pp. 107, 184). Esquibel (1976) found that the overwhelming majority of Chicano administrators at nearly all levels were to be found in four year, rather than two year institutions. This finding is particularly significant in light of the severe maldistribution of Hispanic students in two year institutions.

Summarizing the data presented in this chapter would necessitate

---

* An ISEP analysis of the 1975–76 data (Malott *et al.,* 1976) upon which Van Alstyne based her analysis, suggested that salary scales for Financial Aid Directors vary according to institutional size, rather than to institutional type. I am grateful to Lawrence Gladieux, Director of CEEB, Washington office, for his exchange of correspondence clarifying this point.

** Although two year college enrollments are 49% female (OCR, 1978), women are only a relatively small portion of the administrative ranks in the institutions: 15% in the public sector white coeducational institution, 31% in private (v. 11% in public, 17% in private four year institutions) (Van Alstyne *et al.,* 1977b, p. 40). See, generally, Thurston *et al.,* 1972; Bayer and Astin, 1975; Edsall, 1976.

TABLE 3-36

Job Concentration of Administrators in White Coeducational Institutions 1975–76

Public Institutions (N = 574)

White Male		Minority Male		White Female		Minority Female	
(Total Employed: 9,211)		(Total Employed: 434)		(Total Employed: 1,263)		(Total Employed: 105)	
Chief Business Officer	471	Affirmative Action/Equal Employment Officer	49	Head Librarian	138	Affirmative Action/Equal Employment	25
Chief Academic Officer	439	Director, Student Financial Aid	45	Nursing Dean	138	Head Librarian	11
Director, Physical Plant	433	Chief Student Life Officer	36	Bookstore Manager	112	Director, Student Financial Aid	11
Chief Executive Officer	380	Director, Personnel Services	23	Registrar	81	Nursing Dean	7

Private Institutions (N = 366)

White Male		Minority Male		White Female		Minority Female	
(Total Employed: 4,490)		(Total Employed: 96)		(Total Employed: 977)		(Total Employed: 39)	
Chief Executive Officer	319	Director, Student Financial Aid	11*	Head Librarian	120	Director, Personnel Services	4
Chief Business Officer	294	Chief Student Life Officer	8	Registrar	104	Registrar	4
Director, Physical Plant	286	Affirmative Action/Equal Employment Officer	7	Bookstore Manager	92	Director, Student Placement	4
Chief Development Officer	276	Director, Physical Plant	6	Director, Student Financial Aid	62	Affirmative Action/Equal Employment	3

Source: Van Alstyne et al., 1977a, Table 7.
* Corrected from Table 6.

TABLE 3-37

Race and Gender of Academic Affairs Officers in White Coeducational Institutions (Percentage Distribution) 1975–76

Academic Affairs Officers—Positions	Public Institutions (N = 574)					Private Institutions (N = 366)				
	Number of Administrators	White Male	Minority Male	White Female	Minority Female	Number of Administrators	White Male	Minority Male	White Female	Minority Female
Chief Academic Officer	479	92	3	5	0	281	95	1	4	0
Head Librarian	509	69	1	27	2	317	60	2	38	0
Director; Institutional Research	226	85	4	12	0	51	76	0	22	2
Architecture	42	95	2	2	0	7	100	0	0	0
Agriculture	69	99	1	0	0	0	0	0	0	0
Arts and Sciences	253	92	3	4	0	83	92	1	7	0
Business	247	96	2	3	0	72	92	3	6	0
Dentistry	31	97	0	3	0	10	100	0	0	0
Education	202	89*	7	3	0	66	82	2	17	0
Engineering	115	97	1	1	1	37	97	3	0	0
Extensions	144	94	3	3	0	35	83*	3	11	3
Fine Arts	116	84	4	10	2	38	87	0	13	0
Graduate Programs	158	89	3	8	0	50	84	4	12	0
Home Economics	73	14	1	82	3	7	29	0	71	0
Law	41	100	0	0	0	35	94	3	3	0
Medicine	45	100	0	0	0	11	100	0	0	0
Music	58	95	3	2	0	35	94	0	5	0
Nursing	160	9	1	86	4	39	3	0	95	3
Pharmacy	32	100	0	0	0	6	100	0	0	0
Social Work	64	72*	13	16	0	26	85	0	15	0
Technology	76	96	4	0	0	5	100	0	0	0
Vocational Education	123	93*	4	2	1	4	100	0	0	0

Source: Van Alstyne et al., 1977a; Table 6.   * Less than 95% white.

TABLE 3-38

Proportion of Women as Chief Academic Officers, Deans of Arts and Sciences, and Faculty Members
1972–73

Type of Institution	Chief Academic Officer			Dean of Arts and Sciences			Women on Faculty	
	Total Number[a]	Number of Women	Women in Percentage	Total Number	Number of Women	Women in Percentage	Total Number	Mean Percentage
All Institutions								
Universities	1,819	160	8.8	512	21	4.1	2,051	29.0
Public	80	1	1.3	77	0	0.0	68	17.7
Private	47	0	0.0	45	1	2.2	44	16.8
4-year								
Public	299	3	1.0	180	2	1.1	316	24.5
Catholic	189	74	39.2	30	5	16.7	194	42.0
Protestant	291	19	6.5	21	1	4.8	300	23.4
Independent	256	25	10.0	42	2	4.8	307	22.9
2-year								
Public	503	15	3.0	112	9	8.0	644	30.4
Private	154	23	14.9	4	1	20.0	178	44.4

Source: Astin, 1977b, Table 5.

[a] HEGIS 1972–73. Institution's reporting sex of incumbents.

TABLE 3-39

Chicanos as a Percentage of Higher Education Administrators in Southwestern Institutions 1974–75

State	Total Number of Institutions	Total Number of Administrators	Number of Chicano Administrators	Number of Other Administrators	Percentage of Chicano Administrators	Number of Institutions with No Chicano Administrators	Percentage of Institutions with No Chicano Administrators
Arizona	21	252	8	243	3.1	12	57.2
California	244	2,997	69	2,928	2.3	162	66.4
Colorado	39	446	9	437	2.0	22	56.4
New Mexico	22	164	15	149	9.1	14	66.6
Texas	144	1,845	44	1,801	2.4	120	83.4
Southwest Total	470	6,303	145	6,158	2.3	332	71.5

Source: Esquibel, 1976, Table 2. Includes presidents, vice presidents, deans or equivalent.

considerable repetition of findings essentially similar. This portion of the book has attempted to refute the myth and commonly held assumption that there is adequate representation of minorities in two year institutions; namely, that these colleges, unlike their elite and more selective counterparts, represented the communities from which their students and resources were drawn. Confronted with the available data on faculty, trustees, and administrators, one is forced to concede Moore's indictment: "The two year college system in the United States is a system *of whites,* is controlled and operated *by whites,* and reserves its major rewards *for whites*" (Moore, 1976b, p. 42) [emphasis in the original].

Chapter 4

Academic Programs and Support Services

ツ ツ ツ

Jerome Karabel's classic analysis of stratification in community colleges is a most thoughtful and provocative essay (Karabel, 1972), one that gives credence to what many critics of the two year college movement had felt, namely, that these institutions perpetuate class distinctions (and implicitly, racial and ethnic distinctions). To be sure, minorities have been hit harder by the educational inflation described by Karabel, especially as their enrollments have increased, as is argued in chapter two, only in selected strata of postsecondary education. Further, as argued forcefully by Arce (1976, 1978), only when governmental pressures have served to increase opportunities for majority students have minorities benefited significantly.

Karabel is less convincing, however, in his linking the class stratification two year colleges with race and ethnicity, despite the obvious and disheartening overrepresentation of minorities in the lower economic classes of American society. Indeed, he cites few data to support his thesis that minorities tend to enroll in technical or vocational (i.e., nontransfer) curricula: "Black students show themselves to be considerably more likely than white students to enroll in community college vocational programs" (p. 541). Offered as evidence was a 1969 study of student program enrollments at 63 community colleges, a study that demonstrated caucasian students' low rate of enrollment in technical and vocational curricula and a correspondingly higher minority ("Negro, Oriental, other") enrollment in these programs.

His conclusions coincide with many commonly held perceptions of the "tracking" into lower status career paths alleged to occur in two year institutions. In reference to Chicano students in these institutions, Barron (1973) notes that they are " 'counseled' into what I refer to as a 'minority' curriculum—a vocational program" (p. 23). Gleazer (1973) likewise notes the presumption that minority students are funneled into the lower tracks (see especially chapters 2 and 6). King (1977) has shown that black high school students in college preparatory courses perceive that "vocational training is a device used by the white man to keep blacks out of higher status jobs" (p. 439), and has shown that their parents are more likely to encourage them to attend college than are parents of high school students enrolled in vocational schools.

These perceptions find apparent support in explicit governmental policies establishing tiered systems of postsecondary education, which, through tuition or admissions practices, result in significant minority enrollments only in the institutions at the low end of the continuum, i.e., those two year institutions with technical and vocational program offerings. The New York and California public institutions typify this pyramidal policy of higher education. However, when one looks more closely *within* the lowest stratum, evidence is less convincing that there is "tracking," however perceived.

Indisputably, minority students constitute a disproportionately large share of total enrollments in these institutions, most of which have dual curricula: academic transfer and technical-vocational. This crisis of maldistribution severely limits traditional views of access and diversity, at least for minority students. Claiming that minority students are tracked within the universe of postsecondary education, though, is not the same as claiming that they are tracked within two year institutions. Indeed, enrollment patterns in two year colleges exhibit a semblance of equality and distribution not in evidence for minority students in other sectors of postsecondary education. Observers should not be naive, however, in underestimating the severity of minority maldistribution throughout the entire system, for a reasonable distribution in the lowest stratum of the system does not mean that the entire system has accorded access to minorities.

This point needs to be reiterated, lest this evidence of distribution within restricted access lull policymakers, however well-intentioned, into practices that would adversely affect minorities at the low end of the continuum. The data presented in the chapter should be read with a major caveat in mind, namely, that they show limited progress and that they mask the skewing effect within the postsecondary universe. This chapter will examine two year college enrollment patterns and minority student representation in area enrollments, associate degree patterns in two year institutions, receipt of associate degrees by minority students, associate degree programs in minority institutions, ethnic studies enrollments in two year colleges, racial and ethnic enrollment patterns in noncollegiate proprietary institutions, and two year academic provisions for remedial and honor students.

Academic Programs

ENROLLMENT PATTERNS

Enrollment data limitations include incomplete records and fluctuations in defining "transfer" and "terminal." Moreover, concurrent enrollments by students in transfer and terminal programs preclude exact, mutually exclusive counts, and even counts by program emphasis. What trend is discernable is the increase in vocational enrollments, both in absolute numbers, and as a percentage of all enrollments. These figures indicate the extent to which transfer and technical enrollments have grown, as well as the extent to which the technical emphasis has increased in two year colleges. Parker (1974, 1975), Wilms (1974), Freeman (1976), and others have documented the increasing orientation toward technical career education in these institutions. In reviewing state and federal policies accounting for the increase, one researcher has noted "the surge of occupational education":

> The turning point for occupational education came sometime during the middle 1960s. Not only did occupational enrollment increase in numbers, but it increased at a higher rate than either total enrollment or transfer enrollment. There is no question about the durability of the phenomenon. No matter what the unit of measurement—first-time freshman enrollment, head count, full-time equivalent (FTE), student credit hours, majors, graduates, faculty—the steep upward movement is unmistakable (Lombardi, 1978b, p. 58).

Not only did both curricular emphases grow, but program offerings within each emphasis proliferated, as specialization and fragmentation reached into the two year colleges—mirroring the senior college course proliferation (see, generally, Levine, 1978; Rudolph, 1977).

The following tables indicate the proportions of time for which two year colleges require associate degree students to enroll for academic majors. The high percentages of time spent in courses required for the associate degree, particularly in non-liberal arts curricula, point to the

TABLE 4-1

**Enrollment Increases in Federally Aided Vocational Classes
Selected Years, 1919–20 to 1973–74**

	Number of Students*			
Year	All Programs	Agricul- ture	Home Economics	Trades and Industry
1919–20	265,058	31,301	48,938	184,819
1929–30	981,882	188,311	174,967	618,604
1939–40	2,290,741	584,133	818,766	758,409
1949–50	3,364,613	764,975	1,430,366	804,602
1955–56	3,413,159	785,599	1,486,816	883,719
1957–58	3,629,339	775,892	1,559,822	893,644
1959–60	3,768,149	796,237	1,588,109	938,490
1961–62	4,072,677	822,664	1,725,660	1,005,383
1963–64	4,566,390	860,605	2,022,138	1,069,274
1965–66	6,070,059	907,354	1,897,670	1,269,051
1967–68	7,533,936	851,158	2,283,338	1,628,542
1969–70	8,793,960	852,983	2,570,410	1,906,133
1971–72	11,710,767	896,460	3,445,698	2,397,968
1972–73	12,283,538	927,591	3,516,683	2,702,238
1973–74	13,794,512	976,319	3,702,685	2,824,317

Year	Distri- butive Occupa- tions	Health Occupa- tions	Technical Education	Office Occupa- tions	Other
1939–40	129,433	—	—	—	—
1949–50	364,670	—	—	—	—
1955–56	257,025	—	—	—	—
1957–58	282,558	27,423	—	—	—
1959–60	303,784	40,250	101,279	—	—
1961–62	321,065	48,985	148,920	—	—
1963–64	334,126	59,006	221,241	—	—
1965–66	420,426	83,677	253,838	1,238,043	—
1967–68	574,785	140,987	269,832	1,735,997	49,927
1969–70	529,365	198,044	271,730	2,111,160	354,135
1971–72	640,423	336,652	337,069	2,351,878	1,304,619
1972–73	738,547	421,075	364,044	2,499,095	1,114,265
1973–74	832,905	504,913	392,887	2,757,464	1,803,023

Source: Andersen, ed., 1976, Table 76.129.

* Students in federally aided classes in the U.S. and outlying parts.

TABLE 4-2

State Trends: Credit Enrollment by Program Emphasis

State	Year	Total Enrollment[1]		Occupational Enrollment[2]		Transfer Enrollment[3]	
		Number	Average Yearly Increase	Number	Average Yearly Increase	Number	Average Yearly Increase
Florida	1970	107,630		25,980		78,940	
	1975	169,790	12%	47,400	17%	105,280	7%
Hawaii	1969	8,200		3,660		3,170	
	1976	20,880	22%	9,090	21%	9,980	16%
Illinois	1968	89,530		23,450		49,750	
	1976	325,830	33%	108,330	45%	107,050	14%
Iowa	1968-9	21,440		7,860		9,790	
	1975-6	43,770	15%	21,080	24%	10,580	1%
Massachusetts	1967	11,620		5,090		5,360	
	1974	28,100	20%	16,540	32%	9,000	11%
Mississippi	1972	33,420		10,150		16,230	
	1975	45,750	16%	14,980	16%	20,400	9%
Nevada	1973	2,890		1,790		950	
	1976	4,980	24%	2,130	6%	2,150	42%
Oregon	1968-9	80,940		33,860		22,740	
	1975-6	201,770	21%	72,020	16%	40,760	11%

Source: Lombardi, 1978, Table 1.

[1] Total Enrollment includes Occupational and Transfer, "Other Studies and Undeclared" (Illinois), "Other Reimbursable," "Non-Reimbursable" and "Separate Contract" (Oregon), "Development" (Nevada), etc.

[2] Occupational is synonymous with such other designations used in state reports as: technical, vocational, career education, occupational extension, supplementary vocational.

[3] Transfer is synonymous with such other designations used in state reports as: liberal arts, baccalaureate-oriented, college or university parallel, preprofessional, academic, professional and advanced.

critical need for competent academic advising and career counseling early in the admissions and registration process. The margin for error is much narrower in a two year curriculum than it is in a four year plan.

Earlier studies of academic majors (baccalaureate) suggest that degree requirements have not changed dramatically in the last ten years, despite the increases in number of courses and majors available to students (Dressel and DeLisle, 1969; Blackburn, Armstrong, *et al.*, 1976). These findings are somewhat surprising, given the flux in higher education, general perceptions concerning dilution of quality standards, and rapidly changing demographics (Knoell, 1976). The most rapid change in student enrollments has been the increase in the number of minority students, particularly in the two year colleges.

This change is apparent to anyone examining aggregate enrollment figures; less obvious has been the distribution of minority students *across fields in the aggregate.* The other major sector of minority access in postsecondary education—historically black colleges—reports severe maldistribution problems in enrollments and degrees, with disproportionate numbers of students enrolled in the fields of education and social sciences (Blake, Lambert, and Martin, 1974, pp. 33–45).* Unlike the aggregate figures for historically black college enrollments, however, data for minority students in two year colleges show better distributions

TABLE 4-3

Percentage of Undergraduate Degree Programs Requiring Varying Amounts of Time for Major

Percentage of Time Spent on Major	Degree				
	A.A	A.S.	A.A.S.	B.A.	B.S.
1–10					
11–20	2	3		4	3
21–30	23	7		36	17
31–40	23	6	7	32	18
41–50	18	20	9	17	19
51–60	8	14	9	7	18
61–70	13	18	26	3	13
71–80	7	12	21	1	9
81–90	4	15	19		3
91–100	2	6	9		

Source: Levine, 1978, Table 4.

---

* Associate degree figures for historically black colleges were not reported.

TABLE 4-4

Percentage of Associate Degree Programs
Requiring Varying Amounts of Time for Major

Percentage of Time Spent on Major	Humanities	Social Science	Science	Business	Education	Engineering	Health Science	Trade and Technical Arts
1–10								
11–20	12			2	4			2
21–30	24	26	23	13	12	9	4	9
31–40	24	32	15	11	40	3	5	2
41–50	29	13	18	23	8	13	8	22
51–60	6	16	15	11	4	6	13	7
61–70	6	13	13	17	12	20	20	20
71–80			13	11	12	22	17	11
81–90			3	8	8	19	25	15
91–100				5		3	9	11

Source: Levine, 1978, Table 6.

in the aggregate for both transfer and terminal enrollments, and less severe maldistribution in enrollments by major field.

Goodrich's study of minority enrollments and degrees awarded oversampled institutions with concentrations of minority students, but even this unrepresentative sample of institutions showed evidence of considerable student choice and differentiated enrollments. There is an internal pattern of clustering in traditionally female occupational areas (nursing, data processing, secretarial, and stenography), a pattern with which policy makers should be concerned. Although the two columns are not strictly comparable, the percentages of minorities receiving degrees and those enrolled form a rudimentary indication of retention rates, which seem to be higher in the career programs than in the transfer curricula.

Bushnell's study (1973) reported over 30% minority enrollments in two year colleges, but 15% of his respondents did not indicate race or ethnicity. His figures therefore overstate minority enrollments for 1971 (or any other year), but his enrollment distribution data indicate no skewing of minority enrollment into career curricula. Indeed, with the exception of Oriental American patterns, the minority choices of transfer curricula surpass white transfer enrollment percentages. Census data from 1972 and 1974 are less helpful in gauging program emphases, although they do show low enrollments for blacks in vocational and

TABLE 4-5

**Minority Student Status in Selected Career Education
and Academic/Transfer Programs
1971**

Program	Number of Schools Offering	1971 Graduates	1971 Minority Graduates	1971 Minority Percent of Total Graduates
Agri-Business				
Agri-business	15	44	5	11.3
Ornamental horticulture, landscaping	15	44	6	13.6
Agri-business (management oriented)	15	69	6	8.6
Allied Health				
Dental hygiene	19	190	23	12.1
Dental office assistant	24	167	6	3.5
Medical lab technician	42	240	29	12.0
Medical secretary	38	207	28	13.5
RN nursing	76	2,463	636	25.8
X-ray technician	34	146	12	8.2
Inhalation therapy technician	34	157	65	41.4
Business and Related				
Bookkeeping-accounting	81	1,091	563	51.6
Data processing (programmer)	81	785	171	21.7
Data processing (operator)	50	352	190	53.9
Mid-management (merchandise)	66	572	158	27.6
Secretarial (executive)	91	838	261	31.1
Stenographer	64	673	266	39.5
Applied Arts				
Commercial artist	30	329	42	12.7
Engineering, Science Technology				
Architectural technology	36	128	45	35.1
Automotive technology	53	445	118	26.5
Civil technician	35	260	11	4.2
Drafting technician	77	466	69	14.8
Electronics technician	79	945	137	14.4

Program	Number of Schools Offering	1971 Graduates	1971 Minority Graduates	1971 Minority Percent of Total Graduates
Public Services				
Education aide	44	190	114	60.0
Fire science	37	138	28	20.2
Law enforcement	69	864	239	27.6
Library and audio-visual aides	23	64	21	32.8
Social service technician	30	175	51	29.1
Academic Transfer				
Pre-teaching	73	2,844	296	10.4
Pre-law	55	227	17	7.4
Pre-medicine	59	205	20	9.7
Pre-engineering	69	559	37	6.6
Business	86	3,317	338	10.1
Social science	77	2,303	321	13.9
Math	78	393	62	15.7
English	73	514	175	34.0
General studies	89	4,888	520	10.6

Source: Goodrich, 1977, Table 12.

Number of Graduates By Minority Group*					Fall, 1971 Total Enroll-ment	Fall, 1971 Minority Enroll-ment	Fall, 1971 Minority Percentage of Total Enroll-ment
B	MA	PR	AI	AO			
Agri-Business							
2	1	0	0	2	321	11	3.4
2	4	0	0	0	233	32	13.7
1	5	0	0	0	303	17	5.6
Allied Health							
6	11	0	0	6	1,155	26	2.2
6	0	0	0	0	640	50	7.8
20	7	1	0	1	1,543	176	11.4
22	3	2	1	0	1,360	169	12.4
336	210	24	25	41	13,346	2,364	17.7
9	3	0	0	0	1,198	239	19.9
22	27	5	2	9	1,650	339	20.5

Number of Graduates By Minority Group*					Fall, 1971 Total Enrollment	Fall, 1971 Minority Enrollment	Fall, 1971 Minority Percentage of Total Enrollment
B	MA	PR	AI	AO			
Business and Related							
181	272	15	8	87	12,521	1,914	15.2
83	47	0	4	37	7,259	1,041	14.3
52	106	12	0	20	2,756	602	21.8
47	96	7	2	6	4,620	421	9.1
116	117	0	3	25	7,036	1,315	18.6
178	53	19	2	14	3,882	1,126	29.0
Applied Arts							
20	12	0	2	8	2,454	173	7.0
Engineering, Science Technology							
13	21	0	3	8	2,270	204	8.9
30	70	0	6	12	2,795	547	19.5
2	9	0	0	0	1,968	148	7.5
32	33	0	5	4	2,601	379	14.5
73	48	2	2	12	6,776	709	10.4
Public Services							
96	5	7	2	4	2,148	640	29.7
9	16	0	0	3	1,981	127	6.4
54	178	0	3	4	10,302	1,121	10.8
5	13	2	0	1	724	104	14.3
34	3	12	0	2	2,138	481	22.4
Academic Transfer							
208	74	5	7	2	12,165	2,018	16.5
9	3	0	1	4	1,780	232	13.0
13	4	1	0	2	3,642	463	12.7
12	14	0	1	10	5,352	625	11.6
198	89	14	20	17	21,251	3,383	15.9
196	91	11	4	19	17,006	2,286	13.4
14	31	2	2	13	4,384	471	10.7
95	52	6	1	21	9,030	461	5.1
343	123	6	39	9	59,140	6,785	11.4

* Key: B = Black
MA = Mexican American
PR = Puerto Rican
AI = American Indian
AO = American Oriental

TABLE 4-6

Program Enrollments of 2-Year College Students (by Percent)
1970–71

Type of Program	Afro-American		Mexican/Spanish American		Caucasian		American Indian		Asian-American		Total	
	Male	Female	Male	Female	Male	Female	Male	Female	Male	Female	Male	Female
Career program	17	39	11	30	18	33	11	41	23	25	17	35
College transfer	83	61	89	70	82	67	89	59	77	75	83	65
Total	100	100	100	100	100	100	100	100	100	100	100	100

Source: Bushnell, 1973, Table 2.6.

technical studies; figures for Hispanics are not available for these tables. (For a discussion of difficulties in utilizing Census Bureau minority data, see ISEP, 1976 and Abramowitz, ed., 1976).

The following tables represent the first comprehensive federal data collection of minority enrollments by program emphasis. Unfortunately, the data are not disaggregated by institutional type, but by subject field designators and program level. Thus, it is possible to analyze enrollment patterns in sub-baccalaureate and associate degree curricula, but not to distinguish between two year and four year institutions. Because nearly all associate degrees are awarded by two year institutions (87% in 1972 and in 1974; see Table 4-12), this analysis will concentrate upon associate degree curricula leading to sub-baccalaureate degrees, regardless of institutional type. Receipt of degrees by minority students will be treated separately later in this chapter.

In 1974, minority undergraduate students constituted 14.3% of full and part time undergraduates in all institutions (OCR, 1976, Table 4). As Table 4.8 indicates below, minority student enrollments in sub-baccalaureate technology curricula exceeded their proportion of the undergraduate enrollments; this overrepresentation occurred across the major technology fields (except natural science technologies) and, in varying amounts, across racial and ethnic categories, with the black figures most notable. This macro-analysis does give evidence of minority clustering at program areas and levels generally believed to be least prestigious, and for which graduates receive lower amounts of remuneration or social mobility (see Karabel, 1972; Rodriguez, 1978). More detailed analysis, however, indicates a natural and reasonable "marketplace" effect occurring in two year college minority program enrollments, one somewhat at variance with minority four year undergraduate program enrollments. Severe overrepresentation of minority students in a certain few fields at the baccalaureate levels (Blake, Lambert, Martin, 1974; Nwagbaraocha, 1974) continues to pose a problem, as does the severe underenrollment of minority students in scientific fields and professional schools. In the associate degree programs, however, severe highs and lows are less evident, although data processing and natural science technologies present high and low indices of minority enrollments.*

Special attention will also need to be given to minority enrollments in nontraditional sub-baccalaureate degree institutions, including exter-

---

* The gross aggregation of associate curricula into six areas undoubtedly masks inconsistent figures and disproportionate enrollments within categories. Goodrich's data shown in Table 4-5 indicate variations within the larger groupings.

TABLE 4-7

Undergraduates (14 to 34 Years Old) in 2-Year Institutions, by Program Enrollment 1974

Gender	Total		Agriculture and Forestry		Biological Sciences		Business or Commerce		Education		Engineering	
	Number	Percent	Number	Percent	Number	Percent	Number	Percent	Number	Percent	Number	Percent
					White							
Total	7,781	100.0	102	1.3	305	3.9	1,176	15.1	1,024	13.2	364	4.7
Male	4,367	100.0	87	2.0	178	4.1	834	19.1	272	6.2	343	7.9
Female	3,413	100.0	14	0.4	127	3.7	342	10.0	752	22.0	20	0.6
Total number of 2-year institutions	1,764		22		41		362		125		74	
					Black							
Total	814	100.0	1	0.1	12	1.5	156	19.2	127	15.6	27	3.3
Male	422	100.0	1	0.2	6	1.4	87	20.6	45	10.7	20	4.7
Female	392	100.0	—	—	5	1.3	69	17.6	82	20.9	7	1.8
Total number of 2-year institutions	237	100.0	—	—	—	—	45	19.0	21	8.9	7	3.0

Source: U.S. Bureau of Census [Major Field of Study], 1976, Table 3.

Gender	English or Journalism		Other Humanities		Law		Mathematics or Statistics		Physical or Earth Sciences		Social Sciences	
	Number	Per cent	Number	Per cent	Number	Per cent	Number	Per cent	Number	Per cent	Number	Per cent
White												
Total	234	3.0	371	4.8	254	3.3	149	1.9	126	1.6	681	8.8
Male	100	2.3	188	4.3	196	4.5	90	2.1	91	2.1	379	8.7
Female	134	3.9	184	5.4	58	1.7	59	1.7	35	1.0	302	8.8
Total number of 2-year institutions	26		85		30		24		18		90	
Black												
Total	24	2.9	14	1.7	15	1.8	11	1.4	3	0.4	66	8.1
Male	4	0.9	10	2.4	10	2.4	2	0.5	2	0.5	37	8.8
Female	20	5.1	3	0.8	5	1.3	9	2.3	1	0.3	29	7.4
Total number of 2-year institutions	3	1.3	2	0.8	6	2.5	2	0.8	1	0.4	20	8.4

(continued)

Gender	Vocational/ Technical Studies		Health or Medical Profession		Computer Sciences		Other		Don't Know or Not Reported	
	Number	Per cent	Number	Per cent	Number	Per cent	Number	Per cent	Number	Per cent
White										
Total	206	2.6	694	8.9	60	0.8	1,192	15.3	843	10.8
Male	150	3.4	240	5.5	48	1.1	709	16.2	463	10.6
Female	56	1.6	455	13.3	12	0.4	483	14.2	380	11.1
Total number of 2-year institutions	130		150	8.5	22	1.2	354	20.1	211	12.0
Black										
Total	23	2.8	88	10.8	13	1.6	115	14.1	119	14.6
Male	20	4.7	35	8.3	12	2.8	63	14.9	67	15.9
Female	3	0.8	53	13.5	1	0.3	51	13.0	52	13.3
Total number of 2-year institutions	14	5.9	25	10.5	8	3.4	48	20.3	33	13.9

nal degree programs and proprietary schools.* In a recent study of external degree programs, researchers found one in five bachelor degree students and one in four associate degree students to be non-white. As Table 4-9 shows, there are significant proportions of minority students maldistributed over the areas of study in external (i.e., non-campus-based) degree programs. A 1974 study by Wilms sought to evaluate differences between public and proprietary vocational programming and enrollments. He discovered a relationship between the type of enrollment and race:

> Ethnicity also was significantly related (p < .001) to the type of school a student attended. Whites were more likely to attend public schools while blacks were right on the watershed, choosing public and proprietary schools equally. Students of other ethnicities were more likely to attend proprietary schools. The difference between the kind of school blacks and students of other ethnicities chose was significant (p < .01) (Wilms, 1974, p. 36).

Before turning to an analysis of minority student receipt of associate degrees, two final areas of enrollment patterns require analysis: ethnic studies enrollments, and programs with limited enrollments. During case studies conducted at a number of institutions with majority non-white enrollments, concern was expressed that a disproportionate number of minority students were enrolling in ethnic studies courses and majoring (A.A. or B.A.) in these courses of study. The dual concern was the acknowledged need for minority (and majority) students to be aware of cultural and linguistic characteristics of ethnic and racial groups, and the concomitant fear that these programs would isolate minority students and deter them from other academic fields in which there are shortages of trained minority personnel. A study (Dutton, 1973) of 1972 ethnic studies programs demonstrated that two year colleges had established a significant number of such programs, enrolling over 85,000 students in courses.** Table 4-10 reports the 1972 figures.

Undoubtedly, these enrollments have increased in the six years since the study was conducted, as more institutions have adopted ethnic studies courses as a way of coping with changing student demographics; however, one researcher has noted that white student interest in enrolling in these courses had declined (Mingle, 1978, p. 203). A 1974 study

---

* Examination credit, a widely used means of obtaining credit in two and four year institutions, does not appear to be widely utilized by minority students (Grandy and Shea, 1976, p. 12). (See also Losack, 1978; Wilbur and LaFay, 1978.)

** See also Lombardi, 1971; Morrison, 1973, Table 9.

TABLE 4-8

Undergraduate Minority Enrollments in Sub-Baccalaureate Curricula
1974

Enrollment	American Indian	Black	Asian American
Business and Commerce Technologies			
Full-time	1,462 (0.7%)	27,301 (12.4%)	1,677 (0.8%)
Female	957 (0.8%)	14,786 (12.6%)	1,001 (0.9%)
Male	505 (0.5%)	12,515 (12.3%)	676 (0.7%)
Part-time	781 (0.5%)	15,034 (9.5%)	1,607 (1.0%)
Female	477 (0.6%)	8,309 (10.0%)	878 (1.1%)
Male	304 (0.4%)	6,725 (8.9%)	729 (1.0%)
Total	2,243 (0.6%)	42,335 (11.2%)	3,284 (0.9%)
Female	1,434 (0.7%)	23,095 (11.5%)	1,879 (0.9%)
Male	809 (0.5%)	19,240 (10.9%)	1,405 (0.8%)
Data Processing Technologies			
Full-time	153 (0.6%)	3,928 (16.1%)	304 (1.2%)
Female	85 (0.9%)	1,795 (18.5%)	119 (1.2%)
Male	68 (0.5%)	2,133 (14.4%)	185 (1.3%)
Part-time	98 (0.5%)	2,746 (13.4%)	295 (1.4%)
Female	38 (0.5%)	1,284 (16.3%)	130 (1.7%)
Male	60 (0.5%)	1,462 (11.5%)	165 (1.3%)
Total	251 (0.6%)	6,674 (14.8%)	599 (1.3%)
Female	123 (0.7%)	3,079 (17.5%)	249 (1.4%)
Male	128 (0.5%)	3,595 (13.1%)	350 (1.3%)
Health Services and Paramedical Technologies			
Full-time	985 (0.7%)	14,547 (10.8%)	938 (0.7%)
Female	848 (0.7%)	12,047 (10.6%)	730 (0.6%)
Male	137 (0.6%)	2,500 (11.7%)	208 (1.0%)
Part-time	348 (0.5%)	10,051 (14.2%)	562 (0.8%)
Female	282 (0.5%)	8,687 (14.6%)	408 (0.7%)
Male	66 (0.6%)	1,364 (12.1%)	154 (1.4%)
Total	1,333 (0.6%)	24,598 (11.9%)	1,500 (0.7%)
Female	1,130 (0.7%)	20,734 (11.9%)	1,138 (0.7%)
Male	203 (0.6%)	3,864 (11.9%)	362 (1.1%)

showed black programs had begun to decline in numbers of institutions offering such curricula, while other ethnic curricula had increased (Sedlacek *et al.*, 1974; see also Locke, 1978; Macias *et al.*, 1975).

Another way in which institutions have coped with shifting enrollment

Spanish-Surnamed Americans		Total Minority	All Other Students	Total
		Business and Commerce Technologies		
7,096	(3.2%)	37,536 (17.1%)	182,028 (82.9%)	219,564 (100.0%)
4,311	(3.7%)	21,055 (17.9%)	96,463 (82.1%)	117,518 (100.0%)
2,785	(2.7%)	16,481 (16.2%)	85,565 (83.8%)	102,046 (100.0%)
5,940	(3.7%)	23,362 (14.7%)	135,221 (85.3%)	158,583 (100.0%)
3,263	(3.9%)	12,927 (15.5%)	70,378 (84.5%)	83,305 (100.0%)
2,677	(3.6%)	10,435 (13.9%)	64,843 (86.1%)	75,278 (100.0%)
13,036	(3.4%)	60,898 (16.1%)	317,249 (83.9%)	378,147 (100.0%)
7,574	(3.8%)	33,982 (16.9%)	166,841 (83.1%)	200,823 (100.0%)
5,462	(3.1%)	26,916 (15.2%)	150,408 (84.8%)	177,324 (100.0%)
		Data Processing Technologies		
1,021	(4.2%)	5,406 (22.1%)	19,059 (77.9%)	24,465 (100.0%)
381	(3.9%)	2,380 (24.5%)	7,316 (75.5%)	9,696 (100.0%)
640	(4.3%)	3,026 (20.5%)	11,743 (79.5%)	14,769 (100.0%)
854	(4.2%)	3,993 (19.4%)	16,543 (80.6%)	20,536 (100.0%)
253	(3.2%)	1,705 (21.7%)	6,150 (78.3%)	7,855 (100.0%)
601	(4.7%)	2,288 (18.0%)	10,393 (82.0%)	12,681 (100.0%)
1,875	(4.2%)	9,399 (20.9%)	35,602 (79.1%)	45,001 (100.0%)
634	(3.6%)	4,085 (23.3%)	13,466 (76.7%)	17,551 (100.0%)
1,241	(4.5%)	5,314 (19.4%)	22,136 (80.6%)	27,450 (100.0%)
		Health Services and Paramedical Technologies		
3,848	(2.8%)	20,318 (15.0%)	114,938 (85.0%)	135,256 (100.0%)
2,861	(2.5%)	16,486 (14.5%)	97,463 (85.5%)	113,949 (100.0%)
987	(4.6%)	3,832 (18.0%)	17,475 (82.0%)	21,307 (100.0%)
2,557	(3.6%)	13,518 (19.0%)	57,460 (81.0%)	70,978 (100.0%)
1,993	(3.3%)	11,370 (19.0%)	48,330 (81.0%)	59,700 (100.0%)
564	(5.0%)	2,148 (19.0%)	9,130 (81.0%)	11,278 (100.0%)
6,405	(3.1%)	33,836 (16.4%)	172,398 (83.6%)	206,234 (100.0%)
4,854	(2.8%)	27,856 (16.0%)	145,793 (84.0%)	173,649 (100.0%)
1,551	(4.8%)	5,980 (18.4%)	26,605 (81.6%)	32,585 (100.0%)

(continued)

patterns, specifically with increasing percentages of female students, is to initiate courses and programs in women's studies. In 1977, a monitoring group found 55 two year (and 221 senior) institutions offered

Enrollment	American Indian	Black	Asian American
Mechanical and Engineering Technologies			
Full-time	1,824 (1.1%)	16,919 (10.2%)	1,676 (1.0%)
Female	96 (1.1%)	955 (10.7%)	231 (2.6%)
Male	1,728 (1.1%)	15,964 (10.2%)	1,445 (0.9%)
Part-time	749 (0.6%)	10,751 (9.1%)	1,829 (1.6%)
Female	104 (0.8%)	1,105 (8.4%)	526 (4.0%)
Male	645 (0.6%)	9,646 (9.2%)	1,303 (1.2%)
Total	2,573 (0.9%)	27,670 (9.8%)	3,505 (1.2%)
Female	200 (0.9%)	2,060 (9.3%)	757 (3.4%)
Male	2,373 (0.9%)	25,610 (9.8%)	2,748 (1.1%)
Natural Science Technologies			
Full-time	259 (0.8%)	1,111 (3.3%)	161 (0.5%)
Female	68 (0.7%)	533 (5.4%)	69 (0.7%)
Male	191 (0.8%)	578 (2.4%)	92 (0.4%)
Part-time	93 (0.7%)	724 (5.8%)	76 (0.6%)
Female	38 (0.7%)	454 (8.0%)	44 (0.8%)
Male	55 (0.8%)	270 (3.9%)	32 (0.5%)
Total	352 (0.8%)	1,835 (4.0%)	237 (0.5%)
Female	106 (0.7%)	987 (6.4%)	113 (0.7%)
Male	246 (0.8%)	848 (2.8%)	124 (0.4%)
Public Service-Related Technologies			
Full-time	506 (0.7%)	8,476 (11.2%)	335 (0.4%)
Female	242 (0.8%)	4,109 (13.3%)	144 (0.5%)
Male	264 (0.6%)	4,367 (9.7%)	191 (0.4%)
Part-time	487 (0.6%)	7,713 (10.0%)	524 (0.7%)
Female	287 (0.9%)	4,156 (13.1%)	286 (0.9%)
Male	200 (0.4%)	3,557 (7.9%)	238 (0.5%)
Total	993 (0.6%)	16,189 (10.6%)	859 (0.6%)
Female	529 (0.8%)	8,265 (13.2%)	430 (0.7%)
Male	464 (0.5%)	7,924 (8.8%)	429 (0.5%)

Source: OCR Racial and Ethnic Enrollment Data, 1974, [1976] Table 12.

courses in women's studies; six of the programs offered A.A. degrees (Project on Status, 1978, p. 5). Academic administrators need to walk a fine line in planning such specialized curricula while avoiding stereotypes about student choices and preferences. Faculty and administrators—disproportionately white and male—must exercise sensitivity to such developments in programs and not let such programs become the sole avenue of access for female and minority staff and students.

Spanish-Surnamed Americans	Total Minority	All Other Students	Total
	Mechanical and Engineering Technologies		
9,153 (5.5%)	29,572 (17.8%)	136,274 (82.2%)	165,846 (100.0%)
1,245 (13.9%)	2,527 (28.2%)	6,432 (71.8%)	8,959 (100.0%)
7,908 (5.0%)	27,045 (17.2%)	129,842 (82.8%)	156,887 (100.0%)
11,525 (9.8%)	24,854 (21.1%)	92,882 (78.9%)	117,736 (100.0%)
3,082 (23.6%)	4,817 (36.8%)	8,263 (63.2%)	13,080 (100.0%)
8,443 (8.1%)	20,037 (19.1%)	84,619 (80.9%)	104,656 (100.0%)
20,678 (7.3%)	54,426 (19.2%)	229,156 (80.8%)	283,582 (100.0%)
4,327 (19.6%)	7,344 (33.3%)	14,695 (66.7%)	22,039 (100.0%)
16,351 (6.3%)	47,082 (18.0%)	214,461 (82.0%)	261,543 (100.0%)
	Natural Science Technologies		
417 (1.2%)	1,948 (5.8%)	31,518 (94.2%)	33,466 (100.0%)
114 (1.2%)	784 (8.0%)	9,051 (92.0%)	9,835 (100.0%)
303 (1.3%)	1,164 (4.9%)	22,467 (95.1%)	23,631 (100.0%)
226 (1.8%)	1,119 (8.9%)	11,471 (91.1%)	12,590 (100.0%)
111 (2.0%)	647 (11.4%)	5,024 (88.6%)	5,671 (100.0%)
115 (1.7%)	472 (6.8%)	6,447 (93.2%)	6,919 (100.0%)
643 (1.4%)	3,067 (6.7%)	42,989 (93.3%)	46,056 (100.0%)
225 (1.5%)	1,431 (9.2%)	14,075 (90.8%)	15,506 (100.0%)
418 (1.4%)	1,636 (5.4%)	28,914 (94.6%)	30,550 (100.0%)
	Public Service-Related Technologies		
2,931 (3.5%)	12,248 (16.1%)	63,704 (83.9%)	75,952 (100.0%)
1,183 (3.8%)	5,678 (18.4%)	25,203 (81.6%)	30,881 (100.0%)
1,748 (3.9%)	6,570 (14.6%)	38,501 (85.4%)	45,071 (100.0%)
3,394 (4.4%)	12,118 (15.8%)	64,710 (84.2%)	76,828 (100.0%)
1,689 (5.3%)	6,418 (20.3%)	25,266 (79.7%)	31,684 (100.0%)
1,705 (3.8%)	5,700 (12.6%)	39,444 (87.4%)	45,144 (100.0%)
6,325 (4.1%)	24,366 (15.9%)	128,414 (84.1%)	152,780 (100.0%)
2,872 (4.6%)	12,096 (19.3%)	50,469 (80.7%)	62,565 (100.0%)
3,453 (3.8%)	12,270 (13.6%)	77,945 (86.4%)	90,215 (100.0%)

Given traditional assumptions concerning minority "tracking" into two year vocational programs, assumptions requiring considerable qualification, it will undoubtedly surprise casual observers to discover that many two year colleges have waiting lists and selective admissions policies that restrict the number of students admitted to certain vocational programs. In particular, allied health, nursing, and medical technician

TABLE 4-9

Characteristics of Proprietary School Students

Demographic Characteristics	General Studies	Natural/ Physical Sciences	Behavioral/ Social Sciences	Applied Social Sciences	Humani- ties, Arts	Engineer- ing	Business Administra- tion	Health Services	Semi- Profes- sional	Individual- ized	Not Speci- fied	Total
					Area of Study							
					Proportion Female							
Associate $\bar{X}$	41	50	10	48	73	16	40	86	—	44	59	45
(N)	(13)	(1)	(2)	(7)	(1)	(4)	(11)	(2)	(0)	(10)	(14)	(65)
Bachelor $\bar{X}$	46	55	34	38	41	5	26	81	8	52	58	50
(N)	(37)	(2)	(6)	(14)	(3)	(2)	(20)	(6)	(3)	(47)	(106)	(246)
Total $\bar{X}$	44	54	28	41	49	11	31	82	8	51	59	49
(N)	(50)	(3)	(8)	(21)	(4)	(6)	(31)	(8)	(3)	(57)	(120)	(311)
					Proportion Non-White							
Associate $\bar{X}$	21	33	18	33	64	25	28	4	—	24	25	26
(N)	(10)	(1)	(2)	(7)	(1)	(3)	(9)	(1)	(0)	(9)	(14)	(57)
Bachelor $\bar{X}$	16	49	28	9	38	13	18	15	0	16	22	19
(N)	(32)	(2)	(6)	(14)	(3)	(2)	(14)	(4)	(3)	(45)	(95)	(220)
Total $\bar{X}$	17	44	26	17	44	20	22	12	0	17	22	20
(N)	(42)	(3)	(8)	(21)	(4)	(5)	(23)	(5)	(3)	(54)	(109)	(277)

Proportion Employed

Associate X̄	72	83	85	80	98	94	91	90	90	76	76	82
(N)	(12)	(1)	(2)	(7)	(1)	(2)	(14)	(2)	(1)	(10)	(14)	(68)
Bachelor X̄	86	98	93	88	60	98	91	93	82	76	87	85
(N)	(35)	(2)	(5)	(14)	(3)	(2)	(20)	(6)	(3)	(47)	(106)	(242)
Total X̄	82	93	91	85	70	95	91	92	84	76	86	84
(N)	(47)	(3)	(7)	(21)	(4)	(4)	(34)	(8)	(4)	(57)	(130)	(311)

Proportion Over 30

Associate X̄	61	50	70	61	73	26	57	50	—	50	70	59
(N)	(11)	(1)	(1)	(6)	(1)	(1)	(10)	(1)	(0)	(10)	(12)	(54)
Bachelor X̄	75	94	67	64	69	45	78	63	90	62	71	70
(N)	(36)	(2)	(5)	(13)	(3)	(2)	(18)	(5)	(3)	(46)	(72)	(205)
Total X̄	71	79	68	63	70	39	70	61	90	60	71	68
(N)	(47)	(3)	(6)	(19)	(4)	(3)	(28)	(6)	(3)	(56)	(84)	(259)

Source: Sosdian, 1978, Table 7.

Note: Responding institutions were asked to furnish this information (based on records or on their best estimates) separately for each study area and level. Response rates varied for each item. With a total of 397 degree program areas in the study, the total number of responses was as follows:

311 (for sex of students and proportion employed).
277 (for proportion nonwhite).
259 (for proportion over 30).

Key: N = degree program areas responding.
X̄ = mean proportions rounded to nearest whole number.

TABLE 4-10

Courses and Enrollments in Ethnic/Racial Studies in 2-Year Institutions

Field of Study	Institutions Offering at Least One Course	Course Offerings Fall, 1972	Combined Course Enrollments Fall, 1972	As of the Academic Year '72–'73, Institutions Offering: Major	As of the Academic Year '72–'73, Institutions Offering: Minor	Students Graduated July, '71 to June, '72 with: Major	Students Graduated July, '71 to June, '72 with: Minor
American Indian studies	70	91 (3.8%)	2,315 (2.9%)	0	0	0	0
Asian-American studies	72	119 (5.0%)	3,492 (4.3%)	0	0	0	0
Chinese	48	95 (3.9%)	3,036 (3.7%)	0	0	0	0
Japanese	0	0	0	0	0	0	0
Other	24	24 (1.0%)	456 (.6%)	0	0	0	0
Black studies	385	1,501 (62.4%)	50,407 (62.1%)	36	12	23	0
Spanish-speaking studies	161	497 (20.7%)	16,016 (19.7%)	35	23	12	0
Chicano	161	497 (20.7%)	16,016 (19.7%)	35	23	12	0
Puerto Rican	0	0	0	0	0	0	0
Other	0	0	0	0	0	0	0
White ethnic studies	49	62 (2.6%)	933 (1.1%)	0	0	0	0
Other ethnic studies	23	23 (1.0%)	1,251 (1.5%)	0	0	0	0
Multiethnic studies	67	109 (4.5%)	6,745 (8.3%)	12	0	0	0
Subtotal ethnic studies*		2,293 (95.5%)	74,414 (91.7%)			35	0
Total ethnic studies	514	2,402 (100.0%)	85,159 (100.0%)			35	0

Source: Dutton, 1973, Table 4.　　Note: Sample Number (N) = 1,046.　　* Multiethnic studies are not included in subtotal ethnic studies.

fields, with attendant laboratory and clinical components, have begun to attract many more applications than the institutions have openings (Morgan, 1977). Start-up costs, higher faculty salaries, and laboratory and equipment costs, as well as external accrediting and professional licensing fees combine to make these programs expensive to initiate and maintain.

The increasing number of allied medical positions (Hawthorne and Perry, 1974; Rodriguez, 1978) and excellent salaries for beginning technicians have attracted a significant number of applicants to the limited number of places. The increasing number of female students (Table 4-16) and the tendency of women to seek careers in sub-baccalaureate allied medical and nursing programs have also increased the competition. Elsewhere, it has been argued that selective admission is not a phenomenon exclusive to senior institutions or graduate and professional schools (Morgan, 1977), and that care must be taken by administrators not to employ naive numerical and exclusively quantitative means of judging applications.*

This fear was echoed by health care professionals and minority personnel interviewed in institutions with competitive admissions in technical and laboratory courses. In more than one instance, students with bachelor's degrees (and in some instances, advanced degrees) were applying to, and being accepted into, associate degree programs in allied health. There should be concern that this extreme example of educational inflation does not serve to exclude applications from persons whose highest educational aspiration and achievement will be the associate degree and certificate. Two year colleges are in a unique position to meet pressing health care needs in ghettos, barrios, rural areas, and on reservations; affirmative action and aggressive recruitment of minority students need to be employed in order that minorities not be "tracked out" of consideration for such health care and other highly specialized sub-baccalaureate technical programs.

ASSOCIATE DEGREE PATTERNS

As has been noted throughout this book, no single trait has characterized two year colleges so accurately as growth. Because of the number of part-time and non-degree students enrolled in these institutions, however, enrollment figures portray less well the magnitude of growth

---

* The *Bakke* controlling opinion would probably find Morgan's admissions practice unconstitutional: "Thus 25 persons are chosen for the 28 openings. The remaining three positions are reserved for minority students. They do not compete with the other group; they compete only with each other. Their admission gives them more than 10 percent representation in the program" (Morgan, 1977, p. 69).

than do measurable outputs, such as the number of associate and sub-baccalaureate degrees awarded. By this measure as well, the enrollment growth rate in two year institutions has been phenomenal.

The following tables indicate the number of associate degrees that have been awarded and the rate of increase in that number in the two year sector (Table 4-11). In the years since 1970, sub-baccalaureate and associate degree awards have flourished. These less-than-four-year awards include certificates, licensure awards, and other formal recognitions of credit earned; they may be transfer or terminal, although they are more frequently terminal, and may be two year or one year programs, but are more frequently one year (Table 4-12).

TABLE 4-11

Number of Associate Degrees Awarded
Selected Years 1969–70 to 1974–75

Year	Total Number of Dollars Awarded	Occupational Degrees Awarded	2-Year Institutions	4-Year Institutions
1969–70[a]	206,753	107,908 (52%)	180,697 (87%)	26,056 (13%)
1972–73	319,068	157,777[b] (49%)	277,650 (87%)	41,418 (13%)
1974–75	362,969	224,375[b] (62%)	320,198 (87%)	42,771 (13%)

Source: Baker and Wells (NCES), 1976, Tables 5 and 6; ISEP staff calculations.

[a] Data for this year taken from Gilli, 1975, p. 29.

[b] Data include associate degrees occupational curricula below the technical or semi-professional level.

TABLE 4-12

Other Sub-Baccalaureate Awards, by Institutional Type
and Percentage Occupational

Year	Total	2-Year	4-Year
Awards for Curricula of at Least 2 Years but Less than 4 Years			
1972–73 Occupational	22,217 (89%)	17,043 (77%)	5,174 (23%)
1974–75 Occupational	25,153 (90%)	17,541 (70%)	7,612 (30%)
Awards for Curricula of at Least 1 Year but Less than 2 Years			
1972–73 Occupational	53,901 (97%)	45,257 (84%)	8,644 (16%)
1974–75 Occupational	60,410 (98%)	52,095 (86%)	8,315 (14%)

Source: Baker and Wells (NCES), 1976, Tables 5 and 6; ISEP staff calculations.

Besides the growth pattern, several patterns have emerged in associate degree receipts, including gender-based degree participation and preference, institutional sector trends, and shifting degree area distributions. Once these patterns have been analyzed, this section will focus upon racial and ethnic degree receipt patterns, from the scanty available data. Because federal data collection practices and categorizations have varied over time, and because federal racial and ethnic associate degree data are available only for 1975–76, comprehensive analyses or longitudinal trend comparisons are necessarily limited. Nevertheless, some trends are discernible, showing that minorities have enjoyed mixed success in receiving degrees.

Although female associate degree receipts and two year college enrollments have always lagged behind male patterns, the gap has narrowed, and should close soon. Table 4-13 chronicles the incremental changes in sub-baccalaureate degrees by gender since 1970–71. Women's share of sub-baccalaureate degrees and awards has increased from 42.8% to 46.2% in 1975–76, at a 66.9% growth rate. Men's awards have increased at a slower pace, 45.8%. Women's increasing share is paralleled by the growth rate in degree-credit associate degrees awarded to women: from 1965–66 through 1974–75, women have increased their share from 43% to 47% (Andersen, ed., 1976, Table 76.326).

There have been shifting patterns within aggregate degrees awarded, most notably in women's greater share of occupational curricula sub-baccalaureate awards, where women have increased from 42.4% to 47.0% of the total. Their share of arts and sciences and general program degrees has risen from 43.2% to 45.1% in 1975–76. Of course the aggregate data conceal the severe stereotyping readily evident in the disaggregated, gender-dominant divisions. Women, for example, received degrees ranging from 3.8% in mechanical and engineering technologies to 86.0% in health services and paramedical technologies, which include nursing curricula (Malitz, 1978, Table 1). As was demonstrated in chapter three, a disproportionately large number of white men hold administrative and faculty positions in the institutions, requiring them to exhibit sensitivity to their students, who are more representative of society than are their own professional ranks.

Institutional sector trends turn on two axes: institutional-type and institutional-control. Such sector analysis points clearly to the role of public two year colleges in degree awards, as it did in the enrollment analysis of chapter two. The following tables document the continuing extent to which two year colleges award sub-baccalaureate degrees and the increasing extent to which these institutions lie in the public sector. Table 4-14 reveals that the two year college share of sub-baccalaureate degrees awarded has remained nearly constant since 1970 at 86.4%. The public sector's share of awards has risen slowly so that 87.2% of the

TABLE 4-13

Associate Degrees and Other Formal Awards Conferred, by Gender and Curriculum Category 1970–71 to 1975–76

Curriculum Category and Division	1970–71*		1971–72*	
	Male	Female	Male	Female
All curricula, total	155,979	116,883	178,691	135,066
Arts and science or general programs	84,452	64,317	91,806	69,227
Occupational curricula	71,527	52,566	86,885	65,839
Science/engineering-related	42,123	26,090	49,405	33,664
Data processing technologies	5,156	2,408	5,485	2,356
Health services/paramedical technologies	2,455	21,915	3,616	28,672
Mechanical/engineering technologies	29,761	411	34,058	488
Natural science technologies	4,751	1,356	6,246	2,148
Nonscience/nonengineering related	29,404	26,476	37,480	32,175
Business and commerce technologies	22,067	21,504	26,065	24,938
Public service-related technologies	7,337	4,972	11,415	7,237

Source: Malitz, 1978, Table 3.

* Does not include those below the technical or semiprofessional level.

sub-baccalaureates earned in 1975–76 were from public institutions; concurrently, the number of private two year institutions fell from 251 to 240 (Malitz, 1978, p. 2).

Shifting degree area distribution patterns confirm Lombardi's (1978b) analysis of the surge in occupational programming. As table 4-15 indicates, 1972–73 marked the change of emphasis, when occupational curricula awards outnumbered arts and sciences (transfer) awards. The emphasis has continued, despite the increase in transfer awards since 1970–71 (20.7%). This growth has simply been outstripped by the near doubling of occupational awards in that time. Moreover, shifts in occupational programming reflect both internal and external forces. Internal shifts include the aforementioned changes attendant to women's increasing enrollments and enrollment choices (Table 4-16), the increased competition for baccalaureate-level health and allied medicine admissions, and the entry of minorities into nonscience and nonengi-

1972–73*		1973–74		1974–75		1975–76	
Male	Female	Male	Female	Male	Female	Male	Female
187,105	150,652	203,042	166,901	206,867	181,255	227,483	195,103
92,359	71,297	95,039	73,366	93,169	77,004	98,577	80,908
94,746	79,355	108,003	93,535	113,698	104,251	128,906	114,195
51,789	42,834	57,296	50,036	61,684	56,821	65,742	61,837
5,226	2,414	4,819	2,179	4,600	2,221	4,460	2,716
5,482	37,428	7,346	43,861	8,415	49,528	8,681	53,237
34,047	734	36,802	829	39,713	1,062	43,467	1,702
7,034	2,258	8,329	3,167	8,956	4,010	9,134	4,182
42,957	36,521	50,707	43,499	52,014	47,430	63,164	52,358
27,635	27,676	32,103	33,223	32,714	35,322	39,924	39,255
15,322	8,845	18,604	10,276	19,300	12,108	23,240	13,103

neering degree programs. External forces affecting occupational program trends include the increase in proprietary schools and enrollments, as reflected in the sole decline from 1970—data processing technologies—and concurrent increase in proprietary, not-for-profit data processing enrollments (Bureau of Consumer Protection, 1976, pp. 18–22; Kay, 1976, pp. 14–15). Employment patterns and occupational trends also affect occupational programs, as do governmental and professional pressures and policies, such as national health insurance or employment training legislation.

While occupational trends and labor market developments may be rapid or long-term, student preferences and career choices are slow in developing. Students frequently enroll in institutions in order to find careers and to explore occupational opportunities. Mismatches, false starts, and curricular rigidities are common occurences, as is poor availability of information (Stark, et al., 1977). Again, the need for

TABLE 4-14

Associate Degrees and Other Formal Awards Conferred, by Control and Level of Institution
1970–71 to 1975–76

Control and Level of Institution	1970–71*		1971–72*		1972–73*	
All institutions	274,319	(100.0%)	316,072	(100.0%)	341,290	(100.0%)
4-year	36,258	(13.2%)	39,041	(12.4%)	46,597	(13.7%)
2-year	238,061	(86.8%)	277,031	(87.6%)	294,693	(86.2%)
Public	230,548	(84.0%)	272,765	(86.2%)	297,233	(86.9%)
4-year	21,143	(7.7%)	23,355	(7.4%)	28,330	(8.3%)
2-year	209,405	(76.3%)	249,410	(78.8%)	268,903	(78.6%)
Private	43,771	(16.0%)	43,307	(13.8%)	44,057	(13.0%)
4-year	15,115	(5.5%)	15,686	(5.0%)	18,267	(5.4%)
2-year	28,656	(10.5%)	27,621	(8.8%)	25,790	(7.6%)

Source: Malitz, 1978, Tables 7 and 8.

* Does not include those below the technical or semiprofessional level.

expert career and academic counseling is emphasized, especially in institutions whose students are drawn from high schools with poor or nonexistent counseling services.

Available racial and ethnic data on awards of sub-baccalaureate degrees are available only for 1975–76, and indicate both good and bad news for minority students in two year institutions. The encouraging finding is that minorities are distributed across program types. Nearly all other findings are discouraging, however, including a corollary finding that minorities are even less well-represented at the higher levels. By any yardstick, minority associate degree receipts are disappointing.

For every minority group,* receipt of sub-baccalaureate awards was lower than the group's percentage of total two year college enrollments, indicating a lower success rate, as measured by minority student graduates. As noted in chapter two, transience is exceedingly common in these institutions, requiring analysts to take into consideration varying

---

* As noted in Table 4-18, Hawaii was not included in the OCR data for 1975–76 sub-baccalaureate degrees. The figures for Asians, therefore, are considerably *lower* than they would otherwise have been.

1973–74		1974–75		1975–76		Percent Change 1970–71 to 1975–76
369,943	(100.0%)	388,122	(100.0%)	422,586	(100.0%)	54.0
52,414	(14.2%)	58,105	(15.0%)	57,502	(13.6%)	58.6
317,529	(85.9%)	330,017	(85.0%)	365,084	(86.4%)	53.4
321,985	(87.1%)	339,224	(87.4%)	368,335	(87.2%)	59.8
32,456	(8.8%)	35,536	(9.2%)	30,828	(7.3%)	45.8
289,529	(78.3%)	303,688	(78.2%)	337,507	(79.9%)	61.2
47,958	(13.0%)	48,898	(12.6%)	54,251	(12.8%)	23.9
19,958	(5.4%)	22,569	(5.8%)	26,674	(6.3%)	76.5
28,000	(7.6%)	26,329	(6.8%)	27,577	(6.5%)	−3.8

definitions of program "success" and "output." However, with nearly twenty percent of the *total* two year enrollments, and an even larger share of two year *full time* enrollments, minorities received 13% of technology and 15% of transfer sub-baccalaureate awards in 1975–76 (Table 4-18). White award patterns disclose a disproportionately higher success rate in terms of enrollment percentages, both in total and full-time categories. Nonresident aliens play a relatively smaller role in sub-baccalaureate degree patterns than their substantial share of masters (5.2%) and doctorates (12.0%) (NCES, *Condition of Education, 1978,* Table 3.17).

Thus, minorities are clustered at the lowest stratum of postsecondary education and, by traditional measures of success—however inappropriate to institutional missions—receive fewer degrees than would otherwise be expected in light of their enrollments. This attrition poses an exceptionally serious set of questions for educators: are there systemic, institutional factors that contribute to this lower rate of graduation for minorities? Are there policies and practices that can increase the proportion of minority degrees? The seriousness of these fundamental questions is underscored by the skewness of minority enrollments in these institutions.

TABLE 4-15

Associate Degrees and Other Formal Awards Conferred,*
by Curriculum Category
1970–71 to 1975–76

Curriculum Category and Division	1970–71	1971–72	1972–73
All curricula, total	272,862 (100%)	313,757 (100%)	337,757 (100%)
Arts and science or general programs	148,769 (54.5%)	161,033 (51.3%)	163,656 (48.5%)
Occupational curricula	124,093 (45.5%)	152,724 (48.7%)	174,101 (51.5%)
Science/engineering-related	68,213 (25.0%)	83,069 (26.5%)	94,623 (28.0%)
Data processing technologies	7,564 (2.8%)	7,841 (2.5%)	7,640 (2.3%)
Health services/paramedical technologies	24,370 (8.9%)	32,288 (10.3%)	42,910 (12.7%)
Mechanical/engineering technologies	30,172 (11.1%)	34,546 (11.0%)	34,781 (10.3%)
Natural science technologies	6,107 (2.2%)	8,394 (2.7%)	9,292 (2.8%)
Nonscience/nonengineering-related	55,880 (20.5%)	69,655 (22.2%)	79,478 (23.5%)
Business and commerce technologies	43,571 (16.0%)	51,003 (16.3%)	55,311 (16.4%)
Public service-related technologies	12,309 (4.5%)	18,652 (5.9%)	24,167 (7.2%)

Source: Malitz, 1978, Tables 4 and 5.

* Does not include those below the technical or semiprofessional level.

ACADEMIC CREDIT REMEDIATION AND HONORS COURSES

Predictably, higher education institutions have reacted in various ways and in varying degrees to minority students, particularly in terms of academic credit programming. Mingle reported that the most striking institutional response to black students in white institutions has been

1973–74	1974–75	1975–76	Percent Change 1970–71 to 1975–76
369,943 (100%)	388,122 (100%)	422,586 (100%)	54.9
168,405 (45.5%)	170,173 (43.8%)	179,485 (42.5%)	20.7
201,538 (54.5%)	217,949 (56.2%)	243,101 (57.5%)	95.9
107,332 (29.0%)	118,505 (30.5%)	127,579 (30.2%)	87.0
6,998 (1.9%)	6,821 (1.8%)	7,176 (1.7%)	−5.1
51,207 (13.8%)	57,943 (14.9%)	61,918 (14.6%)	154.1
37,631 (10.2%)	40,775 (10.5%)	45,169 (10.7%)	49.7
11,496 (3.1%)	12,966 (3.3%)	13,316 (3.2%)	118.0
94,206 (25.5%)	99,444 (25.6%)	115,522 (27.3%)	106.7
65,326 (17.7%)	68,036 (17.5%)	79,179 (18.7%)	81.7
28,880 (7.8%)	31,408 (8.1%)	36,343 (8.6%)	195.3

faculty negativism; he reported few for-credit or course option developments (Mingle, 1978). Cross (1976) has reported a significant increase in degree-credit basic skills coursework, although this increase was accompanied by a sharp decline in required remedial work. Snow (1977, in Grant and Hoeber, 1978) confirmed the trend toward lessening of basic skills requirements and expansion of degree basic skills credit.

TABLE 4-16

**Percent Distribution of Associate Degrees and
Other Formal Awards Received by Women
1970–71 to 1975–76**

Curriculum Category and Division	1970–71	1971–72	1972–73	1973–74	1974–75	1975–76
All curricula, total	42.8	43.0	44.6	45.1	46.7	46.2
Occupational curricula	42.4	43.1	45.6	46.4	47.8	47.0
Science/engineering-related	38.2	40.5	45.3	46.6	47.9	48.5
Data processing technologies	31.8	30.0	31.6	31.1	32.6	37.8
Health services/paramedical technologies	89.9	88.8	87.2	85.7	85.5	86.0
Mechanical/engineering technologies	1.4	1.4	2.1	2.2	2.6	3.8
Natural science technologies	22.2	25.6	24.3	27.5	30.9	31.4
Nonscience/nonengineering-related	47.4	46.2	45.9	46.2	47.7	45.3
Business and commerce technologies	49.3	48.9	50.0	50.9	51.9	50.0
Public service-related technologies	40.4	38.8	36.6	35.6	38.6	36.1
Arts and science or general programs	43.2	43.0	43.6	43.6	45.3	45.1

Source: Malitz, 1978, Table 1.

TABLE 4-17

Associate and Other Sub-Baccalaureate Degrees Awarded, by Gender, Control of Institution, and Race
1975–76

Student Gender and Institutional Control	Total	White	American Indian	Black	Asian[a]	Hispanic	Total Minority	Non-resident Alien
Total (NCES)	488,677	413,100 (84.5%)	2,517 (.5%)	40,965 (8.4%)	5,695 (1.2%)	22,714 (4.6%)	71,891 (15.0%)	3,686 (.8%)
Male	256,782	219,019 (85.3%)	1,298 (.5%)	19,163 (7.5%)	3,003 (1.2%)	11,838 (4.6%)	35,302 (14.0%)	2,461 (1.0%)
Female	231,895	194,081 (83.7%)	1,219 (.5%)	21,802 (9.4%)	2,692 (1.2%)	10,876 (4.7%)	36,589 (16.0%)	1,225 (.5%)
Total (OCR)	491,376	413,959 (84.2%)	2,525 (.5%)	40,993 (8.3%)	7,350 (1.5%)	22,801 (4.6%)	73,669 (15.0%)	3,748 (.8%)
Public	432,543 (88.0%)	364,652 (74.2%)	2,313 (.5%)	35,881 (7.3%)	6,975 (1.4%)	20,155 (4.1%)	65,324 (13.3%)	2,567 (.5%)
Private	58,833 (12.0%)	49,307 (10.0%)	212 (0.0%)	5,112 (1.0%)	375 (0.1%)	2,646 (.5%)	8,345 (1.7%)	1,181 (.2%)

Source: NCES, Condition of Education, 1978 Edition; Table 3.17; ISEP staff calculations of OCR unpublished data.

Note: Data do not include U.S. Territories. NCES and OCR data report different totals.

[a] Hawaii was not included in OCR data; these data therefore undercount Asian degree receipts.

TABLE 4-18

Sub-Baccalaureate Degrees Conferred by Major Field, by Race 1975–76

Field	Indian	Black	Asians[a]	Hispanic	Total Minority	White	Non-resident Alien	Total
Business and commerce technologies	403	9,069	1,100	3,423	13,995	79,298	898	
	.00	.10	.01	.04	.15	.84	.01	
Data processing technologies	33	859	111	307	1,310	6,857	90	
	.00	.10	.01	.04	.16	.83	.01	
Health services and paramedical	384	6,937	701	1,879	9,901	71,473	222	
	.00	.09	.01	.02	.12	.88	.00	
Mechanical and engineering technologies	376	4,953	638	2,422	8,389	53,504	431	
	.01	.08	.01	.04	.13	.86	.01	
Nature science technologies	97	701	228	311	1,346	18,001	47	
	.01	.04	.01	.02	.07	.93	.00	
Public service related technologies	192	3,977	326	1,592	6,087	34,000	178	Total
	.00	.10	.01	.04	.15	.84	.00	
All Technologies	1,485	26,505	3,105	9,934	41,028	263,133	1,866	306,037
	.00	.09	.01	.03	.13	.86	.01	
Arts and Sciences or general programs	1,002	14,427	2,482	8,483	26,394	149,549	1,788	177,731
	.01	.08	.01	.05	.15	.84	.01	
Total								483,758

Source: ISEP staff analysis of OCR unpublished data.

Note: Data do not include U.S. Territories.

[a] Hawaii was not included in OCR data; these data therefore undercount Asian degree receipts.

Morrison and Ferrante (1973), in surveying two year colleges' responses to disadvantaged students, noted that 40% of the institutions provided curricular options designed specifically for these students; they did not distinguish between credit and non-credit offerings.

Institutional responses to remedial and honors students are the final consideration of this section; academic provisions and programming are the primary focus, particularly as they affect minority students in two year institutions. Student services administration and student personnel provisions, including non-academic (i.e., extra-curricular and not-for-credit) activities, will be examined in detail in the second half of this chapter: Support Services. Although two year colleges do enroll a significant and disproportionate percentage of minority students, including minority students requiring remedial academic assistance, it is questionable whether such programs originated for minority students, or whether two year institutions have adequate remedial instruction are available. Neither question has been systematically researched, and neither resolved. Moreover, published materials or remedial materials tend to be anecdotal or hortatory, rather than research-based.

The rise in remedial and developmental education programs parallels the increase in minority enrollments, but the increase clearly is not the sole cause or catalyst for such programs, for, increasingly, four year and senior institutions with small proportions of minority enrollments are turning to basic skills curricula and remedial programming (Rouche and Roueche, 1977), and white students do enroll in large numbers in two year remedial courses (Ferrin, 1971). Accompanying the movement to mass higher education and increased access (if not distribution) is the inevitable concern over quality standards and institutional responses to this concern, manifested by curriculum changes and remedial courses, even for traditional and high ability students (Cross, 1976). Initiation of ethnic studies courses (Lombardi, 1971; Dutton, 1973; Locke, 1978) is a more likely and accurate race-specific index of an institutional response to minority students. Roueche and Roueche (1977, p. 8) postulate cynically that such activity on the part of senior institutions marks less an increasing egalitarianism than an increasingly competitive market for students.

Nor is it conceded that two year institutions perform remedial work more ably than do senior institutions, despite the maldistribution of minority students in two year colleges. One critic has openly questioned the institutional commitment toward high-risk students:

Another belief is that the best remedial programs for high-risk students are in two year colleges. This is not necessarily the case. Though there are more community colleges which house remedial programs, the most effective and best-supported remediation programs are located in four year colleges . . . and predominantly black four year colleges . . . (Moore, 1976a, p. 42).

Whatever the institutional motivations or target population, and whether in senior or junior institutions, remedial programming appears to have become firmly entrenched in postsecondary education. Remedial literature has spun off a veritable cottage industry of primers, instructional material, audio-visual devices, and for-hire experts.

Institutional responses to disadvantaged students have centered on programs, courses, and services having both academic and support components. Two profiles of such academic programs have emerged from the research of Morrison (1973) and Cross (1976).

Table 4-19 has extracted academic items from the Cross (1976) questionnaire on developmental services sent to a 20% random sample of the AACJC membership in 1970. Table 4-20 reports Morrison's (1973) academic program findings from his survey of developmental programs conducted in 1971; he used American Council on Education ("ACE National Norms") stratification cells, weighted for representativeness of public two year colleges. Support service elements are analyzed in the second half of this chapter.

TABLE 4-19

Academic Development Services in 2-Year Colleges
1970

1. Does your college have any special provisions for students who do not meet the traditional academic requirements for college work?
   80% Yes
   20% No

2. Special services offered at your college this year.
   92% Remedial or development courses to upgrade verbal or other academic skills.
   20% A total program of recruitment, counseling, courses, etc., with a director.

3. Do you offer any kind of remedial or compensatory courses?
   95% Yes
   5% No

4. Approximately what proportion of the full-time student body is enrolled in remedial courses?
   40% Less than 10 percent.
   39% Between 10 and 25 percent.
   16% Between 25 and 50 percent.
   3% More than 50 percent.

5. What proportion of those taking remedial courses are members of racial minorities?
   64%   Less than 25 percent.
   19%   Between 25 and 50 percent.
   10%   Between 50 and 75 percent
   5%   More than 75 percent.

6. Are remedial courses required for certain students?
   79%   Yes
   19%   No

7. How is eligibility for remedial courses determined? (Answer all that apply.)
   75%   Test scores (Below what percentile? on what test?)
   50%   High school grades (Below C+, C, C−, D+, D, D−) (please circle)

8. Do remedial courses carry?
   25%   No credit.
   29%   Nondegree credit.
   32%   Degree credit.

9. Approximately what proportion of students enrolled in remedial courses later enter regular college courses at your or other institutions?
   11%   Less than 10 percent.
   11%   Between 10 and 25 percent.
   12%   Between 25 and 50 percent.
   45%   More than half.
   18%   Don't know.

10. Academic adjustments.
    58%   Remedial students carry a lighter course load.
    27%   Nonpunitive grading; for instance, pass-no pass.
    58%   Remedial classes smaller than regular classes.
          Other.

11. Instructional methods.
    22%   Team teaching.
    45%   Emphasis on audio-visual aids.
    36%   Skills centers.
    36%   Tutoring by fellow students.
    44%   Programmed instruction.
    3%   "Guaranteed-success" programs.
    7%   Practicum accompanies academic (for instance, New Careers).
    5%   Gaming or psychodrama.
    21%   Use of materials drawn from black and other ethnic cultures.
    31%   "Pacing" methods; emphasis on achievement regardless of time taken.
    7%   Other.

12. Special help with studies.
    48%   Precollege or summer programs.
    39%   Additional intensified study for underprepared students while enrolled in regular classes.
    8%   Other.

13. Faculty.

47%	Instruction of remedial courses restricted to teachers expressing interest.
50%	Most remedial teachers have some special training for work with underprepared students.
9%	Group-sensitivity sessions for faculty.
37%	All expenses paid for attendance at off-campus conferences, workshops.
16%	On-campus in-service training for remedial instructors.
13%	Emphasis on use of racial minorities for faculty.
	Other.

14. Evaluation.

55%	Measurement of changes in test scores.
36%	Measurement of changes in student attitudes.
50%	Follow-up of students on the job or in college.
30%	Formal collection of faculty and student reactions to program.
4%	Other.

Source: Cross, 1976, Appendix C; edited by ISEP staff.

The Cross data revealed a higher percentage of institutions offering remedial coursework (92%) than did Morrison data (46%), although Morrison noted that 99% did offer "special courses for the academically disadvantaged." The discrepancy perhaps lies in the varying definitions assigned to remedial tasks and the degree of formality within institutional structures; Morrison (p. 407) did note the relationship between comprehensiveness of the curriculum and existence of special programs. In short, broadly-designed curricula encompassing technical, transfer, and non-degree offerings were likely to include remedial programs as a formal component of the organization. Common course elements in the academic remedial programs include classes emphasizing basic skills and study techniques—credit and non-credit, smaller class sizes, and tutoring. Administrative provisions, such as reduced course load policies and practices designed to readmit failed students or to extend probationary periods, frequently must contend with funding formulae or financial aid attendance regulations that restrict the flexibility required for those students whose primary learning opportunities occur outside regular, mainstream classes.

Increasingly, such remedial work is being conducted under various rubrics for credit, as general studies or reduced-credit prerequisites to regular coursework. This practice of granting credit for remedial work has been received with mixed reactions from educators. The Carnegie Commission recommended against granting degree credit for remedial education coursework (1970, pp. 17–18), and most states have made no provisions for degree credit reimbursement or for special subsidies to support remedial credit programs.

TABLE 4-20

**Academic Remedial Provisions in Public 2-Year Colleges
1971**

Services	Percent Affirmative	Weighted N
Instructional		
Use of programmed instruction	72	482
Use of reduced course loads	86	640
Liberalized probationary or readmission practices	58	388
Attention to development of study skills	89	628
Stress communication skills	100	774
Stress reading skills	100	732
Stress writing skills	91	652
Stress speaking skills	77	452
Stress listening skills	83	544
Stress the utilization of traditional English	58	358
Stress understanding of student's own dialect	52	352
Develop special courses in ethnic studies	17	102
Other		
Special guidance and counseling	89	554
Special tutoring	91	664
Use of regular faculty in tutoring	95	440
Use of specially trained faculty in tutoring	56	134
Use of regular students for tutoring	77	272
Use of advanced students in program for tutoring	65	212

Source: Morrison, 1973, Tables 8 and 9.

Others have championed credit provisions as providing motivation and reducing attrition (H. Astin *et al.,* 1972; Roueche and Kirk, 1973; Cross, 1970, 1976; Roueche and Snow, 1977; Roueche and Roueche, 1977). Grant and Hoeber (p. 23) have summarized the arguments for those who advocate remedial credit:

> Requiring a student to take basic skills courses but refusing to grant credit certainly causes motivation problems for the student. At bottom, this practice is patently immoral. An institution's admission policy assures the student that he is not being penalized for the quality of academic work up to this point; but then the institution does penalize him by forcing him to pay in money and unrewarded time for that which he has not mastered prior to his admission.

Even if an institution does not require students to take basic skills courses, it should recognize by granting credit not only that the student has mastered a particular course, but also that the student has recognized his deficiency and done something positive on his own initiative—an important step for the basic skills student in improving his academic self-image.

Regardless of degree credit provisions* or grading practices, educators must explore administrative means for loosening strictures of time that force nontraditional students into precisely the same classroom-hour context as regular course instruction, while additional pedagogical methods must be employed in the classrooms. Increasingly, such remediation is being conducted under various administrative structures, combining academic and supportive services. Roueche and Snow (1977), in a national study of developmental education programs, outlined the three major organizational designs for such programming: *isolated developmental courses* within already-existing departmental structures (e.g., a course in developmental mathematics added to mathematics department offerings); *interdisciplinary groups of instructors* who team-teach developmental courses while retaining primary appointments in disciplines; and *comprehensive developmental education* programs as umbrellas for the academic and supportive functions. A fourth, "other" category included various combinations of voluntary and *ad hoc* plans, and derivatives of the three basic designs with institutional variations (Roueche and Snow, 1977).

Choices of provisions for remedial work must, of course, be made to fit institutional characteristics and clienteles. The choice to provide such services, however, must be made. It is a rare open–door institution that can neglect remedial programming and lay claim to serving its community. The demonstrated need for such programs is coincidental with, but not entirely caused by, the rising number of minority enrollments in two year institutions. Nor have minority students been the sole. beneficiaries of remedial coursework.

The increasing heterogeneity of two year institutions has brought not only new types of students, but has probably widened the continuum of traditionally-measured abilities as well. Low cost and proximity have attracted traditional and highly able students as well as students requiring remedial help. To this end, an increasing number of two year colleges have made provisions for honors students. A 1967 attempt to survey two year college honors programs discovered that only 11 of the 270

---

* See Ferrin (1971) for a review of problems connected with transfer of remedial credit.

TABLE 4-21

**Organizational Structures for Remedial Programs
1976**

1. The addition of *isolated developmental courses* in disciplined curricula; that is, adding developmental reading to the list of approved courses in English.
Community colleges = 34%; senior college = 32%.

2. Working with an *interdisciplinary group of instructors* who remain attached to their disciplines organizationally, and who coordinate with instructors from other disciplines and with counselors assigned to compensatory students.
Community colleges = 18%; senior colleges = 11%.

3. Establishment of a *division or department* of developmental studies which plans, coordinates, and allocates funds for instruction, counseling and other support services.
Community colleges = 30%; senior colleges = 24%.

4. Others. Community colleges = 18%; senior colleges = 32%.

Source: Roueche and Snow, 1977, Appendix A.

respondent institutions had honors provisions (Phillips, 1973). By 1975, however, 47 colleges reported formal honors programs, while over 500 reported honors provisions of a curricular or support nature. Fewer than 20% of the institutions reported having no provisions for honors students (Olivas, 1977). In broad form, the special administrative and curricular options resembled remedial program provisions, in that these were programs for a special constituency within a heterogeneous student population.

Table 4-22 indicates the extent to which programming for honors students, however defined, has become entrenched in these institutions. The most common academic provisions included honors classes (50%) and examination credit, including standardized tests (78%) and departmental credit (56%). The significance of honors participation in retention of students has been noted (Astin, 1977a), but little systematic research on traditionally-measured honors students has been undertaken, including the extent to which minority students have participated in such programming. Clearly, honors classes and programs can have disproportionate racial implications for students. Two year institutions would be well-advised to examine K-12 experiences for an indication of the extent to which abused honors programming can negatively affect minorities and institutionalize racial program "tracking."

TABLE 4-22

**Academic Provisions for 2-Year College Honors Program
1975**

Provision	Number of Institutions
Sample Having Honors Elements	511 (80% of total sample, N = 636)
Classes	253 (50% of Table 5, N = 511)
Speakers	60 (12%)
Examination credit	
CLEP, AP	398 (78%)
Departmental	284 (56%)
Honor roll	85 (17%) [question not asked]
Honor Society	270 (53%)
Committee on Honors	83 (16%)

Source: Olivas, 1977, Table 5.

Support Services

The first half of this chapter focused upon courses of instruction and academic affairs. This section will analyze those administrative services that facilitate instruction by enrolling, counseling, advising, and housing students registered for coursework. This latter consideration, support services, is less comprehensive, perhaps, in its scope, though no less crucial in terms of student contact and influence upon all students. Recruiting, admissions, financial aids, scheduling, and registration are the first encounters students have with postsecondary institutions. Intermediate services, including residential living, student programs, advising, and library provisions all affect the academic setting and contribute to the socialization of students. Terminal support services, including transfer or terminal program administration and placement, often form the final impression upon students who leave an institution for whatever reason. This analysis will flow somewhat sequentially, beginning with state-level provisions, or large-scale provisions for special student programming. Institutional-level analysis will include provisions for recruitment and admissions, remedial support services, counseling, and residential facilities. A summary section will review research literatre concerning faculty and student attitudes toward support services.

It has been noted throughout that federal and state governments have played similar significant roles in establishing two year systems, and continue to define, shape, and fund two year institutions (Martorana and McGuire, 1975; Millard, 1976; Mortorana and Nespoli, 1977).

While their major involvement in two year institutions has been in the creating and funding of the institutions, increasingly states are involved in collective negotiations with faculty (Lee, 1978) adult education (Zusman, 1978), and other programs in the two year institutions. Reasons for this trend toward state involvement vary, ranging from systematic responses necessitated by increased educational expenditures and concerns for accountability, to more frivolous, politicized involvement in controversial personnel selection.

State involvement in two year college support services, however, except financial aid, has been minimal, particularly with regard to support services directed at minority student programming. The number of state funding programs designated for disadvantaged or minority students is small, and does not appear to be increasing. Table 4-23 lists the seven states that in 1975 and 1977 funded such programs.

The programs include financial aid provisions explicitly designated for minority groups (e.g., Maine Indian and South Dakota Indian Student Scholarships) or disadvantaged target populations (e.g., Connecticut's 1977 grants "for potentially capable students whose educational achievement is restricted due to special, environmental or economic factors"). Specific support programs targeted for disadvantaged students

TABLE 4-23

**States Having State-Level Programs Designed for
Disadvantaged/Minority Students in Public and
Private Higher Education Institutions
1975 and 1977**

1975[a]	*1977*
California	California
Connecticut	Connecticut
Maine	New Jersey
New Jersey	New York
New York	Pennsylvania
Pennsylvania	South Dakota
Wisconsin	Wisconsin

Source: 1975 data from Millard, 1975, pp. 1–24.
1977 data from Jonsen, 1977, pp. 1–28.

Note: Excludes need-based financial aid programs available to all students, and includes all self-designated disadvantaged/minority programs apart from need-based financial aid programs.

[a] In December 1974, a Washington program and a tuition supplement plan were ruled unconstitutional by the State Supreme Court, due to state constitutional debt limitations and prohibitions on aid to sectarian colleges. The program has been restructured, with no special provisions for minority/disadvantaged students. (ISEP conversation with Council for Postsecondary Education Staff, August, 1978.)

include Connecticut's Talent Assistance Cooperative, designed to identify, recruit, counsel, and place "talented but disadvantaged high school students, dropouts and noncontinuing high school graduates," and Pennsylvania's aid "to institutions for remedial programs for disadvantaged students." Clearly, patterns of state support will reflect a number of considerations, including institutional characteristics, state resources, population demographics, and legislative priorities.

California's state provisions for such special programming are the most comprehensive, and are funded at the highest level (total dollars, not per capita two year college student). Since the initiation of the 1969 Extended Opportunity Programs and Services (EOPS), the financial assistance and support services program serving the community college system (102 colleges) has grown from nearly $3 million to almost $14 million. Nearly 50,000 students (39% of the target disadvantaged population) received financial aid, tutoring, counseling, and/or special instruction through EOPS.

Case studies in California, conducted shortly after the passage of Proposition 13, revealed considerable concern over the fate of such line items in the state budget. Because the programs are need-based, over two-thirds of the students served are minority, while 86% of the campus EOPS directors are minority (Farland *et al.*, 1976, Table 3). Both EOPS personnel and college administrators feared that such programming would be viewed as unimportant and unnecessary by legislators unless the "seed money" nature of special legislation was stressed. Ninety-six percent of the EOPS directors had received supplemental funding (Farland *et al.*, 1976, Table 28) from additional sources, indicating the extent to which state money has enabled the colleges to seek extramural program support (see also Brossman, 1974; Morales, 1977). Visits to two year colleges in other states administering special programming confirmed that the state subsidies enabled personnel to seek federal, other governmental, and private money available for program development and evaluation.

Portions of special program funding frequently went for start-up and admissions costs, understated but exceptionally important components of programs for disadvantaged students (see, for example, H. Astin *et al.*, 1972, pp. 303–317). In a time when senior institutions are employing sophisticated marketing techniques (Leister, 1975; Leister and MacLachlan, 1976) and recruiting increasing numbers of students who might otherwise attend two year colleges (Mundy, 1976), admissions officers in two year institutions may expect their roles to increase in significance, for several trends point to an increasing reliance upon admissions criteria and a need for increasing enrollments, both unfamiliar activities for open–door institutions.

The increased competition for technical and career program admis-

TABLE 4-24

**California EOPS Programming: Students Served,
History of Funding, Expenditures by Category of Service**

History of Students Served in EOPS

School Year	Number of Colleges Participating	Fall Full-Time Enrollment	Students Identified As Eligible	Number of Students Served by EOPS	Students Served as Percent of Eligibles
1969–70	46	259,047	N/A	13,943	N/A
1970–71	67	282,857	N/A	19,725	N/A
1971–72	87	295,620	42,302	19,459	46.00
1972–73	86	284,799	52,819	20,730	39.24
1973–74	94	306,390	69,341	24,341	35.10
1974–75	94	324,277	86,574	23,917	27.62
1975–76	99	374,473	126,136	27,150	21.69
1976–77	100	328,108	127,896	40,724(e)	34.84(e)
1977–78	102	330,000(p)	125,948	48,679(p)	38.85(p)

(*continued*)

Source: Morales, 1977, Tables 2, 3, 4.
Key: e = estimated from approved budgets.
p = projected.

History of Funding and Service

Year	Number of Colleges Participating	Total College Budget Requests	State EOPS Allocation	Percent of Request Granted In Allocation	Number of Students Served	Expenditures Per Student	Expenditure Per Student Adjusted for Inflation (Consumer Price Index On Base Year 1967)
1969–70	46	$10,392,678	$ 2,870,000	28	13,943	$199	$178
1970–71	67	12,296,324	4,350,000	35	19,725	209	179
1971–72	87	15,377,995	3,350,000	22	19,459	163	135
1972–73	86	14,635,668	4,850,000	33	20,730	212	168
1973–74	94	16,453,950	6,170,500	37	24,341	248	182
1974–75	94	16,767,146	6,170,500	37	23,917	258	170
1975–76	99	18,647,146	7,656,018	41	27,150	282	172
1976–77	100	19,784,673	11,484,027	58	40,724(e)	282(e)	162(e)
1977–78	102	26,412,672	13,983,157	53	48,679(p)	287(p)	155(p)

Expenditures of State EOPS Allocation by Budget Category

Year	Part A-Program Administration	Part B-Educational Support Services	Part C-Financial Assistance to Students	Total
1969–70	$ 487,900 (17%)	$ 595,779 (21%)	$1,750,700 (61%)	$ 2,870,000 (99%)
1970–71	435,000 (10%)	983,520 (23%)	2,871,000 (66%)	4,350,000 (99%)
1971–72	301,500 (9%)	928,609 (29%)	2,077,000 (62%)	3,350,000 (100%)
1972–73	388,000 (8%)	1,398,634 (28%)	3,104,000 (64%)	4,850,000 (100%)
1973–74	370,280 (6%)	1,988,422 (33%)	3,764,005 (61%)	6,170,500 (100%)
1974–75	493,640 (8%)	2,076,950 (33%)	3,640,300 (59%)	6,170,500 (100%)
1975–76	535,921 (7%)	2,874,000 (36%)	4,440,490 (58%)	7,656,018 (101%)
1976–77(e)	1,033,562 (9%)	4,881,000 (41%)	5,742,011 (50%)	11,484,027 (100%)
1977–78(p)	1,258,484 (9%)	6,292,420 (45%)	6,432,252 (46%)	13,983,157 (100%)

sions has already begun to require administrative procedures and collegial judgments concerning selection (Morgan, 1977), although it is not clear the extent to which admissions officers will play a role in judgments concerning program applications. Despite the low levels of collegiality in two year faculties (Baldridge *et al.*, 1978) there is every reason to believe selected program admissions will likely be made by technical and career program faculty and departmental heads. Nevertheless, admissions staff members, or departmental administrators and unit staff members, play a formal role in disseminating application materials, assembling applications, and explaining procedures to students; similarly, they play an informal role in the preparation of dossiers and presentation of materials to faculty or admissions committees.

This detailed explanation serves as a reminder of the administrative discretion accorded faculty and staff in making judgments, particularly in competitive admissions procedures. While the anticipated need to recruit students into enrollment formula-funded institutions will require different skills and judgments, admission of minority students into two year colleges will require no less sensitivity on the part of admissions personnel. The Van Alstyne (1977a) study of staffing patterns showed that 93% of two year admissions officers were white, and 91% were white men. Institutions, including two year institutions, would do well to examine staffing patterns to see if the minority communities are being reached adequately by present personnel, and if admissions and recruitment activities are effectively reaching minority community and institutional needs.

The importance of identification, recruitment, and admissions is clear in comprehensive remedial support services, where such initiating activities appear commonplace. The following tables summarize several aspects of supportive programming, including emphases upon admissions, remedial guidance and counseling, and financial aid; the data, together with academic remedial programming, condensed in tables 4-19 to 4-21, provide a more complete portrait of comprehensive remedial programs and support services. The elements, variously assembled, are common denominators in two year college retention policies.

Tables 4-25 and 4-26 indicate the extent to which two year institutions are providing special* support services for remedial students. These figures, gathered and reported in the early 1970's, undoubtedly underrepresent the spread of such programming, as extended access to postsecondary education has had the concomitant effect of attracting

---

* Betances (1974, p. 35) discourages description of such programs as "special" because the designation implies that they are marginal and unimportant: " 'special' assumes that such needs are not essential." This book makes no such assumption.

TABLE 4-25

Elements of Support and Remedial College Programs

1. Special services offered *this year*:

  64% Efforts to recruit students who would not ordinarily seek a college education.
  76% Financial aids designed especially for disadvantaged students.
  61% Special counseling programs.
  92% Remedial or developmental courses to upgrade verbal or other academic skills.
  20% A total program of recruitment, counseling, courses, etc., with a director.

2. Recruitment of students:

  70% Visits to high schools in disadvantaged areas.
  60% Specific requests to high school counselors.
  58% Work with community agencies and leaders.
  52% Use of students to help in recruiting.
  24% Use of a special recruitment program such as Talent Search, NSSFNS, Upward Bound.
  14% Other recruitment techniques.

3. Admissions:

  81% Open admissions.
   4% Attempt to attract a certain number from racial minorities—use of a quota.
  19% Relaxation of test scores or high school grades for underprepared students.

4. Financial aid:

  63% Available to needy students regardless of academic standing; for instance, may retain grant while on probation.
  71% "Need" used as a major criterion of eligibility for funds.
  59% Use of a federally funded program designed for disadvantaged students; EOP.
  38% College has some funds of its own for poorly prepared students.

5. Counseling services

  22% Separate counseling office for underprepared students.
  33% Use of group interaction or group counseling.
  36% Program of teacher counselors.
  17% Use of students as counselors.
  40% Diagnostic testing.
  12% Other.

6. Evaluation:

  55% Measurement of changes in test scores.
  36% Measurement of changes in student attitudes.
  50% Follow-up of students on the job or in college.
  30% Formal collection of faculty and student reactions to program.
   4% Other.

Source: Cross, 1976, pp.191–195. Edited by ISEP staff.

TABLE 4-26

Elements of Support and Remedial Programs

Element	Percent Affirmative	Weighted N
Admissions, Recruiting		
Recruitment teams	36	266
Use of community contacts	75	464
Counseling Services		
Personal counseling	99	774
Academic counseling	99	774
Vocational-occupational counseling	99	774
Job placement counseling	95	750
Job placement follow-up counseling	72	562
Guidance, Tutoring		
Special guidance and counseling	89	554
Special tutoring	91	664
Use of regular faculty in tutoring	95	440
Use of specially trained faculty in tutoring	56	134
Use of regular students for tutoring	77	272
Use of advanced students in program for tutoring	65	212

Source: Morrison, 1973, Tables 3, 4, 6, 7, 8, 10.

non-traditional students with non-traditional academic and supportive needs (Munday, 1976). There is evidence that comprehensive programming, accounting for only 20% of the Cross study (p. 192) and 37% of the Morrison sample (p. 407), is increasing both in frequency and comprehensiveness (Deluca, 1974a; Moore, 1976a; Roueche and Roueche, 1977).

Single elements within limited-focus or comprehensive programs include identification and contact with minority K-12 students, admissions policies or practices characterized (in a limited sense) as open–door, supplemental provisions for financial aid, counseling aimed at integrating nontraditional students into the institutional mainstream, academic assistance and tutoring, or variations of these elements. Each of these elements, whether provided singly by institutions or as components of a well-coordinated program, requires special sensitivities from institutional and program administrators, because institutional and program goals, overlapping to a great extent, can be at cross purposes with one another.

It could be asked, for example, whether two year institutions have a proper mandate to recruit students at all. Clearly, as community schools, they have the responsibility to serve needs as articulated by community representatives, whether they be voters, boards of trustees, legislators, or students. But can open door institutions recruit students, and should they? Should developmental education programs counsel bright minority high school students to attend the two year college, where retention rates are lower and where residential living opportunities may be absent? Enrollment-based financing is undermined by the need to enroll more students (or to alter the support formulae) in order to expand programs. Two year institutions have grown in ways that suggest successful recruiting (and packaging). It has been suggested in this chapter that in some areas of programming, competition for admissions already exists, calling into play a crucial role for developmental support services in assuring that minority students are not routinely screened out of consideration for limited access positions, even in open door colleges. It appears, then, that there are justifications, based upon institutional and program rationales, for undertaking recruitment efforts, provided that appropriate matching occurs between student and institution. The most obvious rationale in employing such efforts is to bring college-going to the attention of students who have requisite skills but inadequate information.

The second common element in support services, not unrelated to the first—recruiting and admissions practices—is a policy of flexible admissions criteria, an underemphasized component of support services for minority students, even in institutions characterized as open door. While both Cross (81%) and Morrison (86%) found evidence of openly stated free access, there was also considerable evidence of additional requirements for admission, including grade point averages, test scores, interviews, and letters of recommendation. These traditionally acceptable indices of admissions, long in use in senior and graduate institutions, have filtered into two year institutional practices as well. Open door institutions must guard against overreliance upon superficially neutral admissions criteria for limited-space programs, lest there be an entrenched, genuine two track system of access developed within two year colleges: traditional quantitative indices designed to admit traditional students into competitive programs, and open door for all other programs. The potential for abuse is perhaps greater in two year colleges even than in graduate and professional schools, where nearly all candidates present test scores and baccalaureate degrees. Nontraditional students, including a large number of minority students, will not have had a chance to develop competitive credentials, particularly should baccalaureate degree holders begin to apply in greater numbers to allied health and other highly competitive programs (Morgan, 1977).

The role of remedial programs in assisting institutions to assemble representative student bodies should be clear. Less certain is the role of

TABLE 4-27

2-Year College Admissions Criteria

Admissions Criteria	Percent	Weighted N
High school diploma or equivalent	86	696
Minimum age	27	214
High school grade average	0	0
Test scores	28	218
Interview	7	54
Letter of recommendation	16	122
Physical examination	41	322
Require high school diploma or certificate only	34	264
Require minimum age only	5	42
Require only high school diploma or minimum age	55	434

Source: Morrison, 1973, Table 3.

support services in providing counseling. Inasmuch as other remedial functions cluster around academics and support services—tutoring, instructing, advising, even financing—which are attendant to academics, counseling, at least theoretically, is affective and personal (Moore, 1976a). There are approaches, including promising and successful programs (e.g., Garfield and McHugh, 1978), that combine instructional and guidance services for remedial students, but these appear to be rare. Visits to institutions, even minority institutions, gave indication of frequent bifurcation of counseling and academic programs, and frequent turf fights, even within comprehensive remedial programs.

Although some internal bifurcation is perhaps inevitable, the fragile nature of special programming cannot withstand frequent bloodletting. To be sure, larger programs serving multiple needs will develop problems of control and coordination, particularly if overall program funding is uncertain and vulnerable, or if institutional authorities are not fully supportive. But, other things being equal, larger, comprehensive programs become more entrenched and are less likely to be eradicated than small, isolated programs without centralized control; a corollary is that special programs serving a disadvantaged clientele must move to traditional, mainstream sources of support and funding. (For research in support of this apparent anomaly of increased size bringing *increased* autonomy, see Baldridge *et al.*, 1978.) No single model or program, however comprehensive, could hope to incorporate sufficient institutional detail to be applicable to all two year institutions, even those presently not serving minority community needs. However, institutional administrators and faculty can ensure that all such programs be given adequate support, especially in times of retrenchment, to perform the academic and supportive tasks not being completed in mainstream classroom instruction.

It could be argued that financial aid, or the inability to pay for college costs, is an even more fundamental threshhold barrier than admissions policies or the availability of remedial programs, academic or supportive, particularly for students of low income families, a disproportionate number of whom are minority. Financial reasons for attrition have been found to be more common among minority students than among whites (Institute for the Study of Educational Policy, 1976), while visits to financial aid offices in minority institutions, particularly institutions that conducted exit interviews with students, have confirmed that large numbers of students who drop out do so for financial reasons. Unfortunately, the recent passage of Proposition 13 in California, the heavy reliance of the state community colleges upon property taxes, and the disproportionately heavy concentration of minorities in the system may create a laboratory experiment for testing the effect of tuition upon college attendance of minorities.

Available federal financial aid provisions are generally underused by two year colleges (Gladieux, 1975), and a significant number of institutions have coordinated or incorporated financial aid counseling and program administration with remedial services administration. Cross (1976, p. 194) reported that 59% of her sample institutions had federally funded financial aid programs for disadvantaged students, while over 90% of Morrison's (1973, p. 409) institutions had such programs. For informational purposes, if not for administrative reasons, it is essential that coordination between financial aid officers and remedial and support services personnel be maintained.* Developmental programs and ethnic studies programs should be involved in this and other support services in order that administrative procedures for students (and their parents) be minimized and facilitated. For example, translation of financial aid forms into languages other than English (or, perhaps more frequently, English into understandable English) could be a regular and essential cooperative activity between administrators, students, and parents; such services become especially necessary when the students are first-generation college-goers and parental income information is required (see, generally, Casso and Roman, eds., 1976; Perez, ed., 1977).

Suggestions for administering financial aid programs seem somehow unimportant in the larger context of the current debate over equity issues in financial aid programs and the national debate over tuition tax

---

* It will be recalled from chapter three that minorities constitute a relatively large share of financial aid officers (Van Alstyne et al., 1977).

credits. These debates and resulting legislation will, however, determine institutional policies and practices regarding availability and disbursement of federal funds for student aid. Tuition (or more accurately, the absence or amount of tuition) appears to be a fundamental determinant of college attendance for all students, although in varying degrees for different groups (Munday, 1976; Bishop, 1977; Bishop and Van Dyk, 1977) and with varying distributional impacts and equity implications (Nelson, 1978a; Vredeveld, 1978). This chapter, indeed this book, makes no evaluation of the various schemes for determining public subsidies or for delivering financial aids.

Although chapter two does report receipt of financial aid by minority groups (Table 2-19) in available federal programs, it can only draw limited inferences. However, several guiding principles for distributing financial aid in two year colleges seem appropriate.

1. Need-based programs of financial aid will continue to distribute large sums of money to minority students. Matching student needs with available funds is a problem resulting from students', particularly minority students', lack of information. Therefore, comprehensive programs to disseminate financial aid information should be undertaken as a regular component of recruitment and admissions. These programs should make use of channels of minority community information, formal or informal, such as minority press, radio, church, and civic groups.

2. It is imperative that parents of minority students be assisted in completion of appropriate forms. Bilingual counselors should be employed if the community is bilingual.

3. Financial aid officers, in making awards to eligible students, should design packages that will not require minority students to incur debts at higher levels than majority students. Similarly, all aid programs should be regularly evaluated for racial and ethnic distributional impacts.

4. Institutions should pursue aggressively all available private and public sources of financial aid and student support.

These general recommendations are institution-directed, and must be adapted to institutional realities. However, until equality of opportunity, however defined, filters down to minority students and accords distribution as well as access, tuition costs and provisions for financial aid will remain a factor in college attendance, one likely to be a substantial barrier to poor and minority students.

Discussions of financial aid are often devoid of information on expenses other than tuition and fees. Gladieux has hypothesized that neglect of other educational expenses, chiefly housing and eating costs, accounts for some of the disproportionately low receipt of financial aid funds by two year institutions (1975, pp. 2–3). Even excluding foregone wages, a major consideration for part time students in two year institutions, there are costs incurred by commuters for which no financial aid provisions are made. This affects two year students primarily, because of the commuter nature of the institutions.

But the commuter nature of two year colleges presents other problems for educators besides the financial aid provisions. Most notably, there are negative implications for retention, socialization, and campus employment stemming from the lack of residential facilities in two year colleges. It will be recalled that less than nine percent of all public two year college facilities are residential, in comparison to thirty percent in universities and nearly forty percent in four year colleges (see Figure 2-1); more recent data on freshman students indicate that 14% of public two year freshmen live on campus, in comparison to 56% of private two year freshmen, 66% of four year freshmen, and 77% of university freshmen.

Research findings almost unanimously agree that residential living increases the likelihood that students will stay in college (e.g., Richardson, 1956; Stark, 1965; Feldman and Newcomb, 1973, pp. 196–226; Chickering, 1974; Astin, 1975a; Astin, 1977a), although phenomena of retention are extraordinarily complex. It is clear, however, that opportunities for campus-based social interaction, informal socialization, and

TABLE 4-28

Weighted National Norms for Freshman Residence on Campus
(in Percentages)
1976

Residence Planned During Fall Term	All 2-Year	Public 2-Year	Private 2-Year	All 4-Year	All Universities
With parents or relatives	69.8	71.9	35.3	28.7	19.0
Private home or apartment	12.5	12.8	7.2	4.1	3.0
Dormitory	15.1	12.8	52.9	63.8	73.9
Fraternity/sorority	.2	.2	.2	1.1	1.7
Other campus housing	1.1	1.0	3.4	1.6	1.9
Total on campus*	[16.4	14.0	56.5	66.5	77.5]
Other	1.3	1.3	1.0	.7	.4

Source: Astin, King, Richardson, 1976, p. 20.

* ISEP calculations of dormitory, Greek, other campus housing.

free time are reduced when students live at home. While these opportunities may be of secondary interest or importance to two year (or four
year) students, and while part time or older students may be developing
such opportunities apart from campus, a significant number of full time
two year students (including minority students) may unwittingly deny
themselves social and informal reinforcement of their academic development by attending these institutions.

Of course, many commuter institutions (two and four year) have
developed large, comprehensive student affairs programs, mitigating
somewhat the lack of social interaction opportunities.* These programs
may enable students to become involved in organizations and to develop
leadership skills normally afforded students in residential institutions,
and they may even generate work-study or other employment opportunities similar to those in dormitories and other campus housing, but
the time spent in social interaction is obviously less than it is in residential
living, and the opportunities for institutionalized programs are similarly
reduced.

It may be politically impossible for two year colleges, particularly in
times of retrenchment or no-construction phases, to reconcile their
accessibility to commuters and part-timers with the demonstrable needs
of residential students. Inasmuch as the former constituencies are less
expensive to serve, their needs have superseded those of residential
students (or students who would be residential if the institutions provided
housing). If construction of dormitories is impossible, then two year
college administrators could at the least seek to provide adequate
surrogates for residential programs by making available cultural and
supportive educational programs, including ones that will involve students and institutional personnel. Further, increasing involvement with
the community by students and staff would tend to enlarge the impact
of the institution upon the community, including students within the
community.

This chapter has attempted to review state-subsidized and institu-
tionally-based academic and support services, concentrating upon minority student participation and institutional impact upon these students;
federal financial aid policies were also examined, and principles for
institutional administration of financial aid were proposed. Throughout
previous chapters, an underlying theme has been the dissonance and
incongruity between groups within two year institutions: trustees felt
their demographics represented the community; faculty members
wanted their students better prepared; administrators wanted to exert

---

* And of course, dormitory experiences of minority students are not always
positive, and frequently are negative (Hedegard, 1972; Epps, ed., 1972; Peterson
et al., 1978).

more authority; legislators wanted education delivered as inexpensively as possible. Conflict, a natural part of any organization (Baldridge, *et al.*, 1978), is at the core of the task that two year colleges face. Differing perceptions over the effectiveness of student services, therefore, are to be expected, as students and faculty view these programs quite differently. As the following table notes, there are significant variations in the perceived value of two year college support services, with students in each case perceiving them as less worthwhile than do faculty members. There is also a disturbing pattern of nonparticipation by students in some of the support service areas, most notably, financial aid. This failure to use existing financial aid provisions could partly explain Gladieux's (1975) finding that financial aid is underused in the institutions. A corollary could be that the offices are not advertising their wares.

Students themselves differ in their needs, and even those with similar needs will vary in their disposition to seek assistance and to involve themselves in institutional programs (see, for example, Richards and Braskamp, 1969). As was noted in chapter two, two year students participate less in extracurricular activities than do other students (Fenske and Scott, 1973, Table C-3), although this may be a result of the fewer extracurricular activities and limited residential facilities available at these institutions. This finding seems reasonable, given the attraction of two year institutions to part-time students. It is this array of student needs and institutional missions that points to the increased necessity for planning.

As was noted in the sections on academic programs and support services designed for remedial students, the most successful programs appear to be comprehensive, cooperative efforts that involve institutional staff (H. Astin *et al.*, 1972; Garfield and McHugh, 1978) and students (Reed, 1973). These efforts are aimed at providing for student needs, and, if performed by sensitive, competent staff, would theoretically assist retention of minority and majority students (Astin, 1975b). This concept, that integrated and comprehensive services will assist many constituencies, should make such programs more acceptable to administrators. Surely, the faculty will support efforts to assist students, but this support should be participatory, and efforts at remedial programs should not be sloughed off onto support services components alone (Alfred, 1975).

Evaluation, a popular catchword for institutional self studies, must become serious, searching exercises and not mere public relations gestures. The multiple constituencies within two year institutions may scare off serious evaluation as inapplicable or unwieldly. To some extent, fear would be justified, if each group were separate. But many of the problems overlap, and require dispassionate evaluation. In some situations (as in California), evaluation may be forced upon institutions.

TABLE 4-29

Student and Faculty Perceptions of College Services (in Percentages)

Type of College Service	Student or Faculty Perceptions	Extremely Valuable	Worthwhile	Of Little Benefit	Never Used	Not Offered or Available	Total
Academic advising service (assistance in selecting courses, adjusting schedules, planning programs, etc.)	S	25	38	22	13	2	100
	F	36	48	15	...	1	100
Counseling service (assistance in choosing a major, vocational planning, resolving personal problems, etc.)	S	21	31	22	24	2	100
	F	30	51	17	1	1	100
Orientation service (assistance in getting started in college—learning the ropes, getting acquainted, overcoming apprehensions, etc.)	S	16	29	25	24	6	100
	F	23	47	25	1	4	100
Developmental education services (improvement of reading, study skills, spelling, etc.)	S	13	17	9	53	8	100
	F	41	41	7	3	8	100
Financial needs service (assistance in obtaining a scholarship, loan, part-time job; or assistance in budgeting and controlling expenses)	S	19	15	12	51	3	100
	F	48	46	4	1	1	100

Source: Bushnell, 1973, Table 2.26.

Others, anticipating problems, make contingency administrative plans. At the least, institutions can evaluate new programs or consider cuts with impact in mind: will cutting X program negatively affect minority students? How will proposed program Y help minority students? If such evaluation is seen as integrative, it would improve the situation for minorities in the only stratum of postsecondary education to which they presently have access.

Chapter 5

Conclusion,
Recommendations

ᛄᛄᛄ

The dilemma is clear: do two year institutions provide opportunities for minorities, or do they perpetuate inequities? The data examined in this book suggest that the answer to both questions is a qualified "yes." To the extent that easily-available institutions do increase access, opportunities are provided to all who would enroll. However, to the extent that full time access for minorities occurs predominantly in the public two year college sector, it cannot be said that this system represents an equitable distribution. This dilemma is perhaps inevitable in a system of education that grew from access for the privileged few to access for all who choose to attend college. It was all the more inevitable when access was originally by law and practice, exclusively for white men. Further, the tremendous growth in access was possible only because lower cost commuter institutions were constructed.

This dilemma, however, does not preclude isolated solutions to specific problems or the fine tuning of programs designed to assist minority students. And while it is difficult to be sanguine concerning systemwide changes for increasing access, occasions such as the passage of Proposition 13 in California will cause systemwide changes certain to *decrease* access and services for minority students. It becomes more crucial, in times of retrenchment, to assess cutbacks with respect to the disproportionate impacts they will have upon sectors or systems which provide educational access to minority students. The perverse logic of "last hired, first fired" has applicability although recent, incremental minority gains have not been sufficiently consolidated to withstand major budget cutbacks. Yet, in this increasingly conservative climate programs designed to assure opportunities for minorities, always on the periphery of higher education interests, are threatened first. Not only are such programs viewed as nonessential, but few minorities are in positions where they have substantial impact upon budgets.

Those who argue that wholesale, radical restructuring of the postsecondary system is necessary, and those who argue that the system works well are of one voice on proposed solutions. In effect, opponents and proponents conclude that the system is the worst possible, except for all the other systems. Thus Jerome Karabel concludes, "Even if the community colleges were to undergo a major transformation, little change in the system of social stratification would be likely to take place" (Karabel, 1972, p. 558) and Chester Finn concludes, "self control, flexibility, patience, and circumspection—these do not seem to be a very exciting set of prescriptions by which to guide the future relationship between higher education and the federal government. The main reason is that the patient is not very ill. The academy is basically healthy" (Finn, 1978, pp. 224–225).

To be sure, Karabel's conclusion is pessimistic, arrived at only after discarding as impractical several possible reforms. Among these reforms is the reversal of existing funding policies in order to invest proportionately more dollars in two year colleges; he rejects this suggestion as unlikely to effect radical change. Another potential reform is to upgrade two year institutions to baccalaureate institutions; he feels this would merely relegate the newly transformed senior colleges to the low end of the baccalaureate scale. Moreover, in a time of incremental enrollment growth, building larger or more comprehensive institutions makes little economic sense. A third reform examined and rejected by Karabel is the suggestion that two year institutions focus solely upon vocational education; he contends that this proposal would continue to perpetuate class-based access in the lowest stratum.

Whether one believes the system is terminally ill or basically sound, it is difficult to prescribe changes, or even to diagnose ailments. Any radical changes, even if they are likely to work, would be prohibitively expensive; indeed, radical changes, if they occur, are likely to result from massive retrenchment occasioned by fiscal conservatism, as in Californa's Proposition 13. Second, while there is no comprehensive federal policy regarding higher education, there is even less federal direction concerning two year colleges. The highest ranking federal education official with a specific portfolio for two year college issues is a grade 17 appointment in the U.S. Office of Education with no statutory program responsibilities, save Title X, which has never been funded. Third, programs designed to help minority students or institutions enrolling minority students are increasingly looked upon with suspicion and are subject to extraordinary political disputes. As an example, efforts to increase the two year setaside in Title III affect black colleges' share of the money—and the statutory ceiling for appropriations—has been met for several years. This internecine competition tends to isolate minority education concerns, as the amount of effort expended over the minority-sensitive Titles, however esssential to institutional survival, is considerable. Finally, institutional needs vary widely, depending upon a number of factors, including the stability of funding sources, competition for students, the health of the local economy, demographic elements, and other characteristics affecting the colleges and their environments. Therefore, policies aimed at one institution's set of circumstances would not necessarily assist another college, or could do considerable damage to yet another.

These drawbacks notwithstanding, several suggestions follow, including policy recommendations addressed to policy makers, from those at the federal level to those who head institutional and departmental units, to those who lead high schools. Several recommendations focus upon curricular matters, while other focus more upon the periphery, as in those aimed at improving racial and ethnic data. All derive from findings discussed or policies analyzed earlier in the three central, substantive chapters. None would radically change existing systems, although several are aimed at rooting out systemic inequities or reducing systemic problems disproportionately affecting minority students. The two-fold common denominator of each suggestion is of particular concern for students in two year institutions and providing a means to assess and meet their needs. Recommendations are ordered from the federal level to the institutional and organizational levels.

1. *Congress and the Office of Education should consider the feasibility of removing the two-year college setaside from Title III and designating an authority for developing two year institutions under Title X. This revised Title X should be reauthorized, and Congress should appropriate a sum above the amount presently set aside in Title III.*

In the current reauthorization of the Higher Education Amendments, several proposals have been promoted to reduce the friction between two year and four year institutional competition in Title III (Strengthening Developing Institutions). Those proposals most likely to assist minority students are those that incorporate increased support to two year colleges while retaining the primary emphasis upon baccalaureate institutions that serve minority and low income students. Increased authorization and appropriations levels will be necessary, as the program has reached its $120 million ceiling. Competition between institutional types could be diminished by separate authorities for two and four year colleges, such as with a revised Title X, or by separate parts within Title III for two and four year colleges.

2. *The director of the Community College Unit, Bureau of Higher and Continuing Education, should be given larger responsibilities within the Bureau to coordinate federal policies toward two year colleges.*

The existing directorship is a symbolic appointment without specific, designated responsibilities to advocate for its designated constituency. Title X, the sole earmarked two year college legislation, has never been funded, and is unlikely to be funded in its present form. The director should be given authority, by statute or regulations, to coordinate programs and setasides for two year institutions and to provide technical assistance. The director should regularly assess USOE programs for their impact upon two year colleges, and should provide drafting assistance to legislative liaison staff in order to assure two year college eligibility for funded programs.

3. *To increase two year college shares of federal programs, two year college personnel should be more extensively involved in competitive proposal reading.*

Existing programs, through design or practice, tend to favor graduate or baccalaureate institutions. This is so in part because of meritocratic competition, in part because of proposal selection processes that involve senior college participants, and in part because two year institutions have not perceived proposal writing or development activities as essential missions. The director, with or without additional portfolio, should convene a task force to remedy this underparticipation in federal programs (see Appendix J). Similarly, the Bureau of Student Financial Assistance should take steps to assure more active participation by two year colleges. For instance, programs that would enable students and parents to understand and complete financial aid forms should be identified and strengthened.

The director should monitor emerging legislation and triggered-funding programs to ensure that two year colleges participate fully in such programs. For example, Title VI, of the National Defense Education

Act (1958)*, authorizing "Grant Programs to Promote Cultural Understanding," was triggered for funding only after $15 million had been expended for earlier sections. Fiscal year 1979's appropriations have triggered this funding mechanism, and the considerable multicultural activities conducted by two year colleges would make them eligible for the grant program.

4. *The Bureau of Higher and Continuing Education should evaluate all statutes, regulations, and internal procedures to assure full and fair participation by two year colleges and minority institutions in federal programs.*

Because minorities continue to be underrepresented in decisionmaking levels of federal education agencies, it is essential that the work product be reviewed for its calculated or inadvertantly negative impact upon two year colleges and minority institutions. The liaison for Women and Minorities and the director of the Community College Unit should work together to monitor this process.

5. *States should systematically gather, analyze, and disseminate institutional racial and ethnic enrollment, faculty, and program data.*

Throughout this book, the vagaries of existing data systems have been noted. Because states bear a major responsibility for providing equality of access and opportunity, they appear to be major policymakers concerning racial and ethnic data. Yet, an ISEP survey indicated scant attention being paid to this aspect of systemwide planning. The USOE State Commissions staff should use its 1202 planning authorization to oversee and coordinate this responsibility, and to serve as technical advisers to NCES data gathering efforts.

6. *States should review their two year college financing policies to ensure equitable distribution of state tax resources and to stabilize funding sources for higher education.*

Proposition 13, and its property tax implications, has shown the precariousness of financing higher education through local tax bases. Further, the data examined in this study have shown enormous dis-

---

* NDEA (1958), Title VI, Sec. 601–604.

crepancies between public subsidies at two and four year levels of statewide higher education systems. In each case, despite high part time enrollments, two year colleges received strikingly smaller per capita and full time equivalent appropriations. It is only a matter of time before minority groups or public interest groups mount legal challenges against this system of financing public higher education. State authorities would do well to anticipate such challenges by eliminating inequities.

7. *States should be the major consumer advocates of higher education, making available all pertinent institutional information so that students can make informed decisions concerning their enrollment.*

The increased competition for students between public and private sectors, and among institutions, affords states excellent opportunities to gather and disseminate information to assist students in choosing schools, in securing counseling, and in applying for financial assistance. The centralization of this information would reduce costs, provide planning data, and would likely reduce student attrition. Informal and formal minority information systems and community-based organizations should be utilized. To assist students in securing information and in negotiating systems is perhaps the greatest contribution statewide agencies could make to the creation of a more diverse and accessible marketplace.

8. *States should examine existing and proposed statutes, regulations, and practices to assess disproportionate impacts upon two year colleges and minority students.*

In one midwestern state, for instance, an existing residency rule literally prevented migrant workers from enrolling as residential students in state institutions, even though existing supportive programs were intended to assist just such non-traditional students. When the issue was brought to the attention of state officials, an exemption for alternative documentation was devised and is presently in place.

State coordinating or governing boards are in strategic positions to discover and eliminate such systemic barriers to minority participation, and institutions should actively cooperate to bring administrative problems to the attention of state officials. Statewide groups of professionals (e.g., registrars and admissions officials, financial aid officers) should regularly review institutional practices for such unintended barriers and should propose creative equitable means to eliminate these barriers.

9. *Colleges should practice aggressive affirmative action in hiring faculty and administrative personnel.*

This study has documented the surprisingly low proportion of minority faculty and administrators in two year colleges, even in colleges with substantial minority enrollments. As noted in chapter three, this situation is particularly indefensible in two year institutions, where the need for minority leadership and role models is particularly acute, where demand has been high for many years, and where the supply of qualified minorities is greater than the supply of Ph.D.-holders for senior institutions. The historical exclusion of minorities from skilled trades and crafts has resulted in fewer minority faculty for technical curricula, but the striking underrepresentation of minority faculty in transfer programs is inexcusable.

10. *Graduate and professional programs should actively seek minority students and aggressively apply for available federal funding.*

Senior institutions must share the responsibility for the underrepresentation of minorities in administrative and faculty ranks, inasmuch as they serve as training institutions for such personnel. The only means for ending this cycle of exclusion is for senior institutions to cooperate with education and business sectors in identifying minority persons with the desire and capabilities to pursue graduate work. Historically denied such opportunities, many women and minorities fully capable of undertaking graduate work have never been given the encouragement or means to attend college. Majority men have historically competed only with each other for career positions. Institutions, themselves party to these practices, must undertake extraordinary steps to end them.

11. *Institutions must identify underserved clienteles, assess their needs, and move aggressively to meet these needs.*

In some cases, this recommendation means undertaking extensive sensitivity campaigns to eliminate stereotypes, as with mainstreaming handicapped students or with providing in-service training to staff who have little experience with nontraditional students. Two year colleges have moved assertively into this area by arranging class hours and modes of instruction to accomodate new learners. Four year institutions, in need of student enrollments, have similarly moved to market themselves more effectively.

However, providing courses at all hours and teaching courses by newspaper will not adequately reach a major non-traditional clientele already enrolled in institutions: full time minority students, disproportionately enrolled in public, two year, commuter institutions. Counseling, academic advising, and the negotiating of financial assistance are essential to these students, not merely offering rearranged class hours.

Two year institutions need to devote staff and energy to a comprehensive program of supportive services, including development time for aggressive recruitment of federal and private funds for such purposes. When federal programs designed to provide such assistance are threatened two year colleges, located in nearly every congressional district in the country, must involve themselves in attempts to rescue these programs. Two year colleges have not advanced their own interests within Congress and the U.S. Office of Education.

12. *Two year and senior institutions must work together to alleviate problems of transfer between the two levels.*

While this recommendation surely is tired of seeing itself only in print, negotiating transfer constantly appears to be an impediment to baccalaureate completion by students, particularly minority students who are so overwhelmingly clustered in two year institutions. Most senior schools have arrangements for articulation, although this frequently means that registrars merely familiarize themselves with other institutions' catalogs. This is important, but hardly sufficient.

As state professional associations must examine their practices for continuity and fairness, so must admissions officers and advisers communicate concern about their overlapping responsibilities. Case studies conducted for this book revealed a number of transfer horror stories, including sophomores being held in two year colleges for the equivalent of three years of work and branch campus courses not being admitted for purposes of transfer to main campus programs. While these stories are striking as exceptions, the process of transferring from one school to another by definition requires more coordination and planning than does initially enrolling in a baccalaureate institution. Two year college advisers are more important than even four year advisers in this regard, and should be given the resources to link effectively with senior institutions. Academic and administrative officers should make ease-of-transfer a high institutional priority, as they frequently do ease-of-admission. The feeder system of two year and baccalaureate institutions cannot succeed if convenient two year access contrasts sharply with uncoordinated exit practices.

13. *Two year institutions must upgrade financial aid and development offices.*

Several studies analyzed in chapters three and four noted the low esteem in which financial aid offices and development programs were held by two year colleges; indeed, only affirmative action officers are consistently less central to two year institutional administrative hierarchies. This policy seems shortsighted. Although two year tuitions are, in most cases, lower than baccalaureate tuitions, additional fees, books, and other expenses (as well as foregone wages) would qualify many more two year students for federal, state, and private financial assistance. It appears that the low tuition levels have lulled two year administrators into downgrading the need for experienced and capable personnel in financial aid offices. As a result, these institutions do not receive proportional shares of grant, loan, or work study funds. Particularly as tax referenda threaten once secure community-funded institutions, it will behoove administrators to strengthen and upgrade existing offices for seeking aid and for notifying students of its availability.

The same logic applies to the need for development offices: relatively small investments now will result in a more competitive posture for seeking outside funds. If every earlier recommendation concerning two year federal programs were implemented tomorrow, it would still be necessary for two year colleges to upgrade their fund-seeking capabilities in financial aid and development offices—which could be combined in small schools—in order to compete successfully for funds. Comprehensive two year colleges are integral members of their business and academic communities, and many honorable and appropriate fund raising activities flow naturally from this relationship. Few two year colleges do this, or do it well, while baccalaureate and graduate institutions have done it for a long time.

14. *Two year colleges must practice aggressive affirmative action in all programs, particularly in programs for which there are admissions criteria.*

Increasingly, two year college technical and terminal curricula are receiving more applications than there are available spaces in the programs. On many campuses with predominantly minority enrollments, these programs are predominantly white. In some of these programs, significant numbers of college graduates are enrolled to train for alternative careers or to learn technical skills. Because many minority students have poor high school academic preparation, it is important that technical programs use life experiences, community services, and other alternative criteria in determining admissions standards.

There is a tendency to employ numerical indices and quantitative measures when judging large numbers of applications, but administrative convenience must not dictate admissions practices. Because two year students have fewer leadership development opportunities, fewer extracurricular activities, and less time in which to prepare for declared majors than do students in four year institutions, traditional means of evaluating student applications are less appropriate than they are in baccalaureate, graduate, or professional admissions, where fuller dossiers can be compiled. In technical programs designed to meet community professional and paraprofessional needs, minority community personnel needs also should be considered in assembling heterogeneous classes.

15. *High schools should emphasize college attendance for all students who have the capability, and should upgrade academic advising resources to accomplish this purpose.*

It is acknowledged from the outset that not all students want to attend college, or can do college level work. But if schools must err, it should be on the side of encouraging college attendance for those who might choose not to attend, and not on the side of discouraging those who would choose to attend. While the recruiting and skills development necessary for successful athletic programs are widely acknowledged, the aggressive academic advising, networking, and guidance functions are frequently perceived as peripheral to high school missions. Nothing could be further from the truth. College prerequisite courses, particularly science and math, must be begun early. Suburban, college preparatory institutions have always known this, and have devised rigorous precollege counseling programs that give the assistance necessary to coordinate application processes.

Schools not employing such procedures stand in stark contrast. Counselors frequently are assigned to their positions for precisely the wrong reasons, or for incompetence rather than the crucial competencies required for networking. The skills required include an ability to gather essential information, to match students with appropriate institutions, to assist students and their parents in negotiating the awesome application procedures, and to advocate aggressively for these students. Continuity and coordination are essential components of this office, and advising personnel should be given portfolio to accomplish the tasks. At the very least, schools should maintain centralized information files and encourage students to browse regularly through the information. Finally, parents must exert the pressure necessary to assure this function is being emphasized, including aggressive lobbying of appropriate officials for maintaining and expanding local, state, and federal programs designed to assist students in negotiating information.

16. *In performing their responsibilities, high schools should emphasize reading, test-taking, and study skills.*

Once pre-college obstacles have been negotiated and students are enrolled in appropriate schools, the academic needs of students become apparent. The emphasis upon negotiating skills and needs in earlier recommendations has been intended in no way to slight curricular or academic needs. These are basic to college enrollment and completion. The suggestions have been stressed, however, because the external, supportive elements are more easily manipulated and improved by policy recommendations than is the learning process itself.

One additional supportive service essential to college attendance is a well–developed developmental education program, one stressing fundamental reading, test taking, and study skills. While these appear obvious, many otherwise bright students enter college without having mastered these basic habits. All classes should emphasize reading, particularly self-directed reading; in-service workshops and continuing education should be made available to teachers for this purpose. Test taking and reducing test anxiety are other curricular activities that help make high school students more competitive in their applications to colleges. The cost of commercial testing practice courses may be prohibitive even for middle class students, while economies of scale could enable homerooms, study halls, or after class periods to incorporate such skill development. Finally, the non-structured nature of college enrollment frequently gives freshmen excessive free time for which they are not prepared. Basic study skills and time management training could be incorporated into high school pre-college curricula so that the students will not encounter such a counterproductive culture shock when faced with the need for independent study and self direction.

17. *AACJC should acknowledge its role in representing minority student interests, and should advocate for minority affairs.*

AACJC, the umbrella association representing the institutional sector enrolling most minority students, is predominantly white and male in its leadership. While it does have several special interest councils (Council on Black American Affairs, El Congreso Nacional de Asuntos Colegiales, Center for Women's Opportunities), these remain peripheral to the affairs of the association. The Office of Minority Programs has been dismantled without the concomitant mainstreaming of minority interests or the inclusion of minority professionals in decision–making positions. As a result, minority programming is an *ad hoc,* soft–money, occasional concern in an association that officially represents many minority interests in higher education. AACJC should bring minorities into its leadership, and should initiate programs at all levels to sensitize its membership to minority concerns.

18. *AACJC should regularly gather racial and ethnic data from its member institutions.*

The Association has gathered enrollment and program data and published them for a number of years, but has neither regularly gathered nor published racial and ethnic data since 1973. These data were not even collated from federally collected racial and ethnic enrollment data, although such data have been available for 1972, 1974, and 1976. As a result, the recognized advocate for large minority enrollments did not maintain systematic or comprehensive records of its minority membership.

Minority data were gathered for the 1978–79 year, as residual funds for a Native American foundation grant program were diverted to the data gathering project. While the return to gathering such data, already collected by member institutions, is noteworthy, permanent staff and regular funding, not soft money left from another minority program, should be allocated. This task should be part of an aggressive campaign to increase AACJC awareness of its role in minority education.

Listing these suggestions, one cannot help but be struck by how mundane and elementary any such recommendations must seem, even if all were to be implemented fully. It is clear that even well-intentioned institutions often fail to meet the needs of minority students, but it is essential that exerted efforts be undertaken to remedy, at least in part, historical exclusion. These data, discussions, and recommendations can serve to tap the reservoir of good will in the majority. Minorities represent people rich in traditions, cultures, and service. Higher education is poorer for its repeated failure to allow this resource its full development and expression.

Appendices

Appendix A

Structure of Statewide Coordinating/Governing (Central) Agencies

| State and Agency | Planning/Coordinating Statutory Responsibility | | | | |
	Public Senior	Public Junior	Public Voc/Tech	Private	Proprietary
Alabama Commission on Higher Education	X	X	X		
Alaska Board of Regents, University of Alaska	X	X	X		
Commission on Postsecondary Education	X	X	X	X	X
Arizona Board of Regents	X				
Arkansas Department of Higher Education	X	X		X	
California Postsecondary Education Commission	X	X	X	X	X
Colorado Commission on Higher Education	X	X	X	X	[a]
Connecticut Commission for Higher Education	X	X	X	X	X

Source: Berve, 1975, pp. 308–316.

[a] Subject to regulation by State Board for Community Colleges and Occupational Education, which is coordinated by the Commission.

	Planning/Coordinating Statutory Responsibility				
State and Agency	Public Senior	Public Junior	Public Voc/Tech	Private	Proprie-tary
Delaware Postsecondary Education Commission[b]					
Florida State Board of Education Board of Regents	X				
Division of Community Colleges		X			
Georgia Board of Regents, University System	X	X			
Hawaii Board of Regents, University of Hawaii	X	X	X		
Idaho State Board of Education	X	X	X		
Illinois Board of Higher Education	X	X		X	
Indiana Commission for Higher Education	X	X	X	X	
Iowa State Board of Regents	X				
Kansas State Board of Regents	X				
Kentucky Council on Public Higher Education	X	X			
Louisiana Board of Regents[c]	X	X	X		
Maine Board of Trustees, University of Maine	X	X			

[b] 1202 commission; authority is by executive order, not by statute.

[c] Board of Regents became effective January 1974, replacing the Coordinating Council for Higher Education.

State and Agency	Planning/Coordinating Statutory Responsibility				
	Public Senior	Public Junior	Public Voc/Tech	Private	Proprietary
Maryland Council for Higher Education	X	X	X	X	X
Massachusetts Board of Higher Education	X	X			
Michigan State Board of Education	X	X	X		X[d]
Minnesota Higher Education Coordinating Commission	X	X	X	X	X
Mississippi Board of Trustees, Institutions of Higher Education	X				
Missouri Department of Higher Education	X	X	X	X	
Montana Board of Regents of Higher Education	X	X			
Nebraska Coordinating Council for Postsecondary Education[e]					
Nevada	X	X	X		
New Hampshire Postsecondary Education Commission	X	X	X	X	
New Jersey Board of Higher Education	X	X	X	X	
New Mexico Board of Educational Finance	X	X	X	X	X

[d] Licensure authority.

[e] No statutory or constitutional agency; the 1202 commission designated by the governor for one year.

State and Agency	Planning/Coordinating Statutory Responsibility				
	Public Senior	Public Junior	Public Voc/Tech	Private	Proprietary
New York Board of Regents, State University of New York	X	X	X	X	X
North Carolina Board of Governors, University of NC	X	X	X	X	
North Dakota Board of Higher Education	X	X	X		
Ohio Board of Regents	X	X	X	X	
Oklahoma State Regents for Higher Education	X	X	X	X	
Oregon Educational Coordinating Council	X	X	X	X	X
Pennsylvania State Department of Education	X	X	X	X	X
Rhode Island Board of Regents for Education	X	X	X		
South Carolina Commission on Higher Education	X	X	X	X	
South Dakota Board of Regents	X	[ᶠ]			
Tennessee Higher Education Commission	X	X			
Texas Coordinating Board, College and University System	X	X	X	X	
Utah State Board of Regents	X	X	X	X	X

ᶠ No public junior colleges in the state.

State and Agency	*Planning/Coordinating Statutory Responsibility*				
	Public Senior	Public Junior	Public Voc/Tech	Private	Proprietary
Vermont Higher Education Planning Commission[g]					
Virginia State Council of Higher Education	X	X			
Washington Council on Higher Education	X	X		X	
West Virginia Board of Regents	X	X			
Wisconsin Board of Regents, University System	X	X[h]			
Wyoming Higher Education Council	X	X			
District of Columbia Commission on Postsecondary Education					

[g] 1202 commission.

[h] University centers.

Appendix B

Selected Statistics for the 60 College and University Campuses Enrolling the Largest Numbers of Students: United States Fall 1975

Institution	Rank Order[1]	Control[2]	Type[3]
University of Minnesota, Minneapolis-Saint Paul	1	1	U
University of California, Los Angeles	2	1	U
Ohio State University, Main Campus	3	1	U
Michigan State University	4	1	U
University of Texas at Austin	5	1	U
Pennsylvania State University, Main Campus	6	1	U
University of Wisconsin, Madison	7	1	U
Wayne State University (Michigan)	8	1	U
Miami-Dade Community College (Florida)	9	1	T
University of Michigan-Ann Arbor	10	1	U
Arizona State University	11	1	U
University of Illinois, Urbana Campus	12	1	U
University of Maryland, College Park Campus	13	1	U
University of Washington	14	1	U
Northeastern University (Massachusetts)	15	2	U
University of Houston, Main Campus (Texas)	16	1	U
Temple University (Pennsylvania)	17	1	U
University of Cincinnati, Main Campus (Ohio)	18	1	U
San Diego State University (California)	19	1	F
University of California, Berkeley	20	1	U
City University of New York, Brooklyn College	21	1	F
California State University, Long Beach	22	1	F
Indiana University at Bloomington	23	1	U
Long Beach City College (California)	24	1	T
San Jose State University (California)	25	1	F
Rutgers University, New Brunswick (New Jersey)	26	1	U
Orange Coast College (California)	27	1	T
University of Tennessee, Knoxville	28	1	U
University of Pittsburgh, Main Campus (Pena.)	29	1	U
New York University	30	2	U

Source: National Center for Education Statistics, Digest of Education Statistics, 1976 Edition (1977), Table 81.

[1] Institutions ranked by size of total enrollment.

[2] Publicly controlled institutions are indentified by a "1"; privately controlled by a "2".

Total Enroll-ment[4]	Enrollment by Gender		Enrollment by Attendance Status	
	Men	Women	Full-time	Part-time
66,887	36,717	30,170	39,276	27,611
60,127	31,836	28,291	31,887	28,240
50,146	29,356	20,790	43,972	6,174
48,488	25,726	22,762	37,217	11,271
45,429	26,249	19,180	37,882	7,547
40,102	22,719	17,383	29,639	10,463
38,603	22,138	16,465	32,718	5,885
38,073	22,388	15,685	25,856	12,217
37,669	19,478	18,191	19,521	18,148
37,505	22,017	15,488	31,286	6,219
36,976	20,822	16,154	21,577	15,399
36,845	22,459	14,386	31,678	5,167
35,995	19,526	16,469	26,882	9,113
35,972	20,609	15,363	28,122	7,850
35,970	22,904	13,066	16,080	19,890
35,419	21,191	14,228	19,722	15,697
34,950	19,681	15,269	18,182	16,768
34,885	20,996	13,889	20,522	14,363
34,835	18,564	16,271	19,695	15,140
34,809	21,372	13,437	28,020	6,789
34,497	15,690	18,807	19,999	14,498
34,427	18,290	16,137	16,954	17,473
32,651	18,266	14,385	27,509	5,142
32,241	16,520	15,721	6,876	25,365
31,783	16,163	15,620	15,397	16,386
30,993	16,545	14,448	20,542	10,451
30,842	15,566	15,276	7,286	23,556
29,999	17,179	12,820	22,888	7,111
29,729	16,762	12,967	17,316	12,413
29,698	15,890	13,808	13,625	16,073

[3] The types of institutions are identified as follows: "U", universities; "F", other 4-year institutions; "T", 2-year institutions.

[4] Includes resident and extension students whose programs of study are creditable toward a bachelor's or higher degree and also undergraduate students in 1-, 2-, or 3-year occupational programs which are not chiefly creditable toward a bachelor's degree.

Institution	Rank Order[1]	Con-trol[2]	Type[3]
El Camino College (California)	31	1	T
Purdue University, Main Campus (Indiana)	32	1	U
University of Arizona	33	1	U
University of Florida	34	1	U
California State University, Northridge	35	1	F
University of Southern California	36	2	U
City University of New York, Queens College	37	1	F
Brigham Young University, Main Campus (Utah)	38	2	U
Northern Virginia Community College	39	1	T
University of Missouri—Columbia	40	1	U
University of Virginia[5]	41	1	U
City College of San Francisco (California)	42	1	T
California State University, Los Angeles	43	1	F
University of Massachusetts, Amherst Campus	44	1	U
Louisiana State University, Baton Rouge	45	1	U
San Francisco State University (California)	46	1	F
Northern Illinois University	47	1	U
University of Wisconsin, Milwaukee	48	1	F
University of South Carolina, Main Campus	49	1	U
Texas A&M University, Main Campus	50	1	U
Boston University (Massachusetts)	51	2	U
Los Angeles Valley College (California)	52	1	T
State University of N.Y. at Buffalo, Main Campus	53	1	U
University of Oklahoma, Norman Campus	54	1	U
University of Utah	55	1	U
Charles S. Mott Community College (Michigan)	56	1	T
Los Angeles City College (California)	57	1	T
Los Angeles Pierce College (California)	58	1	T
City University of New York, Hunter College	59	1	F
Western Michigan University	60	1	F

[5] Data are for main campus and School of Continuing Education.

Total Enroll-ment[4]	Enrollment by Gender		Enrollment by Attendance Status	
	Men	Women	Full-time	Part-time
29,457	15,355	14,102	7,495	21,962
29,335	18,155	11,180	25,564	3,771
29,149	16,104	13,045	21,227	7,922
28,830	17,911	10,919	23,545	5,285
28,735	14,389	14,346	15,036	13,699
28,074	19,115	8,959	16,802	11,272
28,057	12,089	15,968	15,681	12,376
27,218	13,976	13,242	21,726	5,492
27,198	13,681	13,517	8,079	19,119
26,190	15,340	10,850	21,624	4,566
26,018	12,853	13,165	14,066	11,952
25,975	13,051	12,924	11,662	14,313
25,962	13,694	12,268	11,238	14,724
25,884	14,768	11,116	22,724	3,160
25,617	14,589	11,028	20,527	5,090
25,485	12,027	13,458	13,606	11,879
24,964	12,578	12,386	15,411	9,553
24,961	13,486	11,475	14,837	10,124
24,923	13,579	11,344	16,862	8,061
24,915	17,782	7,133	21,753	3,162
24,292	12,148	12,144	16,624	7,668
24,167	12,206	11,961	8,074	16,093
24,025	14,696	9,329	17,424	6,601
23,995	15,006	8,989	15,988	8,007
23,978	15,354	8,624	17,520	6,458
23,922	10,106	13,816	4,854	19,068
23,904	13,452	10,452	8,694	15,210
23,798	12,822	10,976	8,843	14,955
23,584	6,170	17,414	9,447	14,137
23,238	12,263	10,975	15,105	8,133

Appendix C

Sources of Direct Student Aid
Academic Years 1972–73 to 1974–75

Level of Institution and Source of Aid	Public			Private		
	1972–73	1973–74	1974–75	1972–73	1973–74	1974–75
All Levels						
GI bill	1,534.2	1,772.3	2,658.8	286.0	342.4	445.2
Social security benefits[a]	305.2	319.5	372.7	131.7	138.0	161.0
Basic educational opportunity grants	—	32.9	238.1	—	13.1	87.1
Guaranteed student loan subsidies	192.0	166.0	250.0	109.0	115.0	148.0
State aid	48.7	52.3	[b]	123.8	160.1	[b]
Total	2,080.1	2,343.0	[b]	650.5	768.6	[b]
4-Year Institutions						
GI bill	860.9	852.1	1,051.4	260.9	302.1	381.8
Social security benefits[a]	210.9	217.8	254.1	121.9	130.7	152.5
Basic educational opportunity grants	—	20.5	142.9	—	11.0	75.6
Guaranteed student loan subsidies	159.0	137.0	207.0	98.0	104.0	134.0
Total (excluding state)[c]	1,230.8	1,227.4	1,655.4	480.8	547.8	743.9
2-Year Institutions						
GI bill	673.3	920.2	1,607.4	25.1	40.3	63.4
Social security benefits[a]	94.3	101.7	118.6	9.5	7.3	8.5
Basic educational opportunity grants	—	12.0	93.6	—	1.7	11.2
Guaranteed student loan subsidies	33.0	29.0	43.0	12.0	12.0	16.0
Total (excluding state)[c]	800.6	1,062.9	1,862.6	46.6	61.3	99.1

Source: Nelson, 1978b, Table 2–3.

Note: The basic educational opportunity grants program did not disburse funds until 1973–74.

[a] Additions to total family benefits from eighteen to twenty-one-year-old children attending college.

[b] The Higher Education General Information Survey (HEGIS) financial surveys for 1974–75 do not give a figure for state student aid funds channeled through the institution.

[c] State data are not available by level of nstitution.

Appendix D

Minority Concentration in 2-Year Colleges (in Percentages)

Institution by State	American Indian	Black	Asian	Hispanic	White	Total Enrollment	Rural Urban Suburban
Alabama							
*Lawson State College	0.0	98.8	0.0	0.0	0.2	1,331	U
*Lomax-Hannon Junior College	0.0	99.2	0.0	0.0	0.8	126	R
*SD Bishop State Junior College	0.1	88.0	0.1	0.1	8.3	1,523	U
*Alabama Lutheran	0.0	94.9	0.0	0.0	0.7	137	U
Arizona							
Central Arizona College	7.5	2.8	0.1	16.7	72.9	5,330	U
Cochise College	0.9	4.2	1.7	18.3	73.3	3,676	R
College of Ganado	95.0	0.0	0.0	0.5	4.5	202	R
Eastern Arizona College	9.1	1.9	0.6	18.7	69.7	3,127	R
Maricopa Technical Community College	3.2	12.3	0.6	17.0	66.9	5,628	U
Phoenix College	2.0	3.9	0.9	9.5	83.1	13,617	U
Navajo Community College	90.2	0.1	0.1	0.0	9.6	917	R
Pima Community College	2.2	4.6	0.7	18.2	72.6	15,638	U
Arkansas							
*Shorter College	0.0	95.0	1.5	0.0	3.0	199	U

Source: OCR unpublished Racial/Ethnic Enrollment data, 1976. ISEP staff calculations.

* Historically black 2-year institutions.

Institution by State	American Indian	Black	Asian	Hispanic	White	Total Enrollment	Rural Urban Suburban
California							
Allan Hancock College	1.4	7.0	3.1	9.7	78.9	7,479	U
Bakersfield College	1.7	6.4	2.2	14.7	74.7	11,091	U
Cerritos College	1.3	3.8	1.9	15.5	70.4	12,462	U
Chabot College	1.1	5.9	5.0	7.4	80.3	18,293	U
Chaffey College	0.7	3.0	0.6	13.4	81.2	9,673	S
Citrus College	1.0	3.8	1.5	11.4	82.4	7,529	S
Coast Community College							
Golden West College	1.1	0.7	3.8	3.4	91.1	17,829	S
Orange Coast College	1.1	0.5	2.4	3.6	91.9	15,083	U
Coastline Community College	1.7	0.9	4.7	4.7	88.0	14,872	S
College of the Desert	0.8	3.2	1.2	12.7	81.8	4,797	R
College of the Sequoias	0.8	2.6	1.5	17.4	74.8	5,895	R
Compton Community College	0.2	85.9	1.3	3.8	5.8	6,016	U
Contra Costa Community College							
Diablo Valley College	0.6	2.2	1.6	2.9	92.3	18,991	S
Los Medanos College	1.2	9.5	1.6	10.2	77.3	5,046	S
D-QU	52.6	0.7	0.0	30.9	15.8	152	R
El Camino College	1.4	13.5	5.6	5.6	74.0	28,454	U
Foothill-Deanza Community College							
DeAnza College	14.9	3.8	5.1	5.7	70.1	16,313	S
Fullerton College	0.9	1.2	1.6	9.4	86.7	16,910	S
Glendale Community College	1.0	0.5	4.0	10.5	79.0	6,469	U
Hartnell College	2.4	4.1	9.4	20.1	64.0	5,777	U
Imperial Valley College	1.1	4.3	1.1	45.2	47.1	4,001	R
Long Beach City College	1.2	9.8	4.3	6.6	77.3	31,065	U
East Los Angeles College	1.1	6.2	8.8	60.8	19.1	17,613	U
L.A. City College	1.5	39.2	13.5	14.3	25.3	21,302	U
L.A. Harbor College	2.1	13.8	10.8	14.1	55.8	11,137	U
L.A. Mission College	2.1	13.2	1.8	32.3	48.4	2,721	S
L.A. Southwest College	0.3	91.8	0.8	0.4	1.0	5,609	U
L.A. Trade and Technical College	1.7	42.7	7.8	18.6	23.7	17,904	U

College							
L.A. Valley College	2.6	4.5	3.8	10.7	75.4	22,133	U
W. Los Angeles College	1.1	49.6	6.2	4.7	34.7	7,857	U
Los Rios Community College							
American River College	2.7	6.3	1.6	3.9	85.5	18,640	S
Sacramento City College	2.3	17.1	9.2	11.6	58.0	12,202	U
Merced College	1.3	11.7	1.2	14.5	70.0	6,163	R
Monterey Peninsula College	0.6	15.2	5.4	3.9	73.0	6,516	R
Mt. San Antonio College	0.9	8.9	1.8	20.1	68.2	16,285	S
Nairobi College	0.0	96.3	0.0	3.7	0.0	135	U
Pasadena City College	0.5	15.7	4.9	10.1	66.6	16,393	U
Peralta Community College							
College of Alameda	1.3	45.8	7.3	5.7	39.5	5,723	U
Laney College	1.1	53.0	5.9	5.5	32.7	9,049	U
Merritt College	1.1	39.9	6.5	4.8	47.0	6,511	U
Rio Hondo College	2.2	0.9	2.0	33.8	61.1	8,717	S
Riverside City College	1.5	9.5	4.3	7.9	71.4	11,716	U
San Bernardino Valley College	0.9	12.5	0.8	15.4	69.9	12,240	U
San Diego Community College							
City College	0.9	24.7	4.2	11.1	58.9	6,803	U
Evening College	0.6	15.7	4.3	7.9	71.4	11,717	U
City College of San Francisco	0.9	14.6	20.1	14.9	47.5	23,030	U
San Joaquin Delta College	1.7	7.7	6.5	12.8	70.8	12,797	U
San Jose City College	1.0	2.9	3.0	11.6	80.8	13,734	U
San Mateo Community College							
Skyline College	0.8	8.8	8.6	12.7	66.2	5,675	S
Santa Ana College	1.2	5.6	1.6	13.7	78.0	13,308	U
Santa Barbara City College	3.6	2.6	1.9	10.6	80.2	6,151	U
Santa Monica College	0.7	7.5	6.3	6.8	78.7	13,774	U
Southwestern College	0.8	4.7	6.7	18.6	65.4	10,722	S
State Central Community College							
Fresno City College	1.0	7.4	2.8	20.3	68.1	13,559	U
Oxnard College	1.4	10.1	5.7	20.4	62.3	4,170	S
Ventura County Community College							
Ventura College	1.0	3.5	3.5	15.7	76.2	10,383	U
West Valley College	2.5	1.2	4.1	2.4	89.3	17,641	S

Institution by State	American Indian	Black	Asian	Hispanic	White	Total Enrollment	Rural Urban Suburban
Colorado							
Aims Community College	0.5	0.5	0.6	14.8	83.5	3,398	S
Community College of Denver							
Auroria	2.2	22.1	0.6	16.7	51.3	3,547	U
North Campus	1.2	6.1	0.9	14.1	77.1	3,988	U
Delaware							
Delaware Technical & CC Wilmington	0.0	40.4	7.1	6.3	42.8	1,176	U
Florida							
Miami Dade Community College	0.6	18.5	0.5	26.2	50.6	35,368	S
Georgia							
Atlanta Junior College	0.0	92.9	0.3	0.2	5.0	1,192	U
DeKalb Community College	0.2	17.0	0.2	0.5	81.4	8,423	S
Hawaii							
Honolulu Community College	0.3	1.5	74.5	3.2	17.3	4,075	U
Kapiolani Community College	0.1	0.6	82.2	1.9	13.1	4,356	U
Kauai Community College	0.4	0.0	62.2	10.7	24.0	820	S
Leeward Community College	0.2	1.9	70.4	3.1	21.4	6,010	S
Maui Community College	0.2	0.0	59.6	10.1	26.4	1,333	S
Windward Community College	0.6	1.2	42.3	4.6	47.1	980	S
Illinois							
Central YMCA Community College	0.6	61.7	2.6	9.0	18.3	4,991	U
Kennedy-King	0.3	97.4	0.1	0.3	0.6	8,860	U
Loop College	0.6	58.6	1.8	7.0	31.5	9,246	U
Malcolm X College	0.3	83.6	0.8	4.3	11.0	4,618	U
Olive-Harvey	0.5	94.7	0.0	1.1	1.9	4,641	U
Truman College	1.5	16.4	0.0	13.6	49.8	3,676	U
Kansas							
Donnelly College	0.0	54.7	9.3	4.9	31.1	486	U
Haskell Indian Junior College	100.0	0.0	0.0	0.0	0.0	1,014	S

Institution							
Kentucky							
Alice Lloyd College	90.1	6.4	0.0	0.0	0.0	172	R
Louisiana							
Delgado College	0.2	37.2	1.1	2.0	56.1	9,326	U
*Southern University—Shreveport	0.0	99.9	0.0	0.0	0.1	974	U
Maryland							
Bay College of Maryland	0.0	95.1	0.0	0.0	1.7	1,011	U
Community College of Baltimore	0.1	79.7	0.3	0.2	18.3	9,049	U
Massachusetts							
Roxbury	0.2	67.7	0.0	20.5	0.4	561	U
Michigan							
Highland Park Community College	0.0	97.0	0.1	0.2	2.4	3,095	R
Lewis College of Business	0.0	98.2	0.4	0.0	1.3	225	R
Wayne County Community College	1.8	77.4	0.3	0.7	19.4	11,221	R
Mississippi							
*Coahoma Junior College	0.0	94.2	0.0	0.0	5.8	1,446	R
Ministerial Institute and College	0.0	99.0	0.0	0.0	1.0	297	R
*Prentiss Normal-Industrial Institute	0.0	98.6	0.0	0.0	1.4	139	R
*Utica Junior College	0.0	99.6	0.0	0.0	0.4	994	R
*Mary Holmes College	0.0	100.0	0.0	0.0	0.0	619	R
Missouri							
St. Louis Community College Forest Park	0.3	62.2	0.4	0.4	36.4	6,074	U
New Jersey							
Essex County College	0.3	67.7	0.7	12.9	18.5	6,862	U
Passaic County Community College	0.1	48.5	0.9	19.2	31.1	1,262	U
New Mexico							
New Mexico State University Grants Branch	14.4	0.6	0.0	43.7	41.4	174	R
University of New Mexico Gallup	60.7	1.2	0.7	10.7	26.6	402	R

Institution by State	American Indian	Black	Asian	Hispanic	White	Total Enrollment	Rural Urban Sub-urban
New York							
City University of New York							
Manhattan Community College	1.4	49.2	4.2	27.8	15.8	7,800	U
Bronx Community College	1.1	49.1	2.4	32.9	13.5	9,649	U
Hostos Community College	1.2	22.2	0.6	72.2	2.9	2,562	U
La Guardia Community College	4.7	35.4	1.7	22.3	35.8	3,512	U
New York City Community College	1.3	46.0	5.2	18.0	28.3	13,833	U
Collegiate Institute	0.0	61.1	2.2	14.6	11.1	266	U
Inst. of Design and Construction	0.0	32.4	7.2	9.9	47.7	111	U
Taylor Business Institute	0.0	67.9	2.0	15.9	10.5	535	U
North Carolina							
Durham Technical Institute	0.5	48.3	0.6	0.1	50.1	2,014	U
Edgecomb Technical Institute	0.0	46.4	0.0	0.0	53.6	793	R
Martin Community College	0.3	41.0	0.0	0.0	58.7	608	R
Pamlico Technical Institute	0.0	44.4	0.0	0.0	55.6	135	R
Piedmont Technical Institute	0.3	43.0	0.0	0.3	56.5	781	R
Roanoke-Chowan Technical Institute	0.0	59.0	0.0	0.0	41.0	615	R
Ohio							
Cuyahoga Community College							
Metro Campus	0.5	60.2	1.4	1.5	36.0	11,619	U
Eastern Campus	0.2	37.1	0.4	0.4	61.8	4,669	S
Oklahoma							
Bacone College	57.1	11.7	0.3	0.2	30.4	573	S
Pennsylvania							
Community College of Philadelphia	0.4	59.8	1.5	5.0	33.0	10,874	U

Institution							
South Carolina							
Beaufort Technical Education Center	0.1	55.0	0.0	0.5	44.2	848	R
*Friendship Junior College	0.5	80.7	0.0	0.5	4.2	192	U
Orangebury-Calhoun Technical College	0.1	46.4	0.0	0.1	53.3	1,369	R
Trident Technical College							
Palmer	0.1	66.8	0.1	0.0	33.1	1,706	U
North	0.1	46.3	0.1	0.1	53.4	3,075	S
*Clinton Junior College	0.0	100.0	0.0	0.0	0.0	208	R
Tennessee							
Shelby St. Community College	0.1	76.3	0.2	0.1	22.1	4,159	U
*Morristown College	0.0	98.3	0.6	1.1	0.0	173	S
Texas							
Dallas County Community College							
Elcentro	0.5	43.1	0.1	7.2	41.8	7,233	U
Delmar College	0.2	3.3	0.4	45.1	50.6	7,104	U
El Paso Community College	0.9	6.1	1.1	55.1	36.4	8,741	U
Bee County College	0.0	2.8	0.1	47.1	48.5	2,218	R
Houston Community College	1.5	39.0	2.3	8.3	47.5	6,083	U
Laredo Junior College	0.1	0.2	0.0	88.3	8.9	2,751	R
San Antonio College	0.5	5.9	1.1	39.4	49.9	17,466	U
SW Texas Junior College	0.0	0.4	0.0	63.2	35.4	2,035	R
Texas Southmost College	0.2	0.2	0.5	69.2	19.9	3,446	S
Texas State Technical							
Rio Grande	0.0	0.2	0.0	87.2	12.2	981	U
*Southwestern Christian College	0.0	93.0	0.0	0.0	3.2	341	S
Virginia							
J. S. Reynolds Community College	0.2	41.3	0.2	0.2	57.3	3,723	U
Paul D. Camp Community College	0.1	54.6	0.1	0.0	45.1	734	R
Southside Virginia Community College	0.0	44.0	0.1	0.1	55.7	847	R

Appendix E
Urban 2-Year Racial/Ethnic Enrollments
1976–77

Institution by State	American Indian	Black	Asian	Hispanic	Total Minority Enrollment
Arizona					
Central Arizona College	400	149	5	890	1,444
Maricopa Tech. Community College	180	692	34	957	1,863
Phoenix College	272	531	123	1,294	2,220
Pima Community College	344	719	109	2,846	4,018
California					
Allan Hancock College	105	524	232	725	1,586
Bakersfield College	189	710	244	1,630	2,773
Cerritos College	162	474	237	1,932	2,805
Chabot College	201	1,079	915	1,354	3,549
Orange Coast College	166	75	362	543	1,146
Compton Community College	12	5,168	78	229	5,487
El Camino College	398	3,841	1,593	1,593	7,425
Glendale Community College	65	32	259	679	1,035
Hartnell College	139	237	543	1,161	2,080
Long Beach City College	373	3,044	1,336	2,050	6,803
East L.A. College	194	1,092	1,550	10,709	13,545
L.A. City College	320	8,350	2,876	3,046	14,592
L.A. Harbor College	234	1,537	1,203	1,637	4,611
L.A. Southwest College	17	5,149	45	22	5,233
L.A. Trade and Tech. College	304	7,645	1,397	3,330	12,676
L.A. Valley College	575	996	841	2,368	4,780
West Los Angeles College	86	3,897	487	369	4,839
Sacramento City College	280	2,086	1,122	1,415	4,903
Nairobi College	0	130	0	5	135
Pasadena City College	82	2,574	803	1,656	5,115
College of Alameda	74	2,621	418	326	3,439
Laney College	100	4,796	533	498	5,927

Merritt College	72	2,598	423	313	3,406
Riverside City College	176	1,113	504	926	2,719
San Bernardino Valley College	110	1,530	98	1,885	3,623
San Diego Community College City	61	1,680	286	755	2,782
Evening	70	1,840	504	926	3,340
Community College of San Francisco	207	3,362	4,629	3,431	11,629
San Joaquin Delta College	218	985	832	1,638	3,673
San Jose City College	137	398	412	1,593	2,540
Santa Ana College	160	745	213	1,823	2,941
Santa Barbara City College	221	160	117	652	1,150
Santa Monica College	96	1,033	868	937	2,934
State Central Community College					
Fresno City College	136	1,006	380	2,752	4,274
Ventura College	104	363	363	1,630	2,460
Colorado					
Community College of Denver-Auraria	78	783	21	592	1,474
North Campus	48	243	36	562	889
Delaware					
Delaware Tech. and Community College, Wilmington	0	475	83	74	632
Florida					
*Miami Dade Community College	212	6,543	177	9,266	16,198
Georgia					
Atlanta Junior College	0	1,107	3	2	1,112
Hawaii					
Honolulu Community College	12	61	3,036	130	3,239
Kapiolani Community College	4	26	3,580	82	3,692
Illinois					
Central YMCA Community College	30	3,079	130	449	3,688
Kennedy-King College	27	8,630	9	27	8,693
Loop College	55	5,418	166	647	6,286
Malcolm X College	14	3,861	37	199	4,111
Olive Harvey College	23	4,395	0	51	4,469
Truman College	55	603	0	500	1,158

Institution by State	American Indian	Black	Asian	Hispanic	Total Minority Enrollment
Kansas					
Donelly College	0	266	45	24	335
Louisiana					
Delgado College	19	3,469	103	187	3,778
Maryland					
Bay College	0	961	0	17	978
Community College of Baltimore	9	7,212	27	18	7,266
Massachusetts					
Roxbury	1	380	0	115	496
Michigan					
Highland Park	0	3,002	3	6	3,011
Lewis College of Business	0	221	1	0	222
Wayne County Community College	202	8,685	34	79	9,000
Missouri					
St. Louis Community College					
Forest Park	18	3,778	24	24	3,844
New Jersey					
Essex County Community College	21	4,646	48	885	5,600
Passaic County Community College	1	612	11	242	866
New York					
Manhattan Community College	109	3,838	14	2,168	6,129
Bronx Community College	106	4,738	232	3,175	8,251
Hostos Community College	31	569	15	1,850	2,465
La Guardia Community College	165	1,243	60	783	2,251
New York City Community College	180	6,363	719	2,490	9,752
Collegiate Institute	0	163	6	39	208
Institute of Design and Construction	0	36	8	11	55
Taylor Business Institute	0	644	19	151	814

North Carolina					
Durham Technical Institute	10	973	12	2	997
Ohio					
Cuyahoga Community College, Metro Campus	58	6,995	163	174	7,390
Pennsylvania					
Community College of Philadelphia	43	6,503	163	544	7,253
South Carolina					
Trident Technical College-Palmer	2	1,140	2	0	1,144
Tennessee					
Shelby State Community College	4	3,173	8	4	3,189
Texas					
El Centro College	36	3,117	7	512	3,672
Delmar College	14	234	28	3,204	3,480
El Paso Community College	79	533	96	4,816	5,524
San Antonio College	87	1,030	192	6,882	8,191
Houston Community College	91	2,372	140	505	3,108
Texas State Tech., Rio-Grande	0	2	0	855	857
Virginia					
J. S. Reynolds Community College	7	1,538	7	7	1,559
Urban Total	8,891	188,621	36,439	104,875	338,826
Total 2-year	41,244	429,723	80,418	242,009	793,394
Percent of total 2-year	21%	43%††	45%	43%	42%

Source: (OCR, 1978) preliminary enrollment figures. AACJC location indicators, unpublished data. ISEP staff calculations.

* Miami Dade's central office is located in a suburb; however, its main campuses are urban. ISEP conversation with Miami-Dade Community College staff, July, 1978.

Appendix F

Noncollegiate Postsecondary Schools Offering Occupational Programs
1973 and 1975

Type of School	Total		Public		Private[1]	
	1973	1975[2]	1973	1975[2]	1973	1975[2]
Total	8,846	8,356	893	964	7,953	7,392
Vocational/technical	1,167	1,187	579	594	588	593
Technical institute	215	210	52	38	163	172
Business/commercial	1,242	1,140	1	1	1,241	1,139
Cosmetology/barber	2,405	2,328	4	21	2,401	2,307
Flight	1,483	1,309	6	44	1,477	1,265
Trade	708	723	30	30	678	693
Home study (correspondence)	130	106	1	0	129	106
Hospital	1,247	1,112	170	215	1,077	897
Other	249	241	50	21	199	220

Source: National Center for Education Statistics, *The Condition of Education, 1978 Edition,* Table 3.26.

[1] Includes proprietary (for profit) schools, and hospitals operated by religious groups.

[2] Data include Puerto Rico as well as the 50 States and D.C.

Appendix G
Composition of Financial Aid Packages Received by Entering Full-Time Freshmen*
1972–73

Item	Total	Total From Federal Aid	Federal Aid				Non-Federal Aid
			Grants	College Work-Study	Loan	Benefit	
All aided freshmen	$1,084	$565	$104	$ 76	$304	$ 81	$519
Family income quartile							
Low	1,267	777	198	128	333	118	490
Lower middle	1,083	556	94	77	326	59	527
Upper middle	1,052	516	51	60	341	64	536
High	945	401	82	37	221	61	544
Student ability group							
Low	962	586	109	97	286	94	376
Lower middle	1,099	584	92	70	346	66	525
Upper middle	1,150	558	99	61	316	82	592
High	1,288	507	112	50	287	58	781
Racial/ethnic group							
White	1,052	533	88	65	294	86	519
Black	1,379	874	224	184	411	55	505
Hispanic	1,108	736	222	91	341	82	372
Other	1,272	518	143	99	259	17	754
Institution control and type							
Public 4-year	956	522	118	70	264	70	434
Public 2-year	618	338	65	77	108	88	280
Private 4-year	1,723	785	150	105	459	71	938
Private 2-year	1,044	480	91	76	216	97	564

Source: "Student Financial Aid: Institutional Packaging and Family Expenditure Patterns," by Alan P. Wagner and Lois O. Rice, Table 5.17, NCES, The Condition of Education, 1978 Edition, Table 5.17.

Note: Details may not add to totals because of rounding.

* In the National Longitudinal Study of the High School Class of 1972.

Percentage Distribution

Item	Total	Total From Federal Aid	Federal Aid				Non-Federal Aid
			Grant	College Work-Study	Loan	Benefit	
All aided freshmen	100.0	52.1	9.6	7.0	28.0	7.5	47.9
Family income quartile							
Low	100.0	61.3	15.6	10.1	26.3	9.3	38.7
Lower middle	100.0	51.3	8.7	7.1	30.1	5.4	48.7
Upper middle	100.0	49.0	4.8	5.7	32.4	6.1	51.0
High	100.0	42.4	8.7	3.9	23.4	6.5	57.6
Student ability group							
Low	100.0	60.9	11.3	10.1	29.7	9.8	39.1
Lower middle	100.0	52.2	8.4	6.4	31.5	6.0	47.8
Upper middle	100.0	48.5	8.6	5.3	27.5	7.1	51.5
High	100.0	39.4	8.7	3.9	22.3	4.5	60.6
Racial/ethnic group							
White	100.0	50.7	8.4	6.2	27.9	8.2	49.3
Black	100.0	63.4	16.2	13.3	29.8	4.0	36.6
Hispanic	100.0	66.4	20.0	8.2	30.8	7.4	33.6
Other	100.0	40.7	11.2	7.8	20.4	1.3	59.3
Institution control and type							
Public 4-year	100.0	54.6	12.3	7.3	27.6	7.3	45.4
Public 2-year	100.0	54.7	10.5	12.5	17.5	14.2	45.3
Private 4-year	100.0	45.6	8.7	6.1	26.6	4.1	54.4
Private 2-year	100.0	46.0	8.7	7.3	20.7	9.3	54.0

Appendix H

Undergraduate College Enrollment of Persons 14 to 34 Years Old (in Thousands)
October 1976

Gender and Institution by Type	Total Enrolled	Number				
		14 to 19 Years Old	20 to 21 Years Old	22 to 24 Years Old	25 to 34 Years Old	
All colleges						
Total	8,270	3,216	2,358	1,223	1,472	
Male	4,301	1,496	1,189	725	893	
Female	3,969	1,721	1,170	499	579	
2-year colleges						
Total	2,435	907	444	367	718	
Male	1,272	430	224	204	415	
Female	1,163	478	220	163	303	
4-year colleges						
Total	5,550	2,151	1,873	822	704	
Male	2,882	998	942	497	446	
Female	2,668	1,153	932	325	258	
Type of college not reported						
Total	285	158	41	35	50	

Source: U.S. Department of Commerce, Bureau of the Census, Current Population Reports, *School Enrollment-Social and Economic Characteristics of Students: October, 1976*, Series P-20, No. 319, February 1978.

Percent Distribution

Gender and Institution by Type	Total Enrolled	14 to 19 Years Old	20 to 21 Years Old	22 to 24 Years Old	25 to 34 Years Old
All Colleges					
Total	100.0	38.9	28.5	14.8	17.8
Male	100.0	34.8	27.6	16.9	20.8
Female	100.0	43.4	29.5	12.6	14.6
2-year colleges					
Total	100.0	37.2	18.2	15.1	29.5
Male	100.0	33.8	17.6	16.0	32.6
Female	100.0	41.1	18.9	14.0	26.1
4-year colleges					
Total	100.0	38.8	33.7	14.8	12.7
Male	100.0	34.6	32.7	17.2	15.5
Female	100.0	43.2	34.9	12.2	9.7
Type of college not reported					
Total	100.0	55.4	14.4	12.3	17.5

Appendix I

Tuition and Fees Per Typical Full-Time Student in 2-Year
Institutions
1976–77

State	Public In-State Institutions	Public Out-State Tuition	Private
Alabama	$204	$ 204	$1,029
Alaska	340	940	2,250
Arizona	204	1,267	1,000
Arkansas	221	422	1,246
California	16	1,074	1,784
Colorado	284	1,228	
Connecticut	324	1,025	2,360
Delaware	504	1,080	2,050
Florida	340	733	1,868
Georgia	355	838	1,073
Hawaii	90	910	
Idaho	332	850	660
Illinois	346	1,708	1,672
Indiana	492	893	1,273
Iowa	468	729	1,445
Kansas	349	903	1,355
Kentucky	390	980	1,188
Louisiana	230	878	
Maine	350	700	1,500
Maryland	422	1,556	1,507
Massachusetts	390	894	2,168
Michigan	427	907	1,607
Minnesota	461	1,067	1,713
Mississippi	255	653	784
Missouri	290	973	1,565
Montana	307	682	
Nebraska	329	521	1,290
Nevada	336	1,536	
New Hampshire	461	1,095	1,836
New Jersey	476	1,776	1,677
New Mexico	474	959	
New York	713	1,320	1,941
North Carolina	114	503	1,497
North Dakota	474	777	920
Ohio	640	1,451	1,360
Oklahoma	313	801	1,136
Oregon	342	1,240	1,638
Pennsylvania	824	2,004	1,786
Rhode Island	400	400	
South Carolina	338	608	1,217

State	Public In-State Institutions	Out-State Tuition	Private
South Dakota			1,380
Tennessee	248	1,007	1,078
Texas	221	661	1,076
Utah	370	847	980
Vermont	475	1,255	2,180
Virginia	307	997	1,614
Washington			
West Virginia	297	1,197	1,375
Wisconsin	279	1,606	1,540
Wyoming	264	684	
District of Columbia			1,800

Source: State Higher Education Executive Officers, Education Commission of the States, National Center for Higher Education Management Systems, State Postsecondary Education Profiles Handbook, 1978 Edition. N/A = Not Available.

Appendix J

Participation of Community Colleges in Office of Education Programs
Fiscal Year 1977

Program	Total Number of Awards	Total Amounts	Number of Awards to Community Colleges	Amounts to Community Colleges
Adult education, Indo-Chinese program	65	$10,250,000	12	$ 1,920,940
Bilingual education, teacher training	101	9,300,000	10	893,292
Career education	136	10,135,000	2	212,438
Community education	92	3,500,000	1	33,500
Community service and continuing education, special projects	21	1,300,000	1	45,487
Consumer education	57	3,135,000	3	126,886
Cooperative education	276	12,250,000	150	5,711,386
Educational opportunity centers	18	4,000,000	3	513,100
Environmental education	89	3,500,000	1	18,639
Ethnic heritage studies	64	2,300,000	3	91,593
Fulbright-Hays training grants				
Faculty research abroad	47	605,516	0	0
Foreign curriculum consultants	16	232,875	1	15,577
Group projects abroad	44	2,427,842	1	54,000
Library				
Title II-A	2,591	9,923,414	1,131	4,322,204
Title II-B				
Fellowships	160	1,020,950	5	24,250
Institute projects and traineeships	25	977,650	2	62,500
Research and demonstration projects	18	944,485	1	70,500

Program	Total Number of Awards	Total Amounts	Number of Awards to Community Colleges	Amounts to Comunity Colleges
Metric education	75	2,090,000	2	62,871
Right to read, reading academies	79	4,800,000	17	1,113,787
Special services	372	30,634,715	93	7,218,462
Strengthening developing institutions				
Basic program	190	52,000,000	68	12,480,000
Advanced program	90	58,000,000	28	13,920,000
Talent Search	116	8,904,309	12	790,234
Title VI—equipment	824	7,500,000	228	2,029,174
Undergraduate international studies program	12	825,000	2	98,000
Upward Bound program	345	41,448,324	28	2,949,304
Veterans cost of instruction	1,125	23,750,000	759	16,251,293
Vocational education				
Innovation	65	8,000,000	4	554,294
Research	92	6,250,000	6	265,132
Women's Educational Equity Act grants	72	7,270,000	5	349,945

Source: U.S. Office of Education unpublished data; ISEP staff calculations.

Appendix K

Direct Federal Support to Indian Higher Education

Fiscal Year	Bureau of Indian Affairs Funds for Higher Education (in Thousands)
1952	$ 9
1953	9
1954	9
1955	20
1956	50
1957	64
1958	132
1959	149
1960	231
1961	243
1962	297
1963	574
1964	863
1965	1,242
1966	1,389
1967	1,913
1968	2,246
1969	2,949
1970	3,767
1971	6,050
1972	15,003
1973	18,456
1974	25,784
1975	32,046
1976	32,855

Postsecondary Schools	Per Pupil Cost, 1976			
	Average Daily Membership	School Operations	School Operations and Facilities Management	Total Costs
Haskell Indian Junior College	994.1	$4,052	$ 5,143	$ 5,143
Institute of American Indian Arts	159.2	9,876	10,077	10,272
Southwest Indian Polytechnic Institute	350.6	6,863	9,044	9,044

Source: Report on Indian Education, Final Report to the American Indian Policy Review Commission, 1976, Table 6 and Appendix M.

Appendix L

Treaties Dealing With Indian Education

Treaty of August 18, 1804, with Delaware Tribe, 7 Stat. 81; treaty of August 29, 1821, with Ottawa, Chippewa, and Pottawatamie, 7 Stat. 218; treaty of February 12, 1825, with Creek Nation, 7 Stat. 237; treaty of February 8, 1831, with the Menominee Indians, 7 Stat. 342; treaty of September 21, 1833, with the Otoes and Missourias, 7 Stat. 429; treaty of March 2, 1836, with the Ottawa and Chippewa, 7 Stat. 491; treaty of September 17, 1836, with the Sacs and Foxes, etc., 7 Stat. 511; treaty of October 15, 1836, with the Otoes, etc., 7 Stat. 524; treaty of January 4, 1845, with the Creeks and Seminoles, 9 Stat. 821, 822; treaty of October 13, 1846, with the Winnebago Indians, 9 Stat. 878; treaty of August 2, 1847, with the Chippewas, 9 Stat. 904; treaty of October 18, 1848, with the Menominee Tribe, 9 Stat. 952; treaty of July 23, 1851, with the Sioux, 10 Stat. 949; treaty of August 5, 1851, with the Sioux Indians, 10 Stat. 954; treaty of May 12, 1854; with the Menominee, 10 Stat. 1064; treaty of December 26, 1854, with the Nisqually, etc., Indians, 10 Stat. 1132; treaty of October 17, 1855, with the Blackfoot Indians, 11 Stat. 657; treaty of September 24, 1857, with the Pawnees, 11 Stat. 729; treaty of January 22, 1855, with The Dwamish, etc., 12 Stat. 927; treaty of January 26, 1855, with the S'Klallams, 12 Stat. 933; treaty of January 31, 1855; with Makah Tribe, 12 Stat. 939; treaty of July 1, 1855, with the Qui-nai-elt, etc., Indians, 12 Stat. 971; treaty of July 16, 1855, with the Flathead, etc., Indians, 12 Stat. 975; treaty of December 21, 1855, with the Molels, 12 Stat. 981; treaty of October 18, 1864, with the Chippewa Indians, 14 Stat. 657; treaty of June 14, 1866, with the Creek Nation, 14 Stat. 785; treaty of February 18, 1867, with the Sac and Fox Indians, 15 Stat. 495; treaty of February 19, 1867, with the Sissiton, etc., Sioux, 15 Stat. 505.

Treaty of May 6, 1828, with the Cherokee Nation, 7 Stat. 311; treaty of New Echota, December 29, 1835, with the Cherokee, 7 Stat. 478 (provides for common schools and "* a literacy institution of a higher order***"); treaty of June 5 and 17, 1846, with the Pottowautomie Nation, 9 Stat. 853; treaty of September 30, 1854, with the Chippewa Indians, 10 Stat. 1109; treaty of November 18, 1854, with the Chastas, etc., Indians, 10 Stat. 1122; treaty of April 19, 1858, with the Yancton Sioux, 11 Stat. 743; treaty of June 9, 1885, with the Walla-Wallas, etc., tribes, 12 Stat. 945; treaty of June 11, 1855, with the Nez Perces, 12 Stat. 957; treaty of March 12, 1858, with the Poncas, 12 Stat. 997; treaty of October 14, 1865, with the Lower Brule Sioux, 14 Stat. 699; treaty of February 23, 1867, with the Senecas, etc., 15 Stat. 513; treaty of October 21, 1867, with the Kiowa and Comanche Indians, 15 Stat. 581; treaty of October 21, 1867, with the Kiowa, Comanche, and Apache Indians, 15 Stat. 589; treaty of October 28, 1867, with the Cheyenne and Arapahoe Indians, 15 Stat. 593; treaty of March 2, 1868, with the Ute Indians, 15 Stat. 619; treaty of April 29 et seq., 1868, with the Sioux Nation, 15 Stat. 635; treaty of May 7, 1868, with the Crow Indians, 15 Stat. 649; treaty of May 10, 1868, with the Northern Cheyenne and Northern Arapahoe Indians, 15 Stat. 655; treaty of June 1, 1868, with the Navajo Tribe, 15 Stat. 667; treaty of July 3, 1868 with the Eastern Band Shoshones and Bannock Tribe of Indians, 15 Stat. 673.

Treaty of November 15, 1827, with the Creek Nation, 7 Stat. 307; treaty of September 15, 1832, with the Winnebago Nation, 7 Stat. 370; treaty of May 24, 1834, with the Chickasaw Indians, 7 Stat. 450; treaty of June 9, 1863, with the Nez Perce Tribe, 14 Stat. 647; treaty of March 19, 1867, with the Chippewa of Mississippi, 16 Stat. 719.

Treaty of October 18, 1820, with the Choctaw Nation, 7 Stat. 210; treaty of June 3, 1825, with the Kansas Nation, 7 Stat. 244; treaty of August 5, 1826, with the Chippewa Tribe, 7 Stat. 290; treaty of October 21, 1837, with the Sac and Fox Indians, 7 Stat. 543; treaty of March 17, 1842, with the Wyandott Nation, 11 Stat. 581; treaty of May 15, 1846, with Comanche, etc., Indians, 9 Stat. 844; treaty of June 5, 1854, with the Miami Indians, 10 Stat. 1093; treaty of November 15, 1854, with the Rogue Rivers, 10 Stat. 1119; treaty of November 29, 1854, with the Umpqua, etc., Indians, 10 Stat. 1125; treaty of July 31, 1855, with the Ottowas and Chippewas, 11 Stat. 621; treaty of February 5, 1856, with the Stockbridge and Munsee Tribes, 11 Stat. 663; treaty of June 9, 1855, with the Yakima Indians, 12 Stat. 951; treaty of June 25, 1855, with the Oregon Indians, 12 Stat. 963; treaty of June 19, 1858, with the Sioux bands, 2 Stat. 1031; treaty of July 16, 1859, with the Chippewa bands, 12 Stat. 1105; treaty of February 18, 1861, with the Arapahoes and Cheyenne Indians, 12 Stat. 1163; treaty of March 6, 1861, with the Sacs, Foxes and Iowas, 12 Stat. 1171; treaty of June 24, 1862, with the Ottawa Indians, 12 Stat. 1237; treaty of May 7, 1864, with the Chippewas, 13 Stat. 693; treaty of August 12, 1865, with the Snake Indians, 14 Stat. 683; treaty of March 21, 1866, with the Seminole Indians, 14 Stat. 755; treaty of April 28, 1866, with the Choctaw and Chickasaw Nation, 14 Stat. 769; treaty of August 13, 1868, with the Nez Perce Tribe, 15 Stat. 693.

Treaty of October 16, 1826, with the Potawatomie Tribe, 7 Stat. 295; treaty of September 20, 1828, Potawatamie Indians, 7 Stat. 317; treaty of July 15, 1830, with the Sacs and Foxes, etc., 7 Stat. 328; treaty of September 27, 1830, with the Choctaw Nation, 7 Stat. 333; treaty of March 24, 1832, with the Creek Tribe, 7 Stat. 366; treaty of February 14, 1833, with the Creek Nation, 7 Stat. 417; treaty of January 14, 1846, with the Kansas Indians, 9 Stat. 842; treaty of April 1, 1850, with the Wyandot Tribe, 9 Stat. 987; treaty of March 15, 1854, with the Delaware Tribe, 10 Stat. 1048; treaty of May 10, 1854, with the Shawnees, 10 Stat. 1053; treaty of May 17, 1854, with the Ioway Tribe, 10 Stat. 1069; treaty of May 30, 1854, with the Kaskaskia, etc., Indians, 10 Stat. 1083; treaty of January 22, 1855, with the Williamette Bands, 10 Stat. 1143; treaty of February 22, 1855, with the Chippewa Indians of Mississippi, 10 Stat. 1165; treaty of June 22, 1855, with the Choctaw and Chickasaw Indians, 11 Stat. 611; treaty of August 2, 1855, with the Chippewa Indians of Saginaw, 11 Stat. 633; treaty of August 7, 1856, with the Creeks and Seminoles, 11 Stat. 699; treaty of June 28, 1862, with the Kickapoo Tribe, 13 Stat. 623; treaty of October 2, 1863, with the Chippewa Indians (Red Lake and Pembina Bands), 13 Stat. 667; treaty of September 29, 1865, with the Osage Indians, 14 Stat. 687.

Source: Thompson, ed., 1978, Appendix IV.

Appendix M

TABLE M-1

Administrative Positions of Chicano Administrators in Five Southwestern States 1974–75

Type and Control of Institution, by State	President	Assistant to President	Vice President	Assistant to Vice President	Dean
Arizona					
4-year					
Public	0	0	0	0	0
Private	0	0	0	0	0
2-Year					
Public	0	1	0	0	3
Private	0	0	0	0	0
Total	0	1	0	0	3
California					
4-Year					
Public	0	4	2	2	8
Private	1	2	1	0	4
2-Year					
Public	3	2	3	0	10
Private	1	0	0	0	2
Total	5	8	6	2	24
Colorado					
4-Year					
Public	0	0	0	0	0
Private	1	0	0	0	0
2-year					
Public	0	0	1	0	2
Private	0	0	0	0	0
Total	1	0	1	0	2
New Mexico					
4-year					
Public	1	0	3	0	3
Private	0	0	2	0	1
2-year					
Public	1	0	0	0	0
Private	0	0	0	0	0
Total	2	0	5	0	4

		Administrative Position				
Associate Dean	*Assistant Dean*	*Department Chairperson*	*Registrar*	*Financial Aids Director*	*Other*	*Total*
0	1	2	0	0	0	3
0	0	1	0	0	0	1
2	0	2	1	0	0	9
0	0	0	0	0	0	0
2	1	5	1	0	0	13
11	5	37	1	3	24	97
1	0	8	2	0	9	28
3	2	7	3	4	8	45
0	0	0	3	1	3	10
15	7	52	9	8	44	180
0	3	9	1	3	0	16
0	1	2	0	0	2	6
1	0	2	0	1	1	8
0	0	0	0	0	0	0
1	4	13	1	4	3	30
1	6	14	2	0	2	32
0	0	1	0	1	0	5
0	0	2	0	0	0	3
0	0	0	0	0	0	0
1	6	17	2	1	2	40

| Type and Control of Institution, by State | Administrative Position | | | | |
	President	Assistant to President	Vice President	Assistant to Vice President	Dean
Texas					
4-Year					
Public	0	2	3	0	8
Private	0	0	0	0	1
2-year					
Public	4	0	0	0	10
Private	0	0	0	0	0
Total	4	2	3	0	19
Southwest total					
4-year					
Public	1	6	8	2	19
Private	2	2	3	0	6
2-Year					
Public	8	3	4	0	25
Private	1	0	0	0	2
Total	12	11	15	2	52

Source: Esquibel, 1976, Table 1.

Administrative Position

Associate Dean	Assistant Dean	Department Chairperson	Registrar	Financial Aids Director	Other	Total
1	2	10	2	2	4	34
0	0	3	0	2	1	7
0	0	2	0	3	2	21
0	0	0	0	0	1	1
1	2	15	2	7	8	63
13	17	72	6	8	30	182
1	1	15	2	3	12	47
6	2	16	4	8	11	87
0	0	0	3	1	4	11
20	20	103	15	20	57	327

TABLE M-2

Chicano Deans, Associate Deans, Assistant Deans
1974–75

School/Division	4-Year		2-Year		Total
	Public	Private	Public	Private	
Deans					
Academic	3	0	0	2	5
Liberal arts	0	0	1	0	1
Education	2	0	0	0	2
Graduate school	2	1	0	0	3
Professional studies	1	0	0	0	1
Arts and sciences	1	0	0	0	1
Fine and applied arts	1	0	0	0	1
Instruction	0	0	3	2	5
Health and related professions	1	0	0	0	1
Continuing education	2	0	2	0	4
Evening division	0	0	1	0	1
Applied sciences	0	0	1	0	1
Business administration	0	0	1	0	1
Social economic studies	0	0	1	0	1
Resident dean	1	0	0	0	1
Area and interdiscipline programs	1	0	0	0	1
Community relations	2	0	0	0	2
Social work	1	0	0	0	1
Graduate summer extension program	0	1	0	0	1
Adult education	0	0	1	0	1
Counseling	0	0	1	0	1
Students	1	3	1	1	6
Student services	1	0	1	0	2
Student personnel	0	0	0	1	1
Student affairs	0	0	2	0	2
Women	1	0	0	0	1
Men	1	1	0	0	2
Total	22	6	16	6	50
Associate Deans					
Graduate	2	0	0	0	2
School of letters and science	1	0	0	0	1
School of education	2	0	0	0	2
Academic administration	1	0	0	0	1
Student affairs	1	0	0	0	1
Student services	1	0	1	0	2
Students	3	1	0	0	4
School of social welfare	0	1	0	0	1
Multidiscipline studies	1	0	0	0	1

School/Division	4-Year		2-Year		
	Public	Private	Public	Private	Total
Instruction	0	0	1	0	1
Continuing education	0	0	2	0	2
Men	0	0	2	0	2
Total	12	2	6	0	20
	Assistant Deans				
Students	5	0	0	0	5
Student affairs	5	0	0	0	5
Student services	1	0	0	0	1
Student activities	0	0	1	0	1
Records	1	0	0	0	1
Financial aids	0	0	1	0	1
Arts and sciences	1	0	0	0	1
Medical school	1	0	0	0	1
Education	1	0	0	0	1
Assistant dean	2	0	0	0	2
Center for experimental studies	1	0	0	0	1
Total	18	0	2	0	20

Source: Esquibel, 1976, Tables 4, 5.

TABLE M-3

Chicano Department Chairpersons
1974–75

Discipline	4-Year		2-Year		Total
	Public	Private	Public	Private	
Chicano studies	14	4	5	0	23
Mexican American studies	12	2	1	0	15
Ethnic studies	4	2	0	0	6
La Raza studies	2	0	0	0	2
Foreign language	6	1	2	0	9
Modern foreign language	2	0	0	0	2
Modern and Classical language	1	0	0	0	1
Spanish	3	0	1	0	4
Hispanic civilization	1	0	0	0	1
Bilingual education	3	0	0	0	3
Cultural awareness	1	0	0	0	1
International studies	1	0	0	0	1
Chemical engineering	1	0	0	0	1
Civil engineering	1	0	0	0	1
Chemistry	2	0	0	0	2
Bacteriology	1	0	0	0	1
Psychobiology	1	0	0	0	1
Plant Science	1	0	0	0	1
Sociology	1	0	0	0	1
Social science	1	0	0	0	1
Behavioral science	1	0	0	0	1
Education	1	1	0	0	2
Physical education	1	0	0	0	1
Cooperative education	1	0	0	0	1
Testing and guidance	2	1	0	0	3
Home economics	0	0	1	0	1
Learning Materials center	0	0	1	0	1
Allied health care services	0	1	0	0	1
Health sciences	1	0	0	0	1
Nursing services	0	1	0	0	1
Nursing	0	0	1	0	1
Medicine	1	0	0	0	1
Humanities	0	0	1	0	1
Art	2	0	0	0	2
Business	1	0	0	0	1
Personnel services	1	0	0	0	1
Special programs	1	0	0	0	1
Political sciences	1	0	0	0	1
Public administration	0	1	0	0	1
Nautical department	1	0	0	0	1
History	0	1	0	0	1
Total	74	15	13	0	102

Source: Esquibel, 1976, Table 6.

Bibliography

Abramomitz, Elizabeth, ed. *Proceedings From the National Institutional Conference on Racial and Ethnic Data.* Washington, D.C.: Institute for the Study of Educational Policy, 1976.

Abramson, Leslie, and Moss, George. "Law School Deans: A Self-Portrait." *Journal of Legal Education* 29 (1977): 6–30.

Advisory Council on Developing Institutions. *Strengthening Developing Institutions: Title III of the Higher Education Act of 1965.* Washington, D.C.: U.S. Office of Education, March 1977.

Alfred, Richard. *Impacts of the Community and Junior College on Students.* Los Angeles: ERIC Clearinghouse for Junior Colleges, 1975.

American Anthropological Association. *The Minority Experiences in Anthropology: Report of the Committee on Minorities and Anthropology.* Washington, D.C.: American Anthropological Association, 1973.

American Association of Community and Junior Colleges. *1976 Community, Junior and Technical College Directory.* Washington, D.C.: American Association of Community and Junior Colleges, 1976.

American Association of Community and Junior Colleges. "Faculty in Two-Year Colleges." *AACJC Fact Sheet,* 1977.

American Indian Higher Education Consortium. [Published membership information]. Denver, Colorado, 1978.

Arce, Carlos H. "Historical, Institutional, and Contextual Determinants of Black Enrollment in Predominantly White Colleges and Universities, 1946–1974." Ph. D. dissertation, the University of Michigan, 1976.

Arce, Carlos H. "Minorities in Higher Education: Recent Advances and Current Problems." in Cynthia J. Smith, ed. *Advancing Equality of Opportunity: A Matter of Justice.* Washington, D.C.: Institute for the Study of Educational Policy, 1978, pp. 165–175.

Association of Governing Boards. "Results of AGB's Third Annual Poll of Board Chairman." *AGB Fact Sheet,* 1975.

Association of Governing Boards. "News Notes." *Association of Governing Boards* 9, No. 4 (April 1978): p. 2.

Astin, Alexander. "Determining Racial Enrollments in Post-secondary Education." in E. Abramomitz, ed. *Proceedings From the National Invitational Conference on Racial and Ethnic Data.* Washington, D.C.: Institute for the Study of Educational Policy, 1976, pp. 16–41.

Astin, Alexander. "The Myth of Equal Access in Public Higher Education." Paper presented at Southern Education Foundation, Atlanta, July, 1975a.

Astin, Alexander. *Preventing Students from Dropping Out.* San Francisco: Jossey-Bass, Inc., 1975b.

Astin, Alexander; King, Margot; and Richardson, Gerald. *The American Freshman: National Norms for Fall 1976.* Los .Angeles: University of Calfornia at Los Angeles, 1976.

Astin, Alexander. *Four Critical Years.* San Francisco: Jossey-Bass, Inc., 1977a.

Astin, Alexander. "Academic Administration: The Hard Core of Sexism in Academe." *UCLA Educator* 19 (Spring 1977b): pp. 60–66.

Astin, Alexander. "Equality of Access for Chicanos in Higher Education." in M. Perez, ed. *Institute on Chicanos in Higher Education.* Pasadena, California: National Association for Equal Educational Opportunities, 1977.

Astin, H.; Astin, A.; Bisconti, A.; and Frankel, H. *Higher Education and the Disadvantaged Student.* Washington, D.C.: Human Science Press, 1972.

Astin, H. S., and Bayer, A. E. "Sex Discrimination in Academe." *Educational Record* (Spring 1972): pp. 101–118.

Atelsek, Frank, and Gomberg, Irene. *Faculty Research: Level of Activity and Choice of Area.* Higher Education Panel Reports, Number 29. Washington, D.C.: American Council on Education, January 1976.

Atelsek, Frank, and Gomberg, Irene. *New Full-Time Faculty 1976–77: Hiring Patterns by Field and Educational Attainment.* Higher Education Panel Reports, Number 38. Washington, D.C.: American Council on Education, March 1978.

Baker, Curtis, and Wells, Agnes. *Associate Degrees and Other Formal Awards Below the Baccalaureate, 1974–75 Summary Data.* Washington, D.C.: National Center for Education Statistics, 1977.

Baldridge, J. Victor, ed. *Academic Governance.* Berkeley: McCutchan Publishing Corporation, 1971.

Baldridge, J. Victor; Curtis, David V.; Ecker, George P.; and Riley, Gary L. "The Impact of Institutional Size and Complexity on Faculty Autonomy." *Journal of Higher Education* 44, (October 1973): pp. 532–547.

Baldridge, Victor; Curtis, David; Ecker, George; and Riley, Gary. "Diversity in Higher Education." *Journal of Higher Education* 48 (July/August 1977): pp. 367–388.

Baldridge, J.; Curtis, D.; Ecker, G.; and Riley, G. *Policy Making and Effective Leadership.* San Francisco: Jossey–Bass, Inc., 1978.

Barron, Jose (Pepe). "Chicanos in the Community College." *AAJC Journal* 42, No. 9 (1972): pp. 23–26.

Barry, Toni, ed. *The Presidents.* Washington, D.C.: American Association of Community and Junior Colleges, 1978.

Baumgart, Neil, and Johnstone, James. "Attrition at an Australian University." *Journal of Higher Education* 58 (September/October 1977): pp. 553–570.

Bayer, Alan. "College and University Faculty: A Statistical Description." *ACE Research Reports* 5, No. 5 (June 1970).

Bayer, Alan. "Teaching Faculty in Academe: 1972–73." *ACE Research Reports* 8, No. 2 (August 1973).

Bayer, Alan E. "College Faculties: Le Plus Ça Change. . . ." *Change* 6, No. 2 (March 1974): pp. 48–49; p. 63.

Begin, James P.; Settle, Theodore C.; and Weiss, Laurie. *Community College Collective Bargaining in New Jersey: Study Report and Recommendations.* New Brunswick, New Jersey: Institute of Management and Labor Relations, Rutgers University, 1977.

Berdahl, Robert. *Statewide Coordination of Higher Education.* Washington, D.C.: The American Council on Education, 1971.

Bernard, J. *Academic Women.* University Park: The Pennsylvania State University Press, 1964.

Berve, Nancy. "Survey of the Structure of State Coordinating or Governing Boards and Public Institutional and Multi-campus Governing Boards of Postsecondary Education As of January 1, 1975." *Higher Education in the States* 4, No. 10 (1975): pp. 297–352.

Betances, Samuel. "Puerto Ricans and Mexican Americans in Higher Education." *The Rican* 1, No. 4 (May 1974): pp. 27–36.

Bishop, John. "The Effect of Public Policies on the Demand for Higher Education." *Journal of Human Resources* 12, No. 13 (Summer 1977): pp. 286–307.

Bishop, John, and Van Dyk, Jane. "Can Adults Be Hooked on College?

Some Determinants of Adult College Attendance." *Journal of Higher Education* 1 (January/February 1977): pp. 39–59.

Blackburn, R.; Armstrong, E.; Conrad, C.; Didham, J.; and McKune, T. *Changing Practices in Undergraduate Education.* Berkeley, California: Carnegie Council on Policy Studies In Higher Education, 1976.

Blackwell, James, and Jamowitz, Morris, eds. *Black Sociologists, Historical and Contemporary Perspectives.* Chicago, Ill.: The University of Chicago Press, 1974.

Blake, Elias, Jr.; Lambert, Linda; and Martin, Joseph L. *Degrees Granted and Enrollment Trends in Historically Black Colleges: An Eight-Year Study.* Washington, D.C.: Institute for Services to Education, October 1974.

Blank, Rolf. "Faculty Support for Evaluation of Teaching, A Test of Two Hypotheses." *Journal of Higher Education* 49 (March/April 1978): pp. 163–176.

Boaz, Ruth. *Participation in Adult Education Final Report 1975.* Washington, D.C.: National Center for Education Statistics, 1978.

Boxley, Russell, and Wagner, Nathanial N. "Clinical Psychology Training Programs and Minority Groups: A Survey." *Professional Psychology* 2 (Winter 1971): pp. 75–81.

Brawer, Florence B. *The Person: A Conceptual Synthesis.* Los Angeles, California: ERIC Clearinghouse for Junior Colleges, March 1970, ED037219.

Brawer, Florence. *Values and the Generation Gap: Junior College Freshmen and Faculty.* Washington, D.C.: ERIC Clearinghouse for Junior Colleges, 1971.

Brawer, Florence B. *A Comparison of the Personality Characteristics of Community College Student Dropouts and Persisters.* Los Angeles: ERIC Clearinghouse for Junior Colleges, 1973.

Breneman, David, and Finn, Chester, eds. *Public Policy and Private Higher Education.* Washington, D.C.: Brookings Institution, 1978.

Brimm, Jack, and Achilles, C. M. "The Reverse Transfer Student: A Growing Factor in Higher Education." *Research in Higher Education* 4, No. 4 (1976): pp. 355–360.

Brooks, Gary D., and Avila, Jose F. "A Descriptive Profile of Junior College Presidents." *Research in Higher Education* 2, No. 2 (1974): pp. 145–150.

Brossman, Sidney. "EOPS Means Opportunity in California." *Community and Junior College Journal* 45, No. 4 (December 1974): pp. 13–15.

Brown, D. G. *The Mobile Professors.* Washington, D.C.: The American Council on Education, 1967.

Brown, George. *Doctoral Degree Awards to Women.* Washington, D.C.: National Center for Education Statistics, 1978.

Brown, James. "Backgrounds and Characteristics of New Full-Time Community College Faculty Members." Los Angeles: ERIC Clearinghouse on Junior Colleges, 1975. ED 112 991.

Bureau of Consumer Protection. *Proprietary Vocational and Home Study Schools, Final Report to the Federal Trade Commission and Proposed Trade Regulation Rule (16CFR Part 438).* Washington, D.C., 1976.

Bushnell, David. *Organizing for Change: New Priorities for Community Colleges.* New York: McGraw-Hill, 1973.

Campbell, Roald, and Newell, L. Jackson. *A Study of Professors of Educational Administration.* Columbus, Ohio: University Council for Educational Administration, 1973.

Caplow, Theodore, and McGee, Reece. *The Academic Marketplace.* Garden City, New York: Doubleday, 1958.

Carnegie Council on Policy Studies in Higher Education. *Making Affirmative Action Work in Higher Education.* San Francisco: Jossey-Bass Publishers, 1975.

Carnegie Commission on Higher Education. *The Open-Door Colleges.* New York: McGraw-Hill Book Company, 1970.

"Carter Signs Labor—HEW Continuing Resolution." *Higher Education Daily* 5, No. 218 (November 11, 1977): p. 1.

Cartter, Allan M. *Ph.D.'s and the Academic Labor Market.* New York: McGraw-Hill Book Company, 1976.

Cartter, Allan M., and Salter, Maurice. "Two-year College Faculty and Enrollment Projections." in Martorana, S. V.; Toombs, W.; and Breneman, D. eds. *Graduate Education and Community Colleges: Cooperative Approaches to Community College Staff Development,* NBGE Technical Report Number Five, Washington, D.C., August 1975, pp. 31–40.

Casso, Henry, and Roman, Gilbert D. eds. *Chicanos in Higher Education.* Albuquerque: The University of New Mexico Press, 1976.

Castro, Barry. "Hostos: Report from a Ghetto College." *Harvard Educational Review* 44, No. 2 (May 1974): pp. 270–294.

Centra, John A. "Types of Faculty Development Programs." *Journal of Higher Education* 49 (March/April 1978): pp. 151–162.

Chavers, Dean. "American Indian Colleges." Unpublished paper. Muskogee, Oklahoma: Bacone College, 1979.

Chickering, Arthur. *Commuting Versus Resident Students.* San Francisco: Jossey-Bass Publishers, 1974.

Christoffel, Pamela, and Rice, Lois. *Federal Policy Issues and Data Needs in Postsecondary Education.* Washington, D.C.: HEW, National Center for Education Statistics, 1975.

Clark, B. R. "The Role of Faculty in College Administration." in L. Wilson and others, eds. *Studies of College Faculty.* Boulder, Colorado: Western Interstate Commission for Higher Education, 1961.

Clark, Burton R. "Faculty Organizations and Authority." in *The Study of Academic Administration.* Boulder, Colorado: Fifth Annual Institute on College Self Study, Western Interstate Commission for Higher Education, 1963.

Cohen, Arthur. "Community College Faculty Job Satisfaction." *Research in Higher Education* 2, No. 4 (1974): pp. 369–376.

Cohen, Arthur, and Brawer, Florence. *The Two-Year College Instructor Today.* New York: Praeger Publishers, 1977.

Cohen, Michael, and March, James. *Leadership and Ambiguity: The American College President.* New York: McGraw-Hill Book Company, 1974.

Cohen, Michael D.; March, James G.; and Olsen, Johan P. "A Garbage Can Model of Organizational Choice." *Administrative Science Quarterly* 17, No. 1 (March 1972): pp. 1–25.

Commission on Academic Tenure in Higher Education. *Faculty Tenure.* San Francisco: Jossey-Bass Publishers, 1973.

Conrad, Clifton, and Cosand, Joseph. *The Implications of Federal Education Policy.* Washington, D.C.: American Association for Higher Education, 1976.

Crain, Robert, and Mahard, Rita. *Desegregation and Black Achievement.* Santa Monica, California: The Rand Corporation, 1977.

Crain, Robert, and Mahard, Rita. *The Influence of High School Racial Composition in Black College Attendance and Achievement Test Performance.* Santa Monica, California: The Rand Corporation, 1978.

Creager, J. A. "General Purpose Sampling in the Domain of Higher

Education." *ACE Research Reports* 3, No. 2. Washington, D.C.: American Council on Education, 1968.

Cross, Patricia. *Beyond the Open Door.* San Francisco: Jossey-Bass, Inc., 1976.

Cross, K. P. "The Role of the Junior College in Providing Postsecondary Education for All." in T. R. McConnell ed. *Trends in Postsecondary Education.* Washington, D.C.: U.S. Government Printing Office, 1970.

Dash, Roger E., and Riley, Gary L. "The Evaluation of an Urban University." in Riley, Gary L., and Baldridge, Victor J., eds. *Governing Academic Organizations.* Berkeley: McCutchan Publishing Corporation, 1977.

Data Book on Illinois Higher Education. State of Illinois Board of Higher Education, May 1977.

de los Santos, Alfredo. "Staffing to Meet the Needs of Spanish Speaking Students." in R. Yarrington, ed. *New Staff for New Students.* Washington, D.C.: AACJC, 1974: pp. 95–105.

Deluca, P. "The Minority Student's Needs." *College and University* 49 (Summer 1974): pp. 711–14.

Drake, Sandra. *A Study of Community and Junior College Boards of Trustees.* Washington, D.C.: American Association of Community and Junior Colleges, 1977.

Dressel, P., and DeLisle, F. *Undergraduate Curriculum Trends.* Washington, D.C.: American Council on Education, 1969.

Dressel, Paul L., and Mayhew, Lewis B. *Higher Education As a Field of Study.* San Francisco: Jossey-Bass Publishers, 1974.

Dutton, Jeffrey. *Courses and Enrollment in Ethnic/Racial Studies.* Washington, D.C.: American Council on Education, August 1973.

Edsall, Shirley. "The Community College Librarian: A Profile." *Community and Junior College Journal* 46, No. 4 (December/January 1976): pp. 32–33.

Education Commission of the States, ECS Evaluation and Improvement of Statewide Planning Project, National Center for Higher Education Management Systems at WICHE, State Higher Education Executive Officers Association. *State Postsecondary Education Profiles Handbook.* Denver, Colorado: Higher Education Services, Education Commission of the States, 1976.

El-Khawas, Elaine H. *Public and Private Higher Education: Differences in*

Role, Character and Clientele. No. 3. Washington, D.C.: American Council on Education, December 1976.

Enarson, Harold L. "A University President: Where Do We Go From Here?" in Kenneth E. Young ed. *Exploring the Case for Low Tuition in Public Higher Education.* Iowa City: American Association of Community and Junior Colleges, American Association of State Colleges and Universities, National Association of State Universities and Land-Grant Colleges, The American College Testing Program, 1974.

"Enrollments in Federally Aided Vocational Classes, by Type of Program Selected Years, 1919–20 to 1973–74." in C. Andersen ed. *A Fact Book on Higher Education.* Washington, D.C.: American Council on Education, 1976.

Epps, Edgar, ed. *Black Students in White Schools.* Worthington, Ohio: Charles A. Jones Publishing Company, 1972.

Epstein, Cynthia F. "Positive Effects of the Multiple Negative: Explaining the Success of Black Professional Women." *American Journal of Sociology* 78, No. 4 (January, 1973).

Esquibel, Antonio. "The Status of Chicano Administrators in Higher Education." in Casso, H., and Roman, G., eds. *Chicanos in Higher Education.* Albuquerque: University of New Mexico Press, 1976, pp. 95–114.

Farland, Ronnald; Rose, Clare; Nyre, Glenn; and Trent, James. *The Study of Extended Opportunity Programs and Services in California Community Colleges.* Sacramento: The Board of Governors, California Community Colleges, April, 1976.

Feldman, Kenneth, and Newcomb, Theodore. *The Impact of College on Students.* San Francisco: Jossey-Bass, Inc., 1973.

Fen, Sing-Nan. "The Faculty of the Sixties." *Change* 5, No. 5 (June 1973): pp. 11–12; 61.

Fenske, Robert, and Scott, Craig. *The Changing Profile of College Students.* ERIC/Higher Education Research Report. Washington, D.C.: American Association for Higher Education, 1973.

Ferrin, Richard. *Developmental Programs in Midwestern Community Colleges.* Evanston, Illinois: College Entrance Examination Board, February 1971.

Fetters, William; Dunteman, George; and Peng, Samuel. *Fulfillment of Short-Term Educational Plans and Continuance in Education, National Longitudinal Study of High School Seniors.* Washington, D.C.: National Center for Education Statistics, 1977.

Finn, Chester. *Scholars, Dollars and Bureaucrats*. Washington, D.C.: The Brookings Institution, 1978.

Fitt, Alfred B. *Social Security Benefits for Students*. Washington, D.C.: Congress of the United States Congressional Budget Office, May 1977.

Fleming, John. *The Lengthening Shadow of Slavery*. Washington, D.C.: Howard University Press, 1976.

Fleming, John; Gill, Gerald; and Swinton, David. *The Case for Affirmative Action for Blacks in Higher Education*. Washington, D.C.: Institute for the Study of Educational Policy, Howard University Press, 1978.

Freeman, Richard B. *Black Elite: The New Market for Highly Educated Black Americans*. New York: McGraw-Hill, 1976.

Fryer, Thomas W., Jr. "New Policies for the Part-Time Faculty." in Roger W. Heyns, ed. *Leadership for Higher Education, The Campus View.* Washington, D.C.: American Council on Education, 1977 (50–59).

Gage, N. L., ed. *Handbook of Research on Teaching*. Chicago: Rand McNally, 1963.

Garbarino, Joseph; Feller, David; and Finkin, Matthew. *Faculty Bargaining in Public Higher Education*. San Francisco: Jossey-Bass Publishers, 1977.

Garfield, Learita, and McHugh, Elizabeth. "Learning Counseling." *Journal of Higher Education* 49 (1978): pp. 382–392.

Garms, Walter. *Financing Community Colleges*. New York: Teacher's College Press, 1977.

Garrison, Roger H. *Junior College Faculty: Issues and Problems, A Preliminary National Appraisal*. Washington, D.C.: American Association of Junior Colleges, 1967.

Gemmell, Suzanne. "Affirmative Action Officers in Higher Education." Ed. D. dissertation, Indiana University School of Education, 1974.

Gilli, Angelo. "Vocational Associate Degrees: Their Place in the Universities." *Community and Junior College Journal* 45, No. 5 (February 1975): pp. 28–29; 34.

Gladieux, Lawrence E. *Distribution of Federal Student Assistance: The Enigma of the Two-year Colleges*. Princeton, New Jersey: College Entrance Examination Board, 1975.

Glazer, Nathan. *Affirmative Discrimination: Ethnic Inequality and Public Policy*. New York: Basic Books, Inc., 1975.

Gleazer, Edmund J. *Project Focus: A Study of Community Colleges*. New York: McGraw-Hill Book Company, 1973.

Gleazer, E. J., Jr. "The Two-Year College." *College and University Business* 36, No. 3 (March 1964): p. 49.

Gleazer, Edmund J., and Yarrington, Roger, eds. *Coordinating State Systems*. San Francisco: Jossey-Bass, Inc., 1974.

Gomberg, Irene and Frank Atelsek. *Composition of College and University Governing Boards*. Washington, D.C.: American Council on Education, August 1977.

Goodrich, Andrew; Lezotte, Lawrence; and Welch, James. "Minorities in Two-Year Colleges." *American Association of Junior Colleges Journal* 43, No. 4 (December 1972/January 1973): pp. 28–31.

Goodrich, Andrew. "Minorities in Community Colleges, 1973–74." Unpublished manuscript. College Park, Maryland [1977].

Grafe, Gale. *The Trustee Profile of 1976*. Washington, D.C.: Association of Community College Trustees, 1976.

Grandy, Jerilee, and Shea, Walter M. *The CLEP General Examinations in American Colleges and Universities*. Princeton: College Entrance Examination Board, 1976.

Grant, Mary Kathryn; and Hoeber, Daniel. *Basic Skills Programs: Are They Working?* Washington, D.C.: ERIC Clearinghouse on Higher Education, 1978.

Greeley, Andrew. *From Backwater to Mainstream*. New York: McGraw-Hill, 1969.

Greeley, Andrew. "On 'Is There an Academic Melting Pot?' (Comment on Wuthnow, SOE, January 1977)." *Sociology of Education* 50, 3 (July 1977): pp. 218–219.

Greeley, A. M., and Rossi, P. H. *The Education of Catholic Americans*. Chicago: Aldine Publishing Company, 1966.

Gross, Edward, and Grambsch, Paul. *Academic Administrators and University Goals*. Washington, D.C.: American Council on Education, 1968.

Halsey, A. H., and Trow, M. *The British Academics*. London: Faber and Faber, 1971.

Halstead, D. Kent. *Statewide Planning in Higher Education*. Washington, D.C.: U.S. Government Printing Office, 1974.

Harcleroad, Fred, ed. *Higher Education: A Developing Field of Study*. Iowa City, Iowa: American College Testing Program, 1974.

Hartnett, R. T. *College and University Trustees: Their Backgrounds, Roles, and Education Attitudes.* Princeton, New Jersey: Educational Testing Service, 1970.

Hawthorne, Mary, and Perry, Warren J. *Community Colleges and Primary Health Care: Study of Allied Health Education (SAHE) Report.* Washington, D.C.: American Association of Community and Junior Colleges, 1974.

Haynes, Leonard. *A Conceptual Examination of Desegregation in Higher Education.* Washington, D.C.: Institution for Services to Education, Inc., 1978.

Hedegard, James M. "Experiences of Black College Students at Predominantly White Institutions." in Epps, Edgar A., ed. *Black Students in White Schools.* Worthington, Ohio: Charles A. Jones Publishing Company, 1972.

Hernandez, J., et al. "Census Data and the Problem of Conceptually Defining the Mexican American Population." *Social Science Quarterly* 53 (March): pp. 671–687.

Hind, Robert R. "Analysis of a Faculty: Professionalism, Evaluation, and the Authority Structure." in Baldridge, J. Victor, ed. *Academic Governance.* Berkeley, California: McCutchan Publishing Corporation, 1971, pp. 264–292.

Hodgkinson, Harold L. *How Much Change for A Dollar? A Look at Title III.* ERIC Higher Education Research Report No. 3. Washington, D.C.: American Association for Higher Education, 1974.

Holmstrom, Engin. *Low Achievers: Do They Differ From "Typical" Undergraduates?* Washington, D.C.: American Council on Education, 1973.

Hudesman, John, and Wiesner, Ezra. "Desensitization of Test-Anxious Urban Community College Students and Resulting Changes in Grade Point Average." *Community Junior College Research Quarterly* 3 No. 3 (April–June 1979): pp. 259–264.

Huther, John W. "Small Market for Ph.D.'s: The Public Two-Year College." *AAUP Bulletin* 58, No. 1 (March 1972): pp. 17–20.

Institute for the Study of Educational Policy. *Equal Educational Opportunity for Blacks in U.S. Higher Education: An Assessment.* Washington, D.C.: Howard University, 1976.

Iwamoto, Carolyn K.; Kaplan, Mario; and Aniloff, Larry. "High School Dropouts, Effects of Hispanic Background and Previous School Achievement." *Urban Education* 11, No. 1 (April 1976): pp. 23–28.

Jencks, Christopher, and Riesman, David. *The Academic Revolution.* New York: Doubleday and Company, Inc., 1968.

Jones, Faustine. *The Changing Mood in America: Eroding Commitment?* Washington, D.C.: Howard University Press, 1977.

Jonsen, Richard. "State Policy and Independent Higher Education Project." *Higher Education in the States* 6, No. 1 (1977): pp. 1–28.

Karabel, Jerome. "Community Colleges and Social Stratification." *Harvard Educational Review* 42, No. 4 (November 1972): 521–562.

Kay, E. R. *Enrollments and Programs in Non-collegiate Postsecondary Schools, 1973–74.* Washington, D.C.: National Center for Education Statistics, 1976.

Kellams, Samuel E. "ASHE Membership Survey Results." *Higher Education Review* 1, No. 1 (Fall 1977): pp. 39–45.

Kelley, W., and Wilbur, L. *Teaching in the Community Junior College.* New York: Appleton-Century-Crofts, 1970.

Kemerer, F. R., and Baldridge, J. V. *Unions on Campus: A National Study of the Consequences of Faculty Bargaining.* San Francisco: Jossey-Bass, 1975.

King, Joe. "The Perceptions of Black High School Students Toward Vocational and Technical Education Programs." *The Journal of Negro Education* 66, No. 4 (Fall 1977): pp. 430–442.

Knoell, Dorothy M. "Changing Enrollment Patterns—Changing Functions." *The College Board Review* No. 99 (Spring 1976): pp. 22–25.

Koos, Leonard V. "Local Versus Regional Junior Colleges." *School Review* 5 (1944): pp. 525–531.

Kreps, Juanita. *Sex in the Marketplace: American Women at Work.* Baltimore: Johns Hopkins Press, 1971.

Kronovet, Esther. "Affirmative Action: Myth or Reality?" in Hollander, Harriet E.; Penney, Sherry; and Haines, John R., eds. *Women, Their Future in the University and the Community.* New York: New York State Citizens Council, Skidmore College and Office of Higher Education Management Services, New York State Education Department, 1974.

Kronovet, Esther. "The Managers of Affirmative Action and Their Role in the Selection Process." Presented at the American Association for Affirmative Action National Conference in Washington, D.C., May 9, 1977.

Ladd, Everett C., and Lipset, Seymour M. "The Politics of American Political Scientists." *Political Science* 4 (Spring 1971): pp. 135–144.

Ladd, E. C., and Lipset, S. M. "Politics of Academic Natural Scientists and Engineers." *Science* 176 (June 1972): pp. 1091–1100.

Ladd, Everett, and Lipset, Seymour. *Professors, Unions and American Higher Education.* Berkeley, California: Carnegie Commission on Higher Education, 1973.

Ladd, Everett, and Lipset, Seymour. "Professors' Religious and Ethnic Backgrounds." *Chronicle of Higher Education* (22 September 1975b), p. 2.

Ladd, Everett C., and Lipset, Seymour M. *The Divided Academy, Professors and Politics.* New York: W. W. Norton and Company, Inc., 1975a.

Ladd, Everett, and Lipset, Seymour. "The Big Differences Among Faculty Unions." *Chronicle of Higher Education* (13 March 1978), p. 14.

Lazarsfeld, Paul F., and Thielens, Wagner. *The Academic Mind: Social Scientists in a Time of Crisis.* Glencoe, Illinois: The Free Press, 1958.

Lee, Barbara. *Collective Bargaining in Four-Year Colleges.* ERIC/Higher Education Research Report. Washington, D.C.: American Association for Higher Education, 1978.

Leister, Douglas V. "Identifying Institutional Clientele: Applied Meta-marketing in Higher Education Administration." *Journal of Higher Education* 46 (July/August 1975): pp. 381–98.

Leister, Douglas, and MacLachlan, Douglas. "Assessing the Community College Transfer Market." *Journal of Higher Education* 47 (November/December 1976): pp. 661–680.

Levine, Arthur. *Handbook on Undergraduate Curriculum.* San Francisco: Jossey-Bass, Inc., 1978.

Lewis, Lionel S. "On Prestige and Loyalty of University Faculty." *Administrative Science Quarterly* 11, No. 4 (March 1967): pp. 629–642.

Lipset, Seymour Martin, and Ladd, Everett C. "Jewish Academics in the United States: Their Achievements, Culture and Politics." *American Jewish Year Book* 72 (1972): pp. 89–128.

Liss, Lara. "Affirmative Action Officers— Are They Change Agents?" *Educational Record* 58, No. 4 (Fall 1977): pp. 418–428.

Locke, Patricia. *A Survey of College and University Programs for American Indians.* Boulder, Colorado: Western Interstate Commission for Higher Education, January 1978.

Lombardi, John. *Black Studies in the Community College.* Washington, D.C.: ERIC Clearinghouse for Junior Colleges, Monograph #14, 1971.

Lombardi, John. *Community Education: Threat to College Status?* Los Angeles: ERIC Clearinghouse for Junior Colleges, 1978a.

Lombardi, John. "The Surge of Occupational Education." *Community College Review* 5, No. 3 (Winter 1978b): pp. 55–65.

Losak, John. "A Validity Study of the General Examinations of the College Level Examination Program." Presented at the American Educational Research Association Annual Meeting. Toronto, Canada, March 1978.

Macias, Reynaldo, and Gomez-Quinones, Juan, eds. *The National Directory of Chicano Faculty and Research*. Los Angeles: Aztlan Publications, Chicano Studies Center, UCLA, 1974.

Macias, Reynaldo Flores; de Macias, Carolyn; De La Torre, William; and Vasquez, Mario. *Educacion Alternativa, On The Development of Chicano Bilingual Schools*. Hayward, California: The Southwest Network, 1975.

MALDEF. *Docket: Litigation Department*. San Francisco: Mexican American Legal Defense and Educational Fund, April 1978.

Malitz, Gerald. *Associate Degrees and Other Formal Awards Below the Baccalaureate: Analysis of Six-Year Trends*. Washington, D.C.: National Center for Education Statistics, 1978.

Malott, Stephen; Mensel, Frank R.; and Boyer, Jeannie. "1975–76 Administrative Compensation Survey Research Report." Washington, D.C.: College and University Personnel Association, 1976.

March, James G., ed. *Handbook of Organizations*. Chicago: Rand McNally, 1965.

Martorana, S. V., and McGuire, Gary W. *State Legislation Relating to Community and Junior Colleges, 1973–75*. University Park, Pennsylvania: Center for the Study of Higher Education, 1975.

Martorana, S. V., and Nespoli, Lawrence. *State Legislation Relating to Community and Junior Colleges*. University Park, Pennsylvania: Center for the Study of Higher Education, 1977.

Martorana, S. V.; Toombs, William; and Breneman, David W., eds. *Graduate Education and Community Colleges: Cooperative Approaches to Community College Staff Development*. National Board on Graduate Education, 1975.

McGuinness, Aims C., et al. *The Changing Map of Post-Secondary Education*. Denver, Colorado: Education Commission of the States, 1975.

Medsker, L. *The Junior College: Progress and Prospect.* New York: McGraw-Hill, 1960.

Menacker, Julius. *From School to College: Articulation and Transfer.* Washington, D.C.: American Council on Education, 1975.

Middleton, Lorenzo. "NAACP Concerned Over 'Racial Isolation' in Cleveland's Community College." *The Chronicle of Higher Education* (19 June 1978), p. 9.

Millard, Richard. *State Boards of Higher Education.* Washington, D.C.: American Association of Higher Education, 1976.

Millard, Richard. "The States and Private Higher Education." *Higher Education in the States* 5, No. 1 (1975): pp. 1–24.

Millett, John. *The Academic Community.* New York: McGraw-Hill, 1962.

Mills, Peter. "Community College Trustees: A Survey." *A Special Report of Association of Governing Board of Universities and Colleges* (December 1972): pp. 30–39.

Mingle, James R. "Faculty and Departmental Response to Increased Black Student Enrollment." *The Journal of Higher Education* 49 (May/June 1978): pp. 201–217.

"Minorities Account for 16.2 Percent of 1976 College Enrollments." *Higher Education Daily* No. 59 (March 27, 1978): pp. 1–2.

Mommsen, K. G. "Career Patterns of Black American Doctorates." Unpublished doctoral dissertation, Florida State University, 1970.

Mommsen, Kent G. "Black Ph.D.'s in the Academic Marketplace: Supply, Demand and Price." *Journal of Higher Education* 45 (April 1974): pp. 253–267.

Montero, Darrel. *The Japanese American Community: A Study of Generational Changes in Ethnic Affiliation.* College Park, Maryland: Institute for Urban Studies, 1978.

Moore, W., Jr. *Against the Odds: The Disadvantaged Student in the Community College.* San Francisco: Jossey-Bass, Inc., 1970.

Moore, W., Jr. *Blind Man on a Freeway: The Community College Administrator.* San Francisco: Jossey-Bass, Inc., 1971.

Moore, William. "The Community College Board of Trustees: A Question of Competency." *Journal of Higher Education* 44 (March 1973): pp. 171–190.

Moore, William, and Wagstaff, Lonnie. *Black Educators in White Colleges.* San Francisco: Jossey-Bass, Inc., 1974.

Moore, William. *Community College Response to the High Risk Student: A Critical Reappraisal.* Washington, D.C.: AACJC/Council of Universities and Colleges/ERIC Clearinghouse for Junior Colleges, 1976a.

Moore, William. "Black Knight/White College." *Community and Junior College Journal* 6, No. 7 (April 1976b): pp. 18–20, 40–43.

Morales, Lilliam. "Extended Opportunity Programs and Services." Staff presentation to Board of Governors of the California Community Colleges (September 30, 1977).

Morgan, Gordon. *The Ghetto College Student.* Iowa: American College Testing Program, 1970.

Morgan, Margaret. "Male University Attrition: A Discriminant Analysis." *Research in Higher Education* 2 (1974): pp. 281–289.

Morgan, Margaret. "Selecting Candidates for Over-subscribed Programs." *Community College Review* 1, No. 2 (Fall 1977): pp. 65–73.

Morrison, James. "The Community College and the Disadvantaged." *Research in Higher Education* 1, No. 4 (1973): pp. 401–413.

Morrison, J. L., and Ferrante, R. "Compensatory Education in the Two-Year College." University Park, Pa: Center for the Study of Higher Education, 1973.

Munday, Leo. "College Access for Nontraditional Students." *Journal of Higher Education* 47 (November/December 1976): pp. 681–699.

Munoz, Daniel, and Garcia-Bahne, Betty. "A Study of the Chicano Experience in Higher Education." Report No. MN 24597-01 National Institute of Mental Health [1977].

Myrdal, Gunnar. *Objectivity in Social Research.* New York: Pantheon Books, 1969.

National Advisory Committee on Black Higher Education and Black Colleges and Universities. *Higher Education Equity: The Crisis of Appearance Versus Reality.* Washington, D.C.: U.S. Office of Education, June 1978.

National Assessment of Educational Progress. *Hispanic Student Achievement in Five Learning Areas: 1971–75.* Denver: National Assessment of Educational Progress, May 1977.

National Board on Graduate Education. *Minority Group Participation in*

Graduate Education. Washington, D.C.: National Board on Graduate Education, June 1976.

National Center for Education Statistics. *The Condition of Education, 1974 Edition.* Washington, D.C.: HEW, 1974.

National Center for Education Statistics. *Digest of Education Statistics, 1976 Edition.* Washington, D.C.: HEW, 1977.

National Center for Education Statistics. *The Condition of Education, 1976 Edition.* Washington, D.C.: HEW, 1976.

National Center for Education Statistics. *The Condition of Education, 1978 Edition.* Washington, D.C.: HEW, 1978.

Nelson, Charles A., and Turk, Frederick J. *Facts About Governing Boards Results of a Survey.* Unpublished survey conducted by Peat, Marwick, Mitchell and Co. for the Association of Governing Boards of Universities and Colleges, 1971.

Nelson, Susan. *The Equity of Public Subsidies for Higher Education: Some Thoughts on the Literature.* Denver: Education Commission of the States, 1978a.

Nelson, Susan C. "Financial Trends and Issues" in David W. Breneman and Chester E. Finn, Jr., eds. *Public Policy and Private Higher Education.* Washington, D.C.: Brookings Institution, 1978b.

Nelson, Susan. *Community Colleges and Their "Share" of Public Student Financial Assistance.* Washington, D.C.: Brookings Institution, 1978c.

Nichols, Richard. "Testimony Before the Subcommittee on Postsecondary Education, Hearings on Title III of the Higher Education Act." American Indian Higher Education Consortium, 29 March 1979.

Nwagbaraocha, Joel O. "Systems Analysis Approach to Academic Planning, Part II." *Research Profile, Institute for Services to Education, Inc.* 2, No. 1 (March 1974).

Office for Civil Rights. *Racial and Ethnic Enrollment Data from Institutions of Higher Education Fall 1974.* Washington, D.C.: HEW, November 1976.

Office for Civil Rights. Unpublished Office for Civil Rights (HEW) data Fall, 1976 [1978], ISEP staff calculations.

Olivas, Michael A. *A Statistical Portrait of Honors Programs in Two-Year Colleges.* Los Angeles: ERIC Clearinghouse on Junior Colleges, 1977, ED 136890.

Olivas, Michael. "Hispanic College Presidents." Unpublished paper. Washington, D.C.: Institute for the Study of Educational Policy, Howard University, 1978.

Oromaner, M. J. "A Note on Analytical Properties and Prestige of Sociology Departments." *American Sociologist* 5 (1970): pp. 240–244.

Palola, Ernest G., and Oswald, Arthur R. *Urban Multi-Unit Community Colleges: Adaptation for the 70's.* Berkeley: Center for Research and Development in Higher Education, 1972.

Pandey, R. E. "A Comparative Study of Dropouts at an Integrated University: The 16 Personality Factor Test." *Journal of Negro Education* 42 (Fall 1973): pp. 447–451.

Pantoja, Antonia; Blourock, Barbara; and Bowman, James. *Badges and Indicia of Slavery: Cultural Pluralism Redefined.* Lincoln, Nebraska: Cultural Pluralism Committee, 1975.

Park, Young. *Junior College Faculty: Their Values and Perceptions.* Washington, D.C.: ERIC Clearinghouse for Junior Colleges, American Association of Junior Colleges, Monograph No. 12, 1971.

Parker, Garland G. *Career Education and Transfer Program Enrollments in Two-year Colleges, 1973–74.* Iowa City, Iowa: American College Testing Program, 1975.

Parker, Garland. *Collegiate Enrollments in the U.S., 1977–78.* Iowa City, Iowa: American College Testing Program, 1978a.

Parker, Garland. *Collegiate Enrollments in American Two-Year Institutions, 1977–78.* Iowa City, Iowa: American College Testing Program, 1978b.

"Participation of Community Colleges in Office of Education Programs, Fiscal Year 1977." *American Education* 14, No. 1 (January/February 1978): pp. 33–34.

Pascarella, Ernest, and Terenzini, Patrick. "Informal Interaction with Faculty and Freshman Ratings of the Academic and Non-Academic Experience of College." *Journal of Educational Research* 70 (1976): pp. 35–41.

Pascarella, Ernest, and Terenzini, Patrick. "Patterns of Student-Faculty Informal Interaction Beyond the Classroom and Voluntary Freshman Attrition." *Journal of Higher Education* 48 (October 1977): pp. 540–552.

Perez, Monte, ed. *Institute on Chicanos in Higher Education.* Pasadena, California: National Association for Equal Educational Opportunities, 1977.

Peterson, Marvin W.; Blackburn, Robert T.; Gamson, Zelda F.; Arce, Carlos H.; Davenport, Rosell W.; and Mingle, James R. *Black Students on White Campuses: The Impacts of Increased Black Enrollments.* Ann Arbor, Michigan: Institute for Social Research, 1978.

Phillips, M. J. "Honors Programs in Higher Education Today: An Overview." *Forum on Honors* 3 (1973): pp. 13–15; 18.

Poinsett, A. "The Brain Drain at Negro Colleges." *Ebony* 25 (October 1970): pp. 74–84.

Pray, Francis C. *A New Look at Community College Boards of Trustees and Presidents and Their Relationships, Suggestions for Change.* Washington, D.C.: American Association of Community and Junior Colleges, 1975.

Project on the Status and Education of Women. "Women's Studies." *Association of American Colleges* No. 20 (June 1978): pp. 5–6.

Rafky, D. M. "The Black Scholar in the Academic Marketplace." *Teachers College Record* 74 (December 1972): pp. 225–60.

Rauh, Morton A. *The Trusteeship of Colleges and Universities.* New York: McGraw-Hill Book Company, 1969.

Reed, Rodney. *Peer-Tutoring Programs for the Academically Deficient Student in Higher Education.* Berkeley: Center for Research and Development in Higher Education, 1973.

Report on Indian Education, Final Report to the American Indian Policy Review Commission. Washington, D.C.: U.S. Government Printing Office, 1976.

Richards, James M., Jr., and Braskamp, Larry A. "Who Goes Where to Junior College." in *The Two-Year College and Its Students: An Empirical Report.* Iowa City: American College Testing Program, Inc., 1969.

Richards, James M., Jr.; Rand, Leonard; and Rand, Lorraine M. "Regional Differences in Junior Colleges." In *The Two-Year College and Its Students: An Empirical Report.* Iowa City, Iowa: The American College Testing Program, Inc., 1969.

Richardson, L. H. "The Commuter College Student's Problem in Synthesizing His Life in a Fragmented Developmental Setting." *Journal of the American College Health Association* 15, No. 4 (April 1956): pp. 302–306.

Richter, Maurice N., Jr. *Science As a Cultural Process.* Cambridge, Massachusetts: Schenkman, 1972.

Riley, Gary, and Baldrige, Victor J., eds. *Governing Academic Organizations.* Berkeley, California: McCutchan Publishing Corporation, 1977.

Rodriguez, Orlando. "Occupational Shifts and Educational Upgrading in the American Labor Force Between 1950 and 1970." *Sociology of Education* 51 (January 1978): pp. 55–67.

Rogers, J. F. *Higher Education As a Field of Study at the Doctoral Level.* Washington, D.C.: American Association for Higher Education, National Education Association, 1969.

Rossi, A., and Calderwood, A., eds. *Academic Women on the Move.* New York: Russell Sage Foundation, 1973.

Roueche, J. E., and Kirk, R. W. *Catching Up: Remedial Education.* San Francisco: Jossey-Bass, 1973.

Roueche, John, and Roueche, Suanne. *Developmental Education, A Primer For Program Development and Evaluation.* Atlanta, Georgia: Southern Regional Education Board, 1977.

Roueche, John, and Snow, Jerry. *Overcoming Learning Problems.* San Francisco: Jossey-Bass, Inc., 1977.

Rudolph, Frederick. *Curriculum, A History of The American Undergraduate Course of Study Since 1636.* San Francisco: Jossey-Bass, Inc., 1977.

Salazar, J. Leonard, and Martorana, S. V. *State Postsecondary Education Planning (1202) Commissions: A First Look.* University Park, Pennsylvania: Center for the Study of Higher Education, June 1978.

Schlesinger, Sue. "Support and Opposition: Community College Faculty Attitudes toward Affirmative Action." *Community Junior College Research Quarterly* 3 (1979): pp. 111–120.

Sedlacek, William; Lewis, Joan; and Brooks, Glenwood. "Black and Other Minority Admissions to Large Universities: A Four-Year National Survey of Policies and Outcomes." *Research in Higher Education* 2 (1974): pp. 221–230.

"Self-Reported Reasons for Withdrawal from Higher Education and Reentry Patterns." *Advance Statistics for Management, National Center for Education Statistics Bulletin* 24 (September 30, 1977).

Snow, Jerry. "What Works and What Doesn't in Community College Developmental Studies Programs." Mimeographed. Austin, Texas: University of Texas at Austin, 1977.

Sosdian, Carol. *External Degrees: Program and Student Characteristics.* Washington, D.C.: Bureau of Social Science Research, Inc., March 1978.

Spady, W. "Dropouts from Higher Education: An Interdisciplinary Review and Synthesis." *Interchange* 1 (1970): pp. 64–85.

Staples, Robert. *Introduction to Black Sociology.* New York: McGraw-Hill, 1976.

Stark, Joan S. and Associates. *The Many Faces of Educational Consumerism.* Lexington, Massachusetts: D.C. Heath and Company, 1977.

Stark, M. "Commuter and Residence Hall Students Compared." *Personnel and Guidance Journal* 44 (1965): pp. 277–281.

Steinberg, Stephen. *The Academic Melting Pot.* New York: McGraw-Hill Book Company, 1974.

Steinberg, Stephen. "On 'Is There an Academic Melting Pot?' (Comment on Wuthnow, SOE, January 1977 and Greeley, SOE, July 1977)" *Sociology of Education* 50, 4 (October 1977): pp. 317–319.

Southwest Network. *Parameters of Institutional Change: Chicano Experiences in Education.* Hayward, California: Southwest Network, 1974.

Sung, Betty Lee. *Statistical Profile of the Chinese in the United States, 1970 Census.* Washington, D.C.: Manpower Administration, U.S. Department of Labor, 1975.

Terenzini, Patrick, and Pascarella, E. "The Relation of Students' Precollege Characteristics and Freshman Year Experience to Voluntary Attrition." *Research in Higher Education* 9 (1978): pp. 347–366.

Thomas, Gail. *Race and Sex Effects on Access to College.* Baltimore: The Johns Hopkins University Center for Social Organization of Schools, Report No. 229, May 1977.

Thomas, G. E.; Alexander, K. L.; and Eckland, B. K. "Access to Higher Education: How Important Are Race, Sex, Social Class and Academic Credentials for College Access?" Baltimore: Johns Hopkins University Center for Social Organization of Schools, Report No. 226, April 1977.

Thompson, Thomas, ed. *The Schooling of Native America.* Washington, D.C.: American Association of Colleges for Teacher Education, 1978.

Thornton, Russell. "American Indian Studies as an Academic Discipline." *The Journal of Ethnic Studies* 5, No. 3 (1977): pp. 1–15.

Thurston, Alice; Zook, Fredrick; Neher, Timothy; and Ingraham, Joseph. *The Chief Student Personnel Administration in the Public Two-Year College.* Washington, D.C.: ERIC Clearinghouse for Junior Colleges, 1972.

Tinto, V. "Dropout from Higher Education: A Theoretical Synthesis of Recent Research." *Review of Educational Research* 45 (1975): pp. 89–125.

Tuckman, Howard P. "Who Is Part-Time in Academe?" *AAUP Bulletin* 64, No. 4 (December 1978): pp. 305–315.

Tuckman, Howard P., and Vogler, William. "The 'Part' in Part-Time Wages" *AAUP Bulletin* 64, No. 2 (May 1978): pp. 70–77.

Turner, William, and Michael, John. *Traditionally Black Institutions of Higher Education: Their Identification and Selected Characteristics.* Washington, D.C.: National Center for Education Statistics, 1978.

U.S. Bureau of Census. *Major Field of Study of College Students: October 1974.* Current Population Reports. Series P-20, No. 289, February 1976.

U.S. Bureau of Census. *Social and Economic Characteristics of Students: October 1974.* Series P-20, No. 286, 1975.

U.S. Bureau of Census. *Social and Economic Characteristics of Students: October 1975.* Series P-20, No. 303, 1976.

U.S. Bureau of Census. *Social and Economic Characteristics of Students: October 1975.* Series P-20, No. 319, 1978.

United States Commission on Civil Rights. *Mexican American Education Study, Report 1: Ethnic Isolation of Mexican Americans in the Public Schools of the Southwest.* Washington, D.C.: U.S. Commission on Civil Rights, April 1971.

United States Commission on Civil Rights. *Social Indicators of Equality for Minorities and Women.* Washington, D.C.: U.S. Commission on Civil Rights, 1978.

Valverde, Leonard A. "Prohibitive Trends in Chicano Faculty Employment" in Casso, Henry, and Roman, Gilbert D., eds. *Chicanos in Higher Education.* Albuquerque: The University of New Mexico Press, 1976.

Van Alstyne, Carol; Withers, Julie; Mensel, Frank; and Malott, Stephen. *Women and Minorities in Administration of Higher Education Institutions: Employment Patterns and Salary Comparisons.* Washington, D.C.: College and University Personnel Association, 1977a.

Van Alstyne, Carol; Withers, Julie; and Elliott, Sharon. "Affirmative Action, The Bottom Line Tells the Tale." *Change* 9, No. 8 (August 1977b): pp. 39–41; 60.

Vasquez, Hector I. "Puerto Rican Americans." *Journal of Negro Education* 38 (1969): pp. 247–256.

Vredeveld, George. "Distributional Impacts of Alternative Methods of

Financing Higher Education." *Journal of Higher Education* 49 (1978): pp. 47–69.

Wagner, Alan P., and Rice, Lois D. "Student Financial Aid: Institutional Packaging and Family Expenditure Patterns." Washington, D.C.: College Board, 1977.

Wilbur, Franklin P., and LaFay, Joseph W., Jr. "The Transferability of College Credit Earned During High School: An Update." Presented at the 1978 Annual Convention of the American Education Research Association, Toronto, Canada, March 30, 1978.

Wilburn, Adolph Y. "Careers in Science and Engineering for Black Americans." *Science* 184 (June 14, 1974): pp. 1148–1154.

Willingham, Warren. W. *Free Access Higher Education.* New York: College Entrance Examination Board, 1970.

Willingham, Warren. *The No. 2 Access Problem: Transfer to the Upper Division.* Washington, D.C.: American Association for Higher Education, July 1972.

Willis, Benjamin C. *Higher Education Part 1: The Chicago Teachers Colleges; Part II: The Chicago City Junior College.* Chicago: Chicago Public Schools, 1964.

Willower, Donald J., and Culbertson, Jack A., eds. *The Professorship in Educational Administration.* Columbus, Ohio: University Council for Educational Administration, 1964.

Wilms, Wellford. *Public and Proprietary Vocational Training: A Study of Effectiveness.* Berkeley, California: Center for Research and Development in Higher Education, 1974.

Wilson, L. *The Academic Man.* New York: Oxford University Press, 1942.

Wilson, R.; Goff, J.; Dienst, E.; Wood, L.; and Bavry, J. L. *College Professors and Their Impact on Students.* New York: Wiley, 1975.

Wispe, L.; Awkard, J.; Hoffman, M.; Ash, P.; Hicks, L.; and Porter, J. "The Negro Psychologist in America." *American Psychologist* (February 1969): pp. 142–50.

Wong, Samuel. *The Changing Universe of Black Colleges.* Washington, D.C.: Institute for the Study of Educational Policy [unpublished paper], 1975.

Wuthnow, Robert. "Is There an Academic Melting Pot?" *Sociology of Education* 50, No. 1 (January 1977): pp. 7–14.

Wuthnow, Robert. "Reply to Steinberg." *Sociology of Education* 51, 1 (January 1978): pp. 72–73.

Zusman, Ami. "State Policy Making for Community College Adult Education." *Journal of Higher Education* 49 (1978): pp. 337–357.

Index